ISSUES IN
CANADIAN
NURSING

ISSUES IN CANADIAN NURSING

Betsy LaSor
M. Ruth Elliott

PRENTICE-HALL OF CANADA, LTD. SCARBOROUGH, ONTARIO

Canadian Cataloguing in Publication Data

Main entry under title:

Issues in Canadian nursing

Includes bibliographical references and index.
ISBN 0-13-506238-1 pa.

1. Nursing—Canada. 2. Nurses—Canada.
I. LaSor, Betsy, 1936-   II. Elliott, Madeleine
Ruth, 1933-

RT6.A1I87   610.73'0971   C77-001258-2

Prentice-Hall, Inc., Englewood Cliffs, New Jersey
Prentice-Hall of Australia, Pty., Ltd., Sydney
Prentice-Hall of India Pvt., Ltd., New Delhi
Prentice-Hall International, Inc., London
Prentice-Hall of Japan, Inc., Tokyo
Prentice-Hall of Southeast Asia (Pte.) Ltd., Singapore

Design: Julian Cleva

ISBN 0-13-506238-1 (pa.)

1 2 3 4 5 W 81 80 79 78 77

Manufactured in Canada by Webcom Limited

Contents

Preface

Canadian nursing has reached a level of sophistication that necessitates dealing with its own health care issues according to the uniqueness of climate, geography, and cultural heritage. When considering
contemporary and historical issues it often becomes necessary to
extrapolate ideas from American and British nursing scenes that do
not accurately reflect the true Canadian picture. A focus is difficult to
establish because of the variety of roles nurses perform and the rapid
changes society imposes upon us. The one definable issue that all
nurses are influenced by is the health care system. "The Governments
of the Provinces and of Canada have long recognized that good
physical and mental health are necessary for the quality of life to
which everyone aspires. Accordingly, they have developed a health
care system which, though short of perfection, is the equal of any in
the world."[1]

The delivery of health care has many facets: the system utilized,
environmental circumstances, formal and informal role expectations,
cultural relatedness, and available education. This comprehensive list
has a unifying effect "on all the participants in decisions which affect
health, bringing together into one common front: the health professions, the health institutions, the scientific community, the educational
system, municipal governments, provincial governments, the federal
government, the business sector and trade unions, the voluntary associations, and the Canadian people as individuals."[2] Both the consumer
and the practitioner are influenced by these considerations.

---

[1] Marc Lalonde. *A New Perspective on the Health of Canadians.* Government of
Canada: Ottawa 1974, p. 5.

[2] *Ibid.* p. 63.

Nursing is a paramount force in health care delivery, and Canadian nursing has enjoyed a prominent position in the world health scene. As nursing has developed and moved through the 20th century, along with the other professions, it has matured. Women, seeing the challenge that nursing offers, have entered the profession from all walks of life and from a variety of social classes. A higher standard of education geared to egalitarian principles has fortified responsibilities as nursing becomes more visible and verbal. Men, recognizing that the potential for care-giving is not peculiar to women, are continuing to enter the profession. These factors have added new dimensions to nursing—clinically, educationally, and professionally.

The most exciting part of this book, for us, was the development not only of the numerous issues but of the total venture. We initially identified 24 critical issues that we felt needed to be either historically reviewed or currently examined. We felt the formulation should be both open and creative. Nursing tends to be fearful of being innovative, sometimes, due to its intense need to be heard and to be recognized. As the book progressed, however, the number of pages began to grow in proportion to the number of ideas. A three-volume series seemed inevitable. Our only alternative was to make a realistic beginning by choosing a few major issues. We are anticipating a second volume that will continue to focus on Canadian nursing contributions.

Of major concern to us was an article that would have dealt with the French and British influences on Canadian nursing development. We fondly titled this proposed chapter "The Fleur de Lis and the Lion" and searched widely for someone to undertake this task. We found, however, that the scope of the paper was of greater magnitude than the resources available to us at this time. Our feelings regarding the importance of this historical review have not changed and we hope the task will be accomplished in the future. One resource person referred to this topic as an anthropological study, so it someday may be the subject of a graduate dissertation.

All of the papers are originals by Canadian nurses. Individual regional participation was our goal. We curbed our enthusiasm for clinical practice because we wanted to start with broader issues. A true picture of Canadian nursing must include those nurses practising in the more isolated parts of this vast country, as well as those practising in the metropolitan areas. Creativity in nursing is becoming more rewarding and fulfilling and should be shared, as well as experienced.

A bonus for us in the preparation of this book was the opportunity to talk with some prominent Canadian nurses. This intensified our respect for the Canadian nursing story. We seem to forget the drama of our growth in nursing with the ever-increasing complexities of our daily roles. Change is not only difficult to experience but frequently is as frightening to review and recall.

As with all books, the writing and the compilation took on enormous proportions but we were encouraged by colleagues, friends and families, too numerous to name individually. Special gratitude should, however, go to Dr. Rae Chittick, Dr. Arthur Elliott, Dr. N. George, Dr. W. S. LaSor, Ms. Elizabeth McCann, Dr. H. K. Mussallem, Dr. J. F. McCreary, Mr. Jonathan Penman, Ms. Margaret Street.

Our students, our patients and our colleagues in the health professions all have been the real impetus for this endeavor.

BETSY LASOR
M. RUTH ELLIOTT

Foreword

The editors and authors of this book have filled a long standing void in nursing education and practice in Canada. The dearth of suitable publications has long exasperated students, teachers and practitioners.

It is said that "the language of science is international," but the reference is really to pure science. While we may have *some* pure science in nursing, most nursing practice is applied science, and its language is not international, or even national. It is cultural. This fact places a distinct limitation on the usefulness of the abundant literature, on nursing and related disciplines coming from the United States. And the very pervasiveness of this literature increases the dangers of misapplications from the limited recording of our activities and the blunted sensitivities to our own milieu.

Canada is a vast country, a federation of ten provinces and two territories. These provinces and regions differ greatly in size, geography, climate, population, resources, economics, law, and politics. Canada is officially bilingual and bicultural but between Atlantic, Pacific, Arctic and southern borders there co-exist many cultures and language groups. John Porter's term "mosaic" is indeed appropriate.

The assignment of health and education to provincial jurisdictions has permitted a great variation in the pace and nature of development of health care systems and services. Multiple approaches and differing emphases provide a rich environment in which professionals can learn from each other. Yet much of this knowledge has come about in a haphazard, circumstantial manner; for example, as by-products at national association and committee meetings. Serious literature about issues in Canadian nursing has been scanty and unorganized. The following words could have been written with this situation in mind.

Upon this gifted age, in its dark hour,
Falls from the sky a meteoric shower
of facts: they lie unquestioned, uncombined,
Wisdom enough to teach us of our ill
Is daily spun, but there exists no loom
To weave it into fabric.

EDNA ST. VINCENT MILLAY

With the publication of this book we begin to see some of the fabric that makes up Canadian nursing today. Assessing that it is a print of varied weave, the editors have made provision for its true nature to emerge through their choice of recognized scholars from all regions of the country.

LUCY D. WILLIS

Introduction

Two very significant aspects of nursing at this time are the celerity with which changes are occurring, and the emphasis being placed on developing the profession more fully. The growth of any professional group has, as a part, (1) the evolution of pertinent issues, and (2) the resolution of, or resistance to, these issues. Nursing education generally acquaints students with a history of their profession and with significant facts about nursing and professional behavior. This is done in a course that is frequently entitled "Trends or Perspectives in Nursing." Because nursing has seen such a rapid growth, its history and dilemmas have taken on a quality that is more than a trend. What we are seeing is the development of pertinent issues that must be disputed, agreed upon, and established. This exercise stresses the need to collect material about nursing that has both historical and contemporary significance in today's demanding society.

Students in Canadian schools of nursing are hindered in their attempts to seek out their heritage by the fact that there is little material available from which to draw information.

The term "issues in nursing" is often confused with the critical comments that nurses frequently engage in when attempting to define their profession more clearly. There is no clear organization of specific issues and few nursing leaders have spoken out about their beliefs.

An issue is a point in question or a matter that is in dispute, the decision of which is special or of public importance; a point at which a matter is ready for decision. Canadian nursing is beginning to state its issues, to discuss conflicting opinions and to arrive at a statement of beliefs. This book presents pertinent issues in Canadian nursing.

We shall emphasize and explore three major areas of the "health care system": legislation and political issues, education, and the practice of nursing. This book is a nursing text, designed for students at all levels in nursing education and practice. The nurse does not function without team members or without clientele and the development of team identity takes time to grow. Comfortable knowledge of who one is comes from an established identity as well as a sound base knowledge. Both these aspects are being developed rapidly in the nursing profession through education, practice, and political expertise.

Health care is an international issue of much study and concern. Because it influences all nurses, it should have more input from nursing. The delivery of health care has many facets; these include the system utilized, environmental circumstances, formal and informal role expectations, and cultural relatedness and available education. Both the consumer and the practitioner are influenced by these considerations. Much money is being spent by provincial and national budgets to fund studies of health care and these reports indicate a need to utilize more wisely those who are responsible for health care. Most educational facilities and most health manpower groups are congregated in large cities. Students in the health care fields frequently remain in the cities to continue their careers. The enormous size of the nation demands that optimum health care be available in a more even distribution.

Canadian nursing has always enjoyed a prominent position in world health, and continuing leadership in this area may be contingent upon identification and resolution of its own significant issues. International conferences in health care are defining issues of importance to third and fourth world nations. This will make our emphasis on defining how we consider ourselves within the context of our own milieu even more significant.

The geographical boundaries of Canada are vast and the cultural mixture is great. Basic preparation of nurses does not include the variety of demands on nursing outside of the urban boundaries. Programs must be established that will assist the nurse in these further challenges—as a practitioner and as a teacher to indigenous helpers.

Education

Preparation of nurses is now almost totally in institutions of higher learning. Curriculum development is a major theme of faculties of nursing. Journals are reporting innovative teaching methods, interdisciplinary courses and expanded practice fields. Qualifications for nurse educators are high, and more nurses are being prepared to fill these positions. Canadian nurses are finding they must return to school to acquire higher degrees in order to compete in the current market. Curricula are being developed that allow for more freedom to move in and out of the educational experience. Many issues arise from this expansion of nursing, and debates are generated around the basic essentials for the education of nurses and what the profession can expect or demand of their members with regard to continuing education. We do not as yet have evaluation methods appropriate and sensitive enough to resolve the dispute concerning the numbers of years of preparation and the consequent levels of practice of nurses.

Everything in the contemporary picture of our profession, as well as in other professions in the health sciences, is leaning toward interdisciplinary education. Medical centers are designing the structures of buildings to encourage the sharing of knowledge and experience. Canada has been quite progressive in establishing Health Science Centers and interdisciplinary education but the realization of this issue is slow and by no means a concept supported by everyone. Nursing has not been aggressively vocal on the pros and cons of an issue that greatly affects its future educational practices.

Research is beginning to shape nursing education and practice, and is seen as an essential component of client care. The ability to engage in research is closely related to the education of nurses. Nursing has, as a part of its history, the adages that "obedience is a virtue" and "ours is not to reason why," and, as rarely as possible, how. However, our nursing education is beginning to encourage open questions of established practices. The emphasis on developing a base knowledge unique to nursing demands that we develop our research skills. The present advances in nursing and in social change, with the altered position of women in society, mean far greater opportunities for nurses to reach out, question, and search for new answers. The development of nurse researchers can give stature to the interdisciplinary nature of nursing care or can isolate nursing from the other health professions by allowing it to become narrow in perspective.

Practice

The practice of nursing is expanding with new, exciting positions and a more definable role. Definitions of various roles, however—nurse practitioner, expanded role, and clinical specialist—are widely challenged over meaning, level of educational preparation, and function. It is not usual to hear nurses talk about job fulfillment, despite the more prevalent indications of exciting job opportunities. What are the discrepancies between what nursing proposes to be as a profession and what nurses feel in the actual work situation? Nursing is becoming a more popular profession to pursue. Men recognize that the potential for giving is not peculiar to women, and increasingly enter the profession.

Nurses are not a homogenous group of people; age, background, education, and motivation are important variables. Therefore the realities of practice rarely synchronize with what is taught in school, and attitudes toward nursing at times become more negative as the nurse becomes more involved in her clinical role. Economic restraints frequently override the level of preparation in the interest of budgets rather than quality of care. Educational requirements in job descriptions are frequently ambiguous, and rather than a reward for more education there are often rejections. In other words, self-improvement is seen as being a deterrent to increased job satisfaction. When fulfillment is found in nursing it is rewarding and is the outcome of an ability to persevere, with a sound background knowledge and a determination to put into practice what is known to be high-quality care.

Those who function in the role of clinical nurse specialist frequently report this type of satisfaction and report they have found new dimensions in nursing; clinically, educationally, and professionally. It is rewarding to read of these experiences and to view Canadian nursing's movement in this direction.

Legislative and Political Issues

Concern that is dealt with by reading and fruitful dialogue is more beneficial than fault finding and withdrawal. Nursing leadership is analogous to the difference between being a politician and a statesman. A politician is one who engages in politics for party ends or for his own advantages, whereas a statesman suggests eminent ability, foresight, and unselfish devotion to the interests of his country. What we seem to have are a few politicians and even fewer statesmen; we need more statesmen in nursing. Perhaps the analogy is inappropriate in that nursing evokes an image far different from that of politics. Nursing has not incorporated in its image what it needs to maintain its place in the health care system; political expertise is an essential component in any developing profession that is so important to the public. Health care and politics are both concerned with issues that affect the management of social institutions, communities, and the welfare of individuals.

Summary

Canadian nursing lacks a recorded history on which to reflect or to challenge. Developing an identity and a tradition is an exciting undertaking. The experience is much like that of seeing an adolescent grow into a productive, independent adult. Parents usually say it was worth all the trials and struggles. In viewing Canadian nursing at this time, we can feel proud of its accomplishments and be proud of the role it is developing. The Lady with the Lamp, who so often symbolizes nursing, has taken up a microphone. She is being heard and listened to, at last.

Canada has a health care system of which to be proud and many countries are studying its successful functioning. Nursing is actively involved in participating in this health care delivery through education, practice, and political involvement. The collection of papers in this book is a beginning focus on this participation. A complete picture can never be obtained, as this would indicate a static condition, and there is too much energy in nursing to allow this. A historical picture now has begun to be available, not only as an indication of the growth of nursing but also as an indication of the development of a nation's response to the health needs of its people. Nursing can stand on its performance and have a record to refer to as an indication of the strides it has taken.

Some of the issues in this book are now commanding prime time in nursing conferences and journals. The papers have not been chosen as a last word from the profession but rather as one statement on a significant issue that can be used in conjunction with other comments. This text does not stand alone as a means of voicing beliefs of the profession but should be a comfortable partner to articles being published elsewhere. The written word promotes thinking and discussion, both of which are needed to establish firm beliefs in Canada's nursing. There are bibliographies that will encourage further study of each subject as well as indicate a collection of useful Canadian references.

BETSY LaSOR
M. RUTH ELLIOTT

I NURSING EDUCATION AND PRACTICE

Nurse educators... are desperate to know what nursing is since this constitutes the major philosophic basis of any nursing education program. If you do not know what nursing is, how can you teach people to become nurses? With the current attempt both to improve and in some circumstances to shorten the period of formal education, it is crucial for the nurse educator to know what nursing is so that essentials will not be overlooked in the multitude of changes.

JOYCE SHROEDER MACQUEEN
Nursing Papers, Fall 1974, "A Phenomenology of Nursing"

Nursing is unique. It is the heart of patient and family care, involved with total life concerns. At the same time, nursing overlaps the other health professions, sharing many of the same goals, including the best possible care for patients and families. Because of the complexity of problems facing nursing in its development toward greater professionalism, questions continue to plague the profession.

Research in nursing remains of fundamental concern to all who work within the health professions. Research is the very epicenter of nursing; it is the thinking process as well as the practice of research that nourishes the profession and aids in its growth and development. Decisions about what is researchable and what is not, and who should do the research, are questions bearing our scrutiny. Stinson identifies six interrelated issues in Canadian nursing research and arguments surrounding better

1

ways and means of achieving the goals of explanation, prediction and control.

Allied with our concern for research is the issue of professionalism in nursing. Is professionalism linked in a direct way to the length of the nursing education program? This question has been carefully researched but still the answer evades us. Schumacher attacks some of the myths about the nature of nursing education—professional and technical—and relates this long-standing debate to the totality of nursing. No guarantee of the quality of professionalism is given, due solely to the setting in which nursing education takes place, be it university-based or community college-based.

Nurses cannot function in professional isolation. The very nature of their role necessitates their interaction with, and their dependency upon, many other members of the health team. One of the characteristics of maturity is the ability to lead as well as to follow, moving easily from one activity to another. On a "maturity scale" of professions, where does nursing fit? Many factors operate which impede nursing functioning as a contributing, effective member of the health team. To deal with these impediments, and to overcome them, nursing first must recognize them. Nursing education must come to grips with the question of the health team and the unique contribution of nursing, as well as the contributions of the other health professions. To ignore this factor is to deny the patient and his family much needed care and assistance.

Elliott has identified factors, positive and negative, influencing the nurse as an effective health team member. New loyalties and skills, other than those generically inherent in the education for the profession, will need to be highlighted and developed. Nurses developing greater confidence in their expertise also must develop their responsibility toward other professionals, through teamwork and cooperation, in order to maximize benefits to both patient and family.

1

Central Issues
in Canadian Nursing
Research

SHIRLEY M. STINSON, R.N., Ed.D.

- ... the first question we should be asking is not, "What is nursing research?" but rather, "What kinds of problems does *nursing* need to solve and what are the appropriate questions that must be posed ... ?"

- The point is not that nurses must do all research connected with nurses and the nursing profession, but do research on problems that only nurses can solve.

- Returning to the idea that all nursing practice should, in effect, be a process of hypothesis testing, the question of where practice ends and research begins is a moot one.

   The goals and issues [of nursing research] are fundamental to the larger issue, "What is nursing?"

Introduction*

What *is* nursing research? why nursing research? How should nursing research and researchers be organized? funded? How should we prepare nurses to do research? And what are the priorities? On the basis of the literature, personal communication with selected nurse researchers across Canada, and the author's own interest and experience in research,[1] these six questions would seem to constitute the central nursing research issues (i.e., matters of controversy, debate) in Canada today. While there is good beginning documentation as to titles, authors, and sources of Canadian nursing research projects to date,[2] literature pertaining to Canadian problems, issues, trends, and the dynamics of research development is sparse. As such, the material presented here must be regarded as highly tentative. An attempt has been made to discuss the issues in a broader context through the use of selected historical references and through making some interprofessional and international comparisons. The approach underlying this chapter is that of a comparative social analysis, using both current and historical data. In this sense, the author is assuming the role, not of historian or sociologist, but rather that of behavioral scientist.

Three final introductory comments. Firstly, a limitation of this chapter is that the focus is only upon *issues*, not upon the *content* of Canadian nursing research. While the two are inextricably linked, for it would seem that "content" factors such as what type of research is done by whom, where, and how, are part and parcel, if not to a great extent the products, of the issues of the day, only a mere fraction of Canadian nursing research is referred to here.

Secondly, recognizing that the nursing practice and research backgrounds and interests of the readers are likely to be considerably varied, the author has attempted to minimize the use of research terms, while at the same time provide the type of technical information and documentation required for adequate precision and substanti-

* The author wishes to express her appreciation to Drs. M. Allen (McGill), M. Cahoon (University of Toronto), J. Flaherty (University of Western Ontario), H. Glass (University of Manitoba), A. Griffin (University of Western Ontario), D. Kergin (McMaster), H. Mussallem (Canadian Nurses' Association), L. Willis (University of Saskatchewan), and, H. Labelle and P. E. Poole (Department of National Health and Welfare). The author also wishes to thank S. Evans and S. Van Haitsma of the University of Alberta Library for their assistance in the search of the literature, and B. Leaver for typing the manuscript.

[1] Including that of Senior National Health Research Scientist (1972), and member of three special research committees of the Canadian Nurses' Association since 1971.

[2] The most outstanding being the *Index of Canadian Nursing Studies* (Ottawa: The Canadian Nurses' Association, August 1974).

ation of the issues at hand. Hopefully, the latter will also provide a helpful basis for further reading for those who wish to probe selected topics more deeply and/or contest the interpretations of the literature cited here.

Lastly, readers are reminded of the importance of distinguishing between what *are* the issues, as reflected primarily by both literature and by the behavior of nurses, researchers inside and outside the health care system, research policy matters, and professional organizations, and what *should be* the issues if one were to analyze nursing research in relation to society's health care needs. The "is" and "should" of issues are not necessarily the same. We shall look at both.

We shall now turn to the first two of our six basic controversies, the "what and why?"

What is Nursing Research?

First and foremost, research is an attitude. This is, and has been a major theme in the literature: being a professional implies being a person who constantly tests ideas and approaches and persistently tries to explain why the ideas are or are not valid, and why some approaches work under certain circumstances and some do not.[3]

In contrast to the above emphasis upon research as an attitude, in the majority of nursing literature, research is treated more as a "thing," a tangible product.[4] Debate seems to center around what kinds of topics, research tasks, and approaches constitute "nursing research," as distinct from non-nursing research. In the author's opinion, one of the most practical ways of making such distinctions lies in asking the question, "Is expertise in *nursing* required to competently generate, design, conduct, analyze, interpret and/or implement such a project?" If "yes," then it is nursing research. Even this technique leaves plenty of room for debate, for there are differing opinions as to

---

[3] Shirley M. Stinson, "Staff Nurse Involvement in Research—Myth or Reality?" *Canadian Nurse*, 69 (June 1973), pp. 28–32, or, in the French language version, "Puis-je Me Lancer dans La Recherche?" *L'Infirmiere Canadienne*, 15e (Septembre, 1973), pp. 26–31. See also H. Marjorie Simpson, "Research in Nursing—The First Step," *International Nursing Review* 18 (No. 3, 1971), particularly pp. 231–47, hereafter cited as Simpson, "First Step"; and Rozella M. Schlotfeldt and Jean Berthold, "Research—How Will Nursing Define It?" *Nursing Research* 16 (Spring 1967), pp. 108–129.

[4] Stinson, June 1973 and September 1973, *op. cit.*

what kinds of research require nursing expertise. Sometimes it is fairly clear-cut. For example, a research project on the topic of determining the nature of corporate ownership of nursing homes need not involve "nursing" input, whereas nursing should be involved integrally in a project aimed at evaluating the quality of patient care in nursing homes. Florence Downs, an American nurse researcher, states, "The first question we should be asking is not, 'What is nursing research?' but, rather, 'What kinds of problems does *nursing* need to solve and what are the appropriate questions that must be posed ... ?[5] Reimann cites as probably "the first national surveys dealing with nursing and nurses ... " the study by Cornet, in 1889, which "dealt exhaustively with the death-rate among nuns of the nursing orders. ... "[6] While it can be argued that these questions—of death-rate and its causes among nurses—needed to be posed, it would seem that this sort of study was, and is, basically an epidemiological one, not "nursing" research.

The point, as this author understands it, is not that nurses must do all research connected with nurses and the nursing profession, but must do research on problems that "only" can be solved by nurses.

Returning to the idea that all nursing practice should be, in effect, a process of hypothesis testing (i.e., asking the question, "I wonder what would happen *if ... ?*"[7]),the question of where practice ends and research begins is a moot one. This is not an issue peculiar to nursing research. Marc Roberts, an economist, distinguishes between non-conceptualized "craft" knowledge learned through apprenticeship, and knowledge evolved through the systematic testing of formally-stated concepts.[8] Ramshorn talks about small studies, "research with a small *r*."[9]

---

[5] "Research in Nursing: The Genie in Florence Nightingale's Lamp," *Nursing Forum* 12 (No. 2 1973), pp. 48 – 57. [Italics mine.]

[6] [Georg] Cornet, "Die Sterblichkeitsverhaltnisse in den Krankenpflegeorden," *Zeitschrift fur Medizinische Mikrobiologie und Immunologie* 6 (1889), pp. 65 – 96, as cited by Christine Reimann, "National Surveys of Nursing and the Nursing Profession," *International Nursing Review* 7 (July 1932), pp. 323 – 8.

[7] Stinson, June 1973, *op. cit.,* pp. 28 – 29; also Pamela E. Poole and Shirley M. Stinson, "Some Aspects of Nursing Research in Canada, 1973," in *Health Care Research Symposium,* D. E. Larsen and E. J. Love, eds. (Calgary: The University of Calgary, 1974), pp. 185 – 8; and Helen M. Elfert, "Clinical Nursing Research," *Nursing Papers* 2 (June 1970), pp. 8 – 12.

[8] Marc J. Roberts, "On the Nature and Condition of Social Science," *Daedalus* 103(Summer 1974), pp. 47 – 64.

[9] Mary T. Ramshorn, "Small *r* in Nursing Research: An Exploratory Study of Patient Experiences in Isolation," *Journal of the New York State Nurses' Association,* (December 1972), pp. 24 – 29.

Two practical questions the author keeps in mind in trying to distinguish between various collections of information and what might accurately be regarded as "research" are, "Was there a formal written plan developed in advance (including delineation of the objectives, clear statement of the research questions, a review of the literature, an outline of the methods and procedures to be used, ethical considerations, and data analysis and collection plans)?"[10] Also the double-barrelled, "Is there a written report available for outside scrutiny?"—for part of the ground rules of research is that investigator(s) must be prepared for critical examination of their questions, methods, findings, and conclusions. One would like to add a third question, "Does the project constitute *sound* research?" for unfortunately in nursing, as in a great many fields of enquiry, there is quite a bit of "rubbish research." That, however, is a value judgment that can be made only *after* the label of research already has been accorded.

Within the definition of "research" there are distinctions to be made between "applied" and "basic" research. Abdellah and Levine regard the former as obtaining "new facts and/or identify[ing] relationships among facts that are intended to be used in a real-life situation," and "basic" as being geared toward "establish[ing] fundamental theories, facts and/or statements of relationships among facts ... that are not intended for immediate use in some real-life situation."[11] Using these definitions, an experiment on the effect of various types of nursing intervention would be applied research; the formulation of theory of nursing intervention would be basic research. Ideally *and* practically speaking, the two types of research are complementary and interdependent: basic research should provide frameworks, guideposts, generalizations to be tested in professional practice situations; insights gained from applied research should, and can, invigorate, vitalize, and provide new insights for basic research.[12] Most nursing research to date is "applied" in its nature, even though most of it is not "implemented"—a situation we will discuss later on.

Further, there is debate as to what constitutes "rationalized" research. "Rationalized" does not necessarily imply that the research is utilitarian, or "practical." Rather, "To rationalize is to use the means available, large or small, to get as close as possible to one's objec-

---

[10] These and other headings are cited by Walter O. Spitzer, "Ten Tips for Preparing Research Proposals," the *Canadian Nurse* 69 (March 1973), pp. 30–33.

[11] Faye G. Abdellah and Eugene Levine, *Better Patient Care Through Nursing Research* (New York: Macmillan Co., 1966), p. 707.

[12] David A. Rodgers, "In Favor of Separation of Academic and Professional Training," *American Psychologist* 19 (August 1964), pp. 675–80.

tives."[13] If one's objectives *are* to carry out basic research, then this can be "rationalized" research. This distinction would help to clarify issues regarding the legitimacy of the two major types of research. To date, nursing literature shows more evidence of concern about increasing and improving nursing research than extensive concern about these kinds of distinctions.

There are other distinctions to be made about what constitutes nursing research, particularly in terms of content and method. These will be discussed in our final section, under "priorities." Let us now look at the "Why"?

Why Nursing Research?

The question "Why?" is really a two-fold one: "Why bother with nursing research?" and "Why is nursing research emerging?"

To put it in the extreme, some nurses take the stance: "Why bother with research, let's just get on with the job." The fact alone that ongoing budgetary provision for nursing research is, as yet, a rarity in Canada's health care agencies would seem to indicate that research is far from being widely considered a necessity for nursing practice. Yet there are those who maintain that nursing practice *must* be based on rational and systematic study, otherwise, we really cannot know what nursing interventions with what kinds of clients create what kinds of effects—with the result that attempts to understand, much less improve, patient care are likely to be meaningless, if not misleading.

Simpson states, "The idea of the nurse using research methods to examine nursing problems is alien, even today, to many people in our society—to nurses, to doctors, to the public."[14] Such debates are not peculiar to any of the helping profession[15] including nursing; indeed, they are basic to society as a whole.

On the one hand, it is clear that most of society's values and

---

[13] Louis-Phillipe Bonneau and J. A. Corry, *Quest for the Optimum*, Vol. 1 (Ottawa: The Association of Universities of Canada, 1972), p. 204.

[14] Simpson, "The First Step," *op. cit.*, p. 233.

[15] Hyman Rodman and Ralph Kolodny, "Organizational Strains in the Researcher-Practitioner Relationship," *Human Organization* 23 (Summer 1964), pp. 171–82; and Calvin W. Taylor *et al.*, "Bridging the Gap Between Basic Research and Educational Practice," *National Educational Association Journal* 23 (January 1962), pp. 23–5. Clergyman Charles R. Fielding, *et al.*, discuss the need for research in relation to the practice of the clergy; *Education for Ministry* (Dayton, Ohio: American Association of Theological Schools, 1966, pp. 103, 158.

activities are *not* "research-based," and, indeed, there would seem to be a real limit to the extent to which society requires "research" as a basis for knowing and/or deciding even major issues. Jacques Barzun, a social analyst, warns against society's excessive dependence on research:

Judging from what is being studied, researched and fact-found all over the world, it is clear that as a civilization we no longer know how to do anything. We can meet no situation, pursue no purpose, without stopping work and studying. ... [16]

On the other hand, "longing to know and understand"[17] is an integral part of "man's search to understand nature and control it,"[18] and research offers a major means of explaining, predicting, and controlling phenomena.[19]

David Rogers underlines the point that in the clinical practice situation, the main thing is for practitioners to be able to come up with usable techniques for specific clients rather than coming up with scientifically-derived generalizations.[20] Yet it is clear that generalizations about such phenomena as child development, and human feelings of grief and loss, form useful bases for exploring usable, workable approaches with specific clients; conversely, learning "what works" at the individual practice level *can* lead to the formation of testable generalizations. In short, while it is not feasible to suggest that *all* practice must, or even can, be researched-based, it is equally untenable to suggest the opposite.

Look at the question "Why nursing research?" in quite another light. Analysts of the phenomenon of professionalization say that the emergence of research is a normal, predictable development in the service-teaching-research sequence which is characteristic of the traditional helping professions.[21] Considered this way, the "Why?" becomes

---

[16] Source unknown; undated newspaper clipping.

[17] Educational Policies Commission, *Education and the Spirit of Science* (Washington, D.C.: National Education Association, 1966), p. 15. Dean Josephine Flaherty warns, however, that those who dare to question, to think, are leaving themselves open to change! See "An Address to the Annual Meeting of the New Brunswick Association of Registered Nurses," May 30, 1974, p. 4. (Mimeographed).

[18] Jacob Bronowski, *The Ascent of Man* (Boston: Little, Brown & Co., 1973), flyleaf, and p. 69; see also Marc J. Roberts, "On the Nature and Condition of Social Science," *Daedalus* 103 (Summer 1974), pp. 47–64.

[19] Marc Roberts, *op. cit.*, p. 48.

[20] David A. Rodgers, *op. cit.*

[21] E.g., see Ernest Greenwood, "Attributes of a Profession," *Social Forces* 2 (July 1957), pp. 44–55; and Shirley M. Stinson, "Deprofessionalization in Nursing?" (Ed.D. dissertation, Columbia University, New York, 1969), pp. 153–4.

more a matter of being a "normal" stage of occupational growth and development, a stage which occurs in any dynamic profession. Thus, if nursing research fails to become an *integral* part of nursing,[22] one might well conclude that nursing, as a profession, is in a state of arrested development.

Organization for Nursing Research

A paradox of modern day research is that it is at once an intensely individual, personal endeavor, yet, if it is to be brought about, much less constitute benefits for society, it is immensely dependent upon organization—and highly complex organization at that. Even half a century ago, natural history researchers could carry out their descriptions and analyses of different organisms on an individual, often amateur, and part-time basis. Today most research, in biology for example, involves complex and expensive laboratory and field equipment, extensive funding arrangements, multiple publication outlets, and a myriad of specialized and sub-specialized professional associations and working groups.

Simpson, a brilliant analyst of nursing research, says very flatly, "Organization for nursing research requires two things: purpose, and money."[23] Whereas, at first glance, one might think money is the prime problem, the literature, including reports of various types of nursing research committees, conferences, and professional government, agency, and association endeavors, would suggest that the delineation of purpose(s) is equally important.

Nursing research organization is in its infancy; indeed, with one or two exceptions, most organizational developments have occurred within the last ten years. This is not to say that many nursing professional associations and university schools of nursing have not, for several decades, been carrying out various research projects; it *is* to say, however, that ongoing, systematic provision for the planning, coordination, structuring, and evaluation of nursing research, and of nursing researchers, only recently has begun to emerge. In the follow-

---

[22] Margaret Scott Wright, the distinguished holder of the only Chair of Nursing in the United Kingdom, maintains that—" 'Research is the mainspring of any group who would call themselves a profession. . . .' " See "Research Urgently Needed, Says Professor of Nursing," *International Nursing Review* 21 (March-April 1974). p. 38.

[23] Statement made at the Third National Conference on Research in Nursing. Toronto. Ontario. May 23 1974.

ing overview, nursing research organization is analyzed first at international and national levels, then, primarily within the Canadian context, at provincial, local, and institutional levels of organization. In each case an attempt is made to utilize historic and current examples to illustrate the nature and significance of professional associations, official and voluntary associations, health care agencies, and interdisciplinary/interorganizational groups as they relate to the topic of organization. Differences and commonalities in issues related to organization are outlined against that backdrop.

INTERNATIONAL

Given nursing's relatively long history of international organization, it may seem strange that the International Congress of Nurses has, to date, played a minimal role in organization for nursing research, and virtually no role in the organization of researchers. Some of its actions have been indirect, e.g., the funding of advanced preparation for selected nurses through the Florence Nightingale International Foundation; upgrading nursing education, service, and socio-economic standards in general; and, maintaining the publication of the *International Nursing Review*, a reference source valuable to nurse researchers.

Nevertheless, some ICN activities have been more directly related to research, such as FNIF funding, and the organizing of two research seminars for nurses in 1956 and 1960;[24] instigating research sessions at the 1969 ICN Congress in Montreal,[25] and providing further sessions at the 1973 Congress in Mexico City.[26] Further, an inherent part of the ICN's mode of operation is that of using survey information to formulate and pursue its objectives, i.e., to some extent ICN "does" research. While such activities are all relevant to nursing research, they do not, as yet, seem to constitute what might be regarded as a viable role in organization for nursing research.

Given the earlier-mentioned principle that the research function of a profession tends to emerge after service and education, and given that many member countries are not only dealing with extreme and very pressing problems in the latter two areas, and do not, as yet, have anything which can be regarded as organization for research within

---

[24] At Sèvres and New Delhi, respectively. See Simpson, *ibid.*

[25] H. Marjorie Simpson, "Nursing Research," *International Nursing Review* 17 (No. 2, 1970), 110 – 34.

[26] Representing the Canadian Nurses' Association, two British Columbia nurses, Sue Rothwell and Helen Garry, and three nurses from the University of Alberta: Patricia Hayes, Margaret Steed, and the author, presented one of the panels, entitled "Research and Reality: Implementation of Nursing Research in Education and Practice," May 16, 1973.

their own countries, ICN's considerable lack of research involvement might well seem explainable, if not defensible. Yet is it? Is systematic provision for ongoing organization for nursing research at the international level not an inherent responsibility of ICN? If increased emphasis upon research would pose an unrealistic financial drain on the ICN's already desperate straits, should member countries see fit to increase their contributions? And/or should money for research organization be obtained from without?

So far as organization of nursing researchers is concerned, an even thornier question, which may at first glance sound heretical, is whether nurse researchers could/should organize themselves at an international level *apart* from ICN?

A striking example of a nursing research activity at an international level was the Pan American Health Organization's interdisciplinary "Task Force on Nursing Systems," created by the PAHO's Chief of Nursing, Margaret Cammaert, a Canadian, in April 1971. The aim was to create a valid research framework for analyzing and comparing nursing "systems" in different countries. The team was comprised of nurses, systems analysts and methodologists, an anthropologist, and two physician-planners.[27]

Another example at the international level is the World Health Organization's move to create a WHO Nurse Researcher position in India.[28] While international ventures of this type are a rarity, they would seem to hold promise for the cooperative sharing of common research problems, resources, and the development of "universal" approaches.

In sum, to date there has been little international development of organization for nursing research or for nurse researchers. One wonders to what extent such developments are limited due to lack of perceived common purpose and/or funds; or, to what extent such developments are limited because of our ignorance of others' skills, and/or that so few health researchers, nurses included, can envision research beyond their own back yards.

NATIONAL

While it is beyond the limits of this chapter to provide a comprehensive nation-by-nation description of nursing research organizational

---

[27] Including an anthropologist from Mexico, a systems methodologist from the United States, and a nurse (the author) from Canada. All other members were PAHO staff, located in either the South America or the Washington office.

[28] Personal correspondence with A. M. Maglacas, Regional Nursing Adviser, WHO Regional Office for Southeast Asia, September 18 1974.

issues, one can scarcely begin to grasp the nature and significance of the Canadian scene without at least beginning to form some comparisons, in this case, that of Britain, the United States, and Canada.[29]

Britain On the basis of her information to date, it is the author's considered opinion that while nursing research in Britain has been a fairly recent (25-year) development, it would seem to be relatively steady, and remarkably integrative and comprehensive in its character. As with nursing research throughout the world, research in Britain by no means seems to have *permeated* the profession; but, it has begun to gain the status of a distinctive and essential component of health services research there. It may be that, given quality leadership in nursing, nationalized health service systems lend themselves to the more systematic development of nursing research and a greater degree and range of integration of nursing with the larger health services research picture than is true for systems based on private finance and/or systems lacking substantial nursing leadership.

Reimann states that as early as 1871, *The Lancet* (medical journal) "investigated the conditions of night nursing in some of the London hospitals."[30] Some twenty years later the Sanitary Commission reported on "duties, pay, diet and recreation of hospital nurses, as deduced from their own testimony."[31] Several other substantial surveys are cited by Johns[32] and Simpson.[33] From an "organization" standpoint, political parties, government, and *The Lancet* in particular, have played an important role in instigating these earlier projects. During the last two decades, however, nurses and various nursing groups have taken more initiative. For example, the Ward Sisters' Section of the Royal College of Nursing sponsored a research report in 1953, and the Dan Mason Nursing Research Committee, in 1956;[34] the RCN has had a nursing research discussion group since 1960;[35] and the first nursing unit within a UK university, the Univer-

---

[29] For some other comparisons see Reimann, *op. cit.*, p. 324 (re: German Nurses' Association); Aila Leminen, "Finnish Nurses Found Their Own Research Institute," *International Nursing Review* 15 (April 1968), pp. 145–51; and P. V. Prabhu and T. Basappa, "Autonomous Institute of Nursing," *Nursing Journal of India* 64 (October 1973), p. 354.

[30] Reimann, *op. cit.*, p. 325.

[31] *Ibid.*

[32] Ethel M. Johns, "Canada Looks at the Neighbors," *Canadian Nurse* 26 (January 1930), pp. 11–13.

[33] Simpson, *op. cit.*, pp. 233-5.

[34] *Ibid.*, p. 233.

[35] H. Marjorie Simpson, "Research in Nursing in the United Kingdom," *International Nursing Review* 17 (No. 2, 1970) pp. 99–100.

sity of Edinburgh Nursing Studies Unit, was established in 1956.[36] Simpson gives great credit to the University of Edinburgh for its organizational support of the development of nursing research.[37] In a further article, she states that "The Department of Health and Social Security has taken a very practical interest in research in nursing, stimulating the training of nurse research workers, commissioning studies, financing research units and encouraging the use of findings."[38]

Currently, a series of twelve research projects on "The Study of Nursing Care" is being administered by the RCN and the National Council of Nurses of the United Kingdom and sponsored by the Department of Health and Social Security.[39] There would seem to be a definitive trend in Britain toward nursing research organized on a multiagency, multidisciplinary basis. This is not to imply that nursing research is not evolving as an entity in its own right; far from it, for it would seem that unless nursing research *is* an entity in its own right, it is not perceived as relevant on an interdisciplinary basis.

The United States Two of the earliest and most outstanding nursing surveys in the United States, the Goldmark and the Burgess studies,[40] were organized under the Committee for the Study of Nursing Education which, as Johns points out, was interdisciplinary/multiorganizational in its character, with membership from "The National League of Nursing Education, The American Nurses Association, The National Organization for Public Health Nursing, The American Medical College, The American College of Surgeons, The American Hospital Association, and The American Public Health Association."[41]

While it would seem evident that the amount and range of nursing research in the United States exceeds that of any other country, to date no one comprehensive analysis of the evolution and organization of its nursing research exists. There are, however, several valuable accounts of various eras and dimensions of nursing research. The *American Journal of Nursing* and *Nursing Research* both contain many

---

[36] Simpson. "The First Step." *op. cit.*

[37] *Ibid.,* p. 234.

[38] Simpson. "Research in Nursing in the United Kingdom." *op. cit.,* p. 100.

[39] J. K. McFarlane. *The Proper Study of the Nurse;* and Evelyn R. Anderson. *The Role of the Nurse* (London: The Royal College of Nursing. 1970 and 1973. respectively).

[40] The Committee for the Study of Nursing Education. *Nursing and Nursing Education in the United States* (New York: The Macmillan Co., 1923). and *Nurses, Patients and Pocketbooks* (New York: The Committee. 1928). respectively.

[41] Johns, *op. cit.,* p. 11–22.

informative articles by such research leaders as Mary M. Roberts, R. Louise McManus, Lucille Notter, Loretta Heidgerken, and Virginia Henderson.[42]

Abdellah's "overview" of nursing research describes the 175 projects "supported in part by the Division of Nursing, National Institutes of Health, U.S. Department of Health, Education, and Welfare [HEW], between 1958 – 1968."[43] This review stands as considerable testimony to the central importance of the federal government in the funding, if not the shaping, of nursing research and the development of nursing researchers in the United States.

The earliest nursing research unit, "The Institute of Research and Service in Nursing Education," was organized in 1953 at Teacher's College, Columbia University, New York, by that venerated nursing leader, R. Louise McManus, under federal funds;[44] this was followed by the development of the Nursing Research Department in the Walter Reed Army Institute of Research, with a focus upon *clinical* nursing research.[45] And the first "center" for nursing research (i.e., an organizational unit in which researchers from various disciplines "work together in pursuit of problems and research interests,") was established at Wayne State University in 1969. Funded by HEW, it was first called "The Center for Nursing Research," and later renamed "The Center for Health Research."[46]

Among centrally important organizational units specifically committed to nursing research are The American Nurses Association's Commission on Nursing Research, established in 1970 for the purpose of giving "appropriate focus and attention to the research needs of the profession";[47] the Council of Nurse Researchers, established by the

---

[42] E.g., see Virginia Henderson, "Overview of Nursing Research," *Nursing Research* 6 (October, 1957), pp. 61 – 71.

[43] Faye G. Abdellah, "Overview of Nursing Research 1955 – 1968, Part I," *Nursing Research* 19 (January-February 1970), "Part II," (March-April 1970), and "Part III," (May-June 1970), pp. 6 – 17, pp. 151 – 62, and pp. 239 – 51, respectively. Abdellah's "The Development of Nursing Research in U.S.A." *Proceedings of The National Conference on Research in Nursing Practice, February 16 – 18, 1971* (Ottawa: Department of Health and Welfare, 1971), pp. 66 – 80, is also instructive.

[44] See E. M. Vreeland, "Nursing Research Programs of the Public Health Service," *Nursing Research* 13 (Spring 1964), 148 – 58; also see Harriet H. Werley, "This I Believe . . . About Clinical Nursing Research," *Nursing Outlook* 20 (November 1972), pp. 718 – 22.

[45] Harriet H. Werley and Fredericka P. Shea, "The First Center for Research in Nursing," *Nursing Research* 22 (May – June 1973), pp. 217 – 31.

[46] *Ibid.*

[47] "House of Delegates Reports 1972 – 1974," 49th Convention of the American Nurses Association, June 9 – 14, 1974, San Francisco (Kansas City, Missouri: The Association, 1974), p. 68.

ANA upon a recommendation of the NR Commission in 1972;[48] and the American Nurses' Foundation, funded by the ANA and the American Journal of Nursing Company, which provides abstracts of studies for *Nursing Research*, awards grants for a wide variety of nursing research and research development purposes, and publishes the ANA's *Nursing Research Report* and the *International Directory of Nurses with Doctoral Degrees*.[49] Also, there is the "American Academy of Nursing," created in 1973, "a working company of scholars committed to the advancement of the profession," which makes systematic provision for the inclusion of nurse researchers.[50] The substantial contribution of the National League for Nursing, particularly by way of its many valuable surveys and its great historic and current contributions to the amassment of data on nurses and nursing and upgrading faculty and student standards, should be regarded as a crucial factor in "organization" for research. Recently, the ANA and its subsidiaries would seem to have made far more specific structural provision for the organization of nursing research and nursing researchers than the NLN.

The ANA's annual "Nursing Research Conferences," started in 1965 and funded by the Division of Nursing (Manpower, NIH), US Department of Health, Education, and Welfare, represent a substantial contribution to the identification, if not organization, of nursing researchers and nursing research. The federal funds have now run out, and the ANA's Commission on Nursing Research is currently attempting to secure monies for "future research conferences for clinical practitioners of nursing, who are those primarily involved in the implementation of research findings."[51]

In the United States there are several regional bodies relevant to nursing research. For example, the Western Interstate Commission for Higher Education, again under funding from the Division of Nursing, sponsored six substantial conferences in the Western United States on "Communicating Nursing Research."[52] When the funding of these conferences was discontinued, nurses at the 1973 meeting of the Western Council on Higher Education for Nursing formed a new society, the Western Society for Research in Nursing. Their goal is "to support nursing research in the West by continuing the annual

---

48 *Ibid.*, pp. 69 – 70.

49 *Ibid.*, pp. 97 – 8.

50 *Ibid.*, 74 – 5.

51 *Ibid.*, p. 69.

52 Marjorie V. Batey, ed., *Communicating Nursing Research: Collaboration and Competition*, Vol. 6 (Boulder, Colorado: WICHE, December 1973).

research conference and a publication of the proceedings."[53] While the new WSRN, "an integral part of WICHEN," can, on the one hand, be looked at as a type of "regional" organization for nursing research, its impact extends far beyond regional parameters. For example, these are essentially the same people who produced the remarkable 1974 compendium of ongoing and completed nursing research in WICHEN schools of nursing in the West;[54] further, under the direction of a nurse researcher, Dr. Carol Lindeman, WICHE is currently compiling a directory of data-collecting instruments relevant to "studies of health care and health care needs,"[55] a project that has national and international potential.

On the wider scene, the United States Department of Health, Education and Welfare has tentatively announced the establishment of National Health Centers for Health Services Research.[56] It will be interesting to see the extent to which nursing research becomes an integral part of such centers.

Canada At the national level in Canada, one of the most comprehensive instructive documents regarding what type of research has been done, by whom, under whose auspices, and where, are *The Proceedings of the [First] National Conference on Research in Nursing Practice,*[57] which contains three central analyses of Canadian nursing research trends: Pamela E. Poole cites "Research Activities Conducted or Sponsored by Government or Service Agencies, 1965 – 1970"; Rose Imai reports on "Professional Associations and Research Activities"; and Dr. Amy Griffin analyzes the quantity and types of "Nursing Research in Canadian Universities."[58] This symposium stands as testimony to the point that Canadian nursing research has received organizational support, if not impetus, from many sources: universities; the CNA and provincial nursing associations; organizations such as the

---

[53] "Nursing Research Society Formed," *WICHE Reports on Higher Education*, 20 (June 1974), p. 2. Membership is open to non-nurses.

[54] *Newly-Initiated and Completed Research, June 1970-July 1973* (Boulder, Colorado: WICHE and WICHEN, May 1974).

[55] "Nursing Research," *WICHE Reports on Higher Education* 21 (November 1974), p. 1.

[56] Announcement, DHEW Publication HRA. 75 – 3128, Rockville, Maryland, 1975.

[57] *Ibid.,* This conference, attended by 380 nurses, was sponsored by the University of British Columbia School of Nursing under the direction of Dr. Floris King, and was funded by the Department of National Health and Welfare.

[58] *Ibid.,* pp. 81 – 8, 89 – 93, and 94 – 122, respectively. Also instructive is the CNA's "List of Nursing Studies and Surveys Conducted or Supported Either by Provincial Nurses' Associations or the Canadian Nurses' Association," (Ottawa: The Association, January 1971), (mimeographed); and the *C.N.A. Index, op. cit.*

VON, the Canadian Medical Association, and the Canadian Red Cross; and government departments at the provincial and federal levels.

There is no up-to-date analysis of the nature of current national organizational sponsorship of nursing research. It is the author's impression that maybe the role of the Department of [National] Health and Welfare in the facilitation of nursing research is of more crucial significance today than it has been at any previous time; and that the CNA, which previously restricted its role largely to conducting survey research of national import, is evolving research policy[59] and is approaching research facilitation more systematically. This is an important trend, for CNA's role in relation to research has been an uneven one.[60] For example, quite apart from the research recommendations made by various standing committees in previous decades, from 1958 to 1971 a total of five *ad hoc* committees met (usually only once) to develop recommendations regarding CNA's role in research.[61] Then, in 1971, the CNA appointed a "Special Committee on Nursing Research" for a two-year term,[62] followed by another two-year Special Committee, whose term ended in 1975. One wonders, will CNA ensure the continuation of its emerging research thrust?

What other bodies are concerned with organization for nursing research in Canada? The Canadian Association of University Schools of Nursing has a research committee, but to date its activities have been limited; further, it includes only nursing educators. The Canadian Nurses' Foundation, while committed to the furtherance of nursing research, has devoted its monies and efforts primarily to scholarships for graduate study.

More recently, the idea of a "Canadian Council of Nurse Researchers" was raised at the 1973 National Conference on Research in Nursing.[63] As we shall discuss below, the issue of how nurse researchers should be organized in Canada is a highly contentious one.

---

[59] See "Policy Statements on Nursing Research," Minutes of the Board of Directors, June 24, 1972, in which four policies were approved: the utilization of research "to provide a comprehensive picture of the profession"; the encouragement of research activities of member associations, agencies, and individual practitioners; the articulation by CNA of nursing research with health care research groups; and the board's use of expert advice on policies and activities related to research.

[60] Apart from developing and maintaining the finest nursing library in the nation, a crucial resource for nurse researchers.

[61] H. Rose Imai, "C.N.A. Committees on Research: 1950 – 1970," (Ottawa: The Association).

[62] It was this Committee which developed recommendations regarding the policies stated above.

[63] Margaret C. Cahoon, as cited, *Nursing Papers* 6 (Fall. 1974), p. 7 – 8.

One other entity which is of extreme importance in the organization of nursing research is the National Research and Development Program.[64] NHRDP funded the First National Nursing Research Conference (1971), the National Nursing Research Colloquium in Montreal (1973), and the "Third National Nursing Research Conference" in Toronto (1974).[65] It should be emphasized that the organization for these conferences was carried out by one British Columbia, three Quebec, and three Ontario university schools of nursing, respectively. NHRDP has sponsored Health Care Evaluation Seminars across the nation which several nurses have attended and it is a prime funding source for nursing research projects and for research training. In short, within a brief period of time this federal program has become of key importance in the facilitation of the communication of nursing research, the constructive criticism of projects, and the funding of research and researchers. The Medical Research Council of Canada, whose terms of reference apply to clinical nursing research (particularly of a biologic nature), has, to date, not figured as a significant force in nursing research.

At the provincial level in Canada, the majority of provincial nursing associations have some form of research committee,[66] although they are not all very active, and several associations are attempting to increase the research component of their annual conventions. The earlier-cited *Proceedings of the 1971 Conference* contains examples of research undertaken by provincial nursing associations. Three provinces have nurses in their health department research and planning divisions,[67] and some provincial systems study groups employ nurse researchers.[68] At the local level, nursing research is not "organized" to any substantial extent in Canada. There are instances of "local" activity such as sporadic nursing research discussion groups, and workshops on nursing research.[69]

---

[64] Formerly known as the National Health Grant program, and still under the Department of Health and Welfare.

[65] For details of the latter, see Amy E. Griffin, as cited, *Nursing Papers* 6 (Fall 1974). pp. 3–6.

[66] One of the activities of the Alberta Association of Registered Nurses' Research Committee is to provide a yearly update of Ada Simm's compendium, "Nursing Research in Alberta: A Beginning Descriptive Study," unpublished major paper, Division of Health Services Administration, University of Alberta, Edmonton, Fall 1972.

[67] Personal communication from Mary E. Wilson, Department of Health and Social Development, Province of Manitoba, August 23, 1974.

[68] E.g., The Hospital Systems Study Group, Saskatoon, Saskatchewan.

[69] E.g., in the spring of 1975 two such workshops were held at the Universities of Calgary and Alberta, with 100 attending.

At the institutional level there is little systematic organizational provision for nursing research. Even within the majority of university schools of nursing, research tends to be done by a small minority, and teaching loads do not reflect aggressive provision for research. A major exception is the McGill School of Nursing's Research Unit.[70] Within individual health agencies, the writer knows of no public health unit which employs a nurse researcher; very few hospitals have any such positions.[71] In short, organizational aims and objectives may often include research, but to date it tends to be limited to the lip service level.[72] Nevertheless, research is being carried out,[73] but it may well be in the absence of active institutional policy and conducive research climates, not because of them.

ISSUES: DIFFERENCES AND COMMONALITIES

On the basis of the above it would seem readily apparent that if one asks, "How should nursing research and nurse researchers best be organized?"—hundreds of controversies surrounding such facets as purposes, objectives, funding, policy control, and communication begin to emerge. Further, these issues extend beyond the parameters of nursing into the broader areas of health services and health services research; as such, it is not simply a matter of nurses working out systems which suit only nurses.

Some of the key issues are the following: should organization for Canadian nursing research be a central function of the CNA? Should all nurses contribute funds for research organization? Should nurse researchers form under the CNA? Should they unite with other health care researchers and not have a separate association? Who should choose nursing research priorities? Is the centralization of funding for nursing research dangerous, regardless of where those funds are? Given that clients' health and illness needs tend to be interprofessional

---

[70] "McGill Sets Up Research Unit in Nursing and Health Care," *Canadian Nurse* 74 (December 1974), p. 8. Of related interest is the newly-established Health Care Research Unit at the University of Western Ontario, which includes provision for nursing research input and nursing research consultation.

[71] Possibly the earliest to do so was the Nursing Department of the Hospital for Sick Children, Toronto (in the early 1960s). A nurse researcher is now employed in their Systems Study Group.

[72] For a description of a systematic attempt to make research a viable component in one educational institution, see Rozella M. Schlotfeldt, *Creating a Climate for Nursing Research* (Cleveland, Ohio: Frances Payne Bolton School of Nursing, Case Western Reserve University, 1973).

[73] Cahoon, *op. cit.*, 7, estimates that [excluding all graduate research] there are currently "well over a hundred Canadian nurses involved in research."

in nature, is it wise to establish separate professional research units, or does the nursing component get overlooked in multidisciplinary units? How active should nursing be in the larger organization of health services research?[74]

The most recent National Conference on Nursing Research was held in Edmonton[75], and was funded through a grant from NHRDP. The Canadian Nurses' Association has agreed to provide secretariat services for the next national conference, likely to be held in 1977. It is probable that for this conference, nurse researchers will have to provide their own funding. Will they do that? If not, who should?

Research Funding

Issues surrounding nursing research funding extend far beyond those simply related to obtaining funds to carry out a specific project, but we shall examine that aspect first, then turn to some of the other key controversies.

FUNDS FOR PROJECTS

The issue of where nursing research funds should come from is a thorny one. For example, in 1932, the editor of the *INR* advocated that funds for nursing surveys should be sought from the community "as nursing is mainly a community service."[76] Yet to what extent is it the profession's obligation to sponsor its own research? In practical terms, the entire budgets of the CNA and the provincial nursing associations could be swallowed up by a few projects. Further, the research that a professional organization might consider a low priority, such as funding a local project with few implications for national nursing, might be a high priority in terms of the problems in a given hospital or health unit; this raises the further question: to what extent do individual health agencies and/or schools of nursing have a responsibility for funding their own research?

In 1930, Ethel Johns stated that the famous *Burgess Report* was

---

[74] E.g., no nurses were involved in the formulation of The Science Council of Canada's *Science for Health Service, Report No. 22* (Ottawa: The Council, October 1974), which deals extensively with the organization and funding of health services research in Canada. Nursing as it relates to health services is all but unmentioned in the report, and nursing research is totally ignored.

[75] Sponsored by the Schools of Nursing of the Universities of Alberta, Calgary, Manitoba, and Saskatchewan.

[76] Reimann, *op. cit.*, p. 328.

estimated to cost $200 000 over a five-year period[77], the funds coming from "various sources," according to Reimann, "but largely from members of the profession."[78] Fidler states that the *Weir Report*, a three-year study, cost approximately $32 000, 70% of which was under-written by the CNA and 30% by the CMA.[79] A review of the above articles would indicate that sources for funds on research on nursing and nurses in Canada and elsewhere were, up to the 1930s, highly varied in nature—ranging from individually undertaken projects, to political parties, government departments, universities, a famous Brit-ish medical journal, and private foundations, to name but a few. That basic characteristic of variety is still true today; but, in terms of money specifically allotted for nursing research projects in Canada, in the last decade there would seem to have been a trend toward increased government funding, primarily at the federal level.[80] However, no systematic and comprehensive analysis of the funding of Canadian *nursing* research projects exists;[81] thus the nature and extent of such a trend really is not known. For example, it must be underlined that, to date, a substantial proportion of Canadian nursing research has been done by graduate students at their own expense, and by nursing faculty and health agency members, often on their own time, and on a non-funded basis. As such, direct cost figures give us only a hint of the time, equipment, supplies, and publication costs of all the nursing research being done.

The Canadian Nurses' Association maintains an up-to-date inven-tory on the various *sources* of funds for nursing research, ranging from private foundations to federal government bodies. It is easier to find funds for some types of projects than for others. For example, it would seem easier to find funds for a study aimed at reducing costs of nursing care than for a historical project. Also, the less local a project is in its character, the more general appeal it tends to have to granting agencies which are of a national order.

---

[77] Johns, *op. cit.*, p. 12.

[78] Reimann, *op. cit.*, p. 327.

[79] Nettie D. Fidler, "Nursing Research in Canada," *Canadian Nurse* 48 (February 1952), pp. 114 – 5.

[80] For example, the very substantial project, Health Sciences Centre, *A Study of the Effects of a Specific Inservice Education Program for Registered Nurses on Patient Welfare and Hospital Operation* (Winnipeg: The Centre, 1974), was funded by the NHRDP.

[81] Partial estimates are reported by Griffin, *Proceedings, op. cit.*, pp. 96 – 7, and Simms, *op. cit.*, pp. 50 – 1. In *Science for Health Services, op. cit.*, p. 80, it is reported that government funding constitutes approximately 60% of all health sciences research and development monies.

At this point in time, the single most viable funding source for nursing research projects is The National Health Research and Development Program. Monies from this source can be applied to a wide variety of nursing research, including studies, demonstration projects, and research training.

The obtaining of research grants is usually a fairly formidable task involving the selection of a topic of particular merit in terms of the granting agency's goals, the careful preparation of research objectives and the methodology, specification of supplies and equipment needed, and the qualifications of the researchers themselves. Recently, an experienced research consultant told the author that the main reason that many nursing (and other health) research projects are not funded is not for lack of good research ideas, but for lack of skill in developing an adequate project proposal. Put another way, "getting funds" is not necessarily a key determinant; having a sound project proposal usually is.

One last point. As Marc Roberts states, availability of outside funding can influence the quality of the research done. But low quality research can also be traced to "a failure of intellectual imagination...."[82]

RESEARCH TRAINING FUNDS

Clearly, the availability of funds for nursing research projects is meaningless if not counterproductive unless there are nurses adequately prepared to *do* research. Until the late 60s, the most extensive "outside" funding for the research preparation of nurses at the graduate level was the Canadian Nurses' Foundation, the money coming from a Kellogg grant and donations from provincial nursing associations and individuals. The CNF funds are now almost depleted, and while other sources such as the Canadian TB and Respiratory Association awards do exist, the most substantial current source of research training funds is the NHRDP.[83]

One of the basic issues underlying the trend toward a single,[84]

---

[82] *Op. cit.*, pp. 59–60.

[83] Funds are available to nurses for research training, at various levels, from post-RN to the post-doctoral level. They also have been applied to national research training conferences for nurse researchers, Health Care Evaluation Seminars for health personnel, including nurses, short-term studentships, and research fellowships for faculty, nursing researchers, and other researchers who wish to devote themselves to nursing research and research consultation on a full-time basis.

[84] I.e., there are many other sources available to Canadians, such as that of the Florence Nightingale International Foundation, but NHRDP is the one massive

massive funding source for research training is whether there should be more regional or more provincial governmental say in the allocation of such funds and/or should nurses, rather than multidisciplinary health research committees which include nurses, have more say in the granting of research training funds to nurses?

While these are important questions, the more important basic fact is that there now is a well-established policy in Canada to provide funds for research training for a substantial number of nurses in a great variety of ways and settings. Further, there is at least some nursing input into the granting of these funds.

FINANCIAL SPONSORSHIP OF RESEARCH FACILITIES

Werley says, "One way to make explicit and give identity to the research function is through the creation of a research center."[85] In one sense, all health science complexes constitute "research facilities," but in Canada to date, the Research Unit in Nursing and Health Care at the McGill School of Nursing is the only unit *specifically* organized to include nursing research.[86] This unit, now in its fifth year, was established through NHRDP funding.

To look at nursing research institutes internationally is to look at a wide variety of forms of sponsorship, both organizational and financial. The first nursing research unit in the world (Teacher's College, Columbia University, New York) was funded federally; and the first clinical nursing practice unit was a US Army venture.[87] In Britain, the first Nursing Studies Unit (University of Edinburgh) and research fellowships were made possible through a grant to the University and the Royal College of Nursing from Boots the Chemist;[88] the World Health Organization is playing a key role in the development of the New Delhi Indian Institute of Nursing;[89] Leminen states that while

---

source. To the author's knowledge, the only nurse to receive research funding from the Canada Council was Margaret M. Street, in relation to her remarkable biography of Ethel Johns, *Watch-fires on the Mountain* (Toronto: University of Toronto Press, 1973). The Medical Research Council is another source rarely tapped by nursing researchers.

[85] Harriet H. Werley, "This I Believe... About Clinical Nursing Research," *Nursing Outlook* 20 (November 1972), p. 722.

[86] The University of Western Ontario's Health Care Research Unit (established in January 1975) provides for input from, and consultation to, a wide variety of disciplines, including nursing, but it was not organized with a specific focus on nursing.

[87] Werley, p. 718.

[88] Margaret Scott Wright, "Progress and Prospects in Nursing Research Occasional Papers," *Nursing Times*, 1:9 (1971), and Simpson, "The First Step," *op. cit.*, pp. 233 –4.

[89] Maglacas, *op. cit.* See also Prabhu and Basappa, *op. cit.*

the "main founders" of the Sponsoring Association which financially guaranteed the Finnish Nursing Research Institute, which began functioning in April 1966, were the Foundation for Nursing Education and the Finnish Federation of Nurses, but about thirty other organizations, including the League of Physicians, the Finnish Red Cross, and about one hundred individual nurses, physicians, sociologists, psychologists, and economists joined the Sponsoring Association.[90] These examples would suggest at least two generalizations that can be made about nursing research institutes or units: they have just begun to emerge; and their financial bases and organizational sponsorship are varied.

In Canada, it would seem that at least in the next five to ten years, most nursing research projects will continue to be done outside of a "unit" setting. At present, while several major hospitals have "systems" or "work" study units, these rarely include nurses with research training, and as previously mentioned, very few hospitals, health units and schools of nursing have money specifically set aside for nursing research facilities and/or nursing research.

In that nursing is, by its very nature, inextricably linked to the larger phenomenon of health care, a key issue is, "Should 'separate' nursing research units be funded?" As implied earlier, those who say "no" argue that nursing researchers should conduct their work mainly in concert with other health care researchers because nursing is only one dimension of health care service; those who say "yes" argue that unless there is a specific unit with funds specifically allocated to *nursing* research, there will be little such research done and/or the research energies of nurses will be siphoned off into projects in which the emphasis on nursing is minimal, if not nonexistent.

THE NURSE AS PRINCIPAL INVESTIGATOR

Do nurse researchers get equitable treatment from granting bodies? "In the effort to secure funding—a male-dominated area—the nurse researcher confronts the problem of being both a woman—i.e., unscientific—and a nurse—i.e., a caretaker, not a researcher." This statement was made by Dr. Patricia MacElween, Professor, School of Nursing, University of Washington, at the Seventh Annual WICHE Communicating Nursing Research Conference in San Francisco, in 1974.[91] The extent to which this "double trouble" is a problem in Canadian nursing research funding is not known, even in the case of highly qualified nurse researchers. The NHRDP policy is that the

---

[90] Leminen, *op. cit.*, pp. 147–8.
[91] "Nurse Researchers Second Class No More," *WICHE Reports in Higher Education* 20 (June 1974), p. 3.

funding of a project depends, among other considerations,[92] upon (1) its merit in terms of a contribution to the health care field, and (2) the capabilities of the principal investigator.[93] But here we encounter some moot points: to what extent can interdisciplinary teams validly appraise the relative worth of *nursing* research ideas? And to what extent is it feasible to apply the same criteria regarding the qualifications and experience of principal investigators to nurse researchers as to other investigators? In the latter regard, there is less than a handful of nurses across Canada who have the paper qualifications and "proven" research ability that in principle can be expected, say, in the field of basic physiological research. Thus, the extent to which Canadian nurses do, and will in the near future, act as principal investigators depends upon granting committees' interpretations of what constitutes the appropriate background for such a role. If the interpretations are rigid, it is reasonable to expect that substantial projects in nursing will be under the control of non-nurses and/or that there will be few such projects developed.

RELATED FUNDING NEEDS

Space does not permit an adequate examination of the trends, issues, and problems surrounding such topics as funds for research consultation, equipment, communicating findings, and writing critiques, to name but a few.

The funding problems in these areas are compounded by a lack of nurses with research expertise: if one can find the funds, very often one cannot find adequately prepared people. This brings us to our next issue: preparation for nursing research.

Preparation for Nursing Research

There is little controversy, in Canada or elsewhere, about the shortage of nursing research manpower. "Lack of trained research personnel" was the problem mentioned most often at the first formal ICN session on research, in Montreal, in 1969.[94] To the author's knowledge, fewer

---

[92] The general terms of reference are outlined in the *National Health Research and Development Manual*, Ottawa: Health and Welfare Canada, the most recent edition to be released early in 1975. Susan R. Gortner, "Research in Nursing: The Federal Interest and Grant Program," *American Journal of Nursing*, 73 (June 1973), explains some of the major federal requirements applied in the United States, pp. 1052–5.

[93] I.e., the person to whom the research funds are awarded.

[94] H. Marjorie Simpson, "Nursing Research," *op. cit.*, p. 110.

than ten nurses in Canada are currently employed on a full-time basis as nurse researchers; most of these nurses have master's degrees. The first nurse to be employed as a full-time nursing research consultant was Pamela E. Poole, in 1965, by the Department of National Health and Welfare.[95]

While all doctoral degrees include preparation for research, that factor does not "guarantee" further research activity. Dean Donna Diers of Yale University maintains that, on the basis of a recent survey of the 676 nurses in the United States with doctoral degrees, "only 21 indicated any real activity in research, although another 171 said research was 'one of my position responsibilities.' "[96]

The preparation issue involves several dimensions; some of the key ones are the following: preparation for what kinds of research functions and roles, and how many? When should research training begin? What research should be taught? How should research be taught? Is there a limit to the amounts and types of preparation needed?

There are many "research roles" in nursing. Ideally, the most universal role is that of utilizer (see Fig. 1), for unless research is reflected ultimately in nursing practice, all the other research roles take on a different, if not irrelevant, social meaning. Closely related to the role of research utilizer are those of problem-suggester and/or data-collector, roles which practicing nurses can fulfill to varying degrees.[97] There seems to be considerable controversy over whether or not research is every nurse's business.[98] Such issues have profound educational implications, for preparation for research and preparation for what Brotherston describes as awareness of the *need* for research (in Simpson's words "research-mindedness") are quite different matters.[99]

A distinction one can make between what might be termed a "technical" nurse and a "professional" nurse is that the former *can*,

---

[95] Corroborated through personal correspondence, September 10, 1974.

[96] Quoted in "Nursing Research: More Studies of Patient Care, Nursing Practice," *WICHE Reports on Higher Education* 20 (November 1973), p. 2.

[97] E.g., see Stinson, "Staff Nurse Involvement," *op. cit.,* p. 30. See also Loretta E. Heidgerken, "Nursing Research—Its Role in Research Activities in Nursing," *Nursing Research* 11 (Summer 1962), pp. 140–3.

[98] E.g., see Margaret Cahoon, "Every Nurse Must Become Involved in Research in Nursing," the *Canadian Nurse* 70 (August 1974), p. 12; and Marjory Hayes, "Nursing Research is Not Everybody's Business," the *Canadian Nurse* 70 (October 1974), p. 17; and subsequent "Letters to the Editor," up to January 1975.

[99] J. H. F. Brotherston, as cited by Simpson in "The First Step," *op. cit.,* p. 233, and Simpson's term, p. 243.

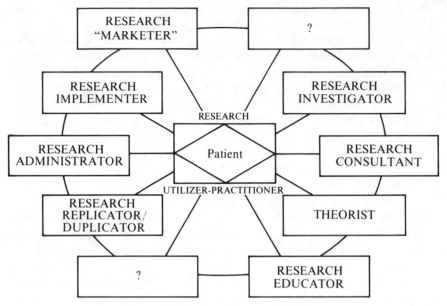

Figure 1. Nursing Research Roles.

conceivably, base her practice on research; the latter *must*. As such, the professional nurse requires, at minimum, what can be thought of as "consumer skills" in research. About this point there seems to be little controversy. But what kinds of preparation does having "consumer skills" involve? There is much debate on this question.

UNDERGRADUATE

Being able to read and recite articles is one thing; being able to examine and analyze them in terms of their validity and their implications for nursing practice is quite another. Nursing literature is filled with examples of unsound research; it contains many examples of "findings" which provide unsound bases for changing one's practice. For these reasons, even preparation at the consumer level is a substantial matter.

The most fundamental "preparation" for research is the desire and ability to think critically and constructively, and the desire and ability to be exploratory. But to what extent can such knowledge, skills, and attitudes be taught? No research course is worth anything if, through it, these elements are not being developed. Conversely, it *can* be argued that the spirit of enquiry can be taught in the absence of research courses as such. The possession of a university degree, even at the doctoral level, does not guarantee that a person is a competent researcher.

Too, one must consider the point that a great deal about research can be learned from participating in increasingly more complex projects. Indeed, in the latter regard, the author knows a British nurse, now in her early fifties, who has no degree whatsoever, yet is a brilliant nurse researcher. She learned largely by studying on her own and doing research under the guidance of skilled UK researchers. Another example is that of the late Kay Sjoberg, the young B.Sc. nurse who made such a substantial contribution to the initial "Levels of Care" research of the Hospital Systems Study Group in Saskatoon. However, there is so much to learn about research that it is only in the rare instance that sound research preparation and high research productivity can occur in the absence of substantial amounts and kinds of formalized instruction.

There seems to be a trend (verbal at least, if not yet realized) in Canadian and US undergraduate nursing programs to systematically teach the elements of nursing research.[100] The central controversies about what undergraduate students should be taught revolve around the extent to which there should be an emphasis on *content*, (an emphasis upon what research questions, findings and conclusions are contained in nursing research articles and reports) and emphasis upon research *methods and statistics* (i.e., the why and how of research). Within the latter area there is debate about the value of nurses' learning general research methods and statistics, as opposed to these areas being taught within a *nursing* framework. Both at the undergraduate and graduate levels there is controversy, too, about the extent to which rigorous skills in the location and critical analysis of literature should be insisted upon, and to what extent skills must be taught regarding the dynamics of research development, including the process of generating funding proposals.

GRADUATE

The above controversies are even more acute at the master's and doctoral levels. While it is agreed in principle that research is an integral part of education at the master's level, some argue that at best only skilled consumers can be prepared at the master's level, others argue that it is possible to prepare a beginning researcher who can design and carry out studies independently. From a practical stand-

---

[100] Simpson, "Nursing Research," *op. cit.*, pp. 112 – 3, reports "some provision" for opportunities for "research-mindedness" for non-graduate nurses in the United Kingdom and Sweden.

point, given the fact that Canada has only some forty nurses with doctorates and fewer than a thousand with master's degrees,[101] the development of nursing research does, and will, depend very heavily upon nurses prepared at the master's level. On this basis alone, sound preparation in nursing research methods and statistics is a must in master's programs. The one-year master's program in nursing with only moderate emphasis upon nursing research is not uncommon in the US. In Canada, the predominant model in the six graduate programs in nursing is the two-academic-year program, with considerable emphasis upon nursing research. Whether or not all master's students should be required to do a thesis is still a controversial point. Most Canadian nursing graduate schools offer a choice between a thesis and a major paper, the latter route involving additional course work. In the United States, the thesis at the master's level would appear to have become the exception rather than the rule; in Britain, the opposite would seem true. The related issue of whether or not it makes sense to have nurses prepared at master's and doctoral levels in fields other than nursing is a crucial one. On the one hand, virtually all realms of knowledge are relevant to the practice of, and thus to research in, nursing. Thus, logically, nurses especially prepared in such areas as sociology, psychology, economics, and others, can bring special expertise to bear on nursing problems. But it can also be argued that such persons tend to have limited substantive nursing expertise so they do *not* view nursing research through a "nursing" lens; rather, they tend to see different research questions and priorities, and tend to utilize research techniques that may not be appropriate for examining what are uniquely "nursing" situations. A related issue, the extent to which *nursing* theory is a requisite for preparation for nursing research, is also unresolved.[102]

RESEARCH ROLES

Referring back to Figure 1 we should emphasize that there is controversy over what kinds of "research roles" are needed in nursing. The circles with question marks are intended to remind readers that we simply do not know what new needs and roles may emerge. The debate over research roles is an important one, for preparation must

---

[101] Canadian Nurses' Association, *Countdown, 1973* (Ottawa: The Association, 1974), p. 48. Even in 1932, Fidler, *op. cit.*, p. 115, noted that Canada had proportionately fewer nurses with research preparation than did the United States.

[102] These issues are not unique to Canadian nursing. For example, see Downs, *op. cit.*, pp. 309 – 404; and Ada Jacox, "The Research Component in the Nursing Service Administration Master's Programs," *Journal of Nursing Service Administration* 4 (March-April 1974), pp. 35 – 9.

be based upon the major functions undertaken by researchers.

Cronbach's analysis of research roles in education would suggest a minimum of three areas of function: the investigator, the developer-tester of research ideas and findings, and the "marketer" or disseminator of research ideas.[103] The complexity of the issue of preparation for research becomes even more apparent when we consider the range and variation of preparation potentially needed *within* any one of the roles cited in Figure 1. For example, a nursing theorest must be knowledgeable not only about nursing, but about theory-building. The research administrator must have not only a sound grasp of how to evolve research program priorities and how to evaluate and fund research proposals, but also must know a great deal about recruiting, rewarding, supporting, and challenging research personnel, setting up research contracts, and so on. Those who take on a full-time role of implementor of nursing research findings must have the ability to tailor the findings of others to fit the needs of particular groups and agencies. The investigator who might be well-prepared to design and carry out a study on nursing staff's attitudes and behaviors toward mothers of still-born infants may well lack the kinds of preparation required to carry out a nurse manpower study; and a nursing research consultant who advises interdisciplinary health research teams must be prepared in much greater breadth than nursing research alone, or she will not be able to grasp the difficulties and/or possibilities regarding the nursing implications of a given project. Added to these vast complexities is the fact that one could have expertise in any one of the above roles in relation to experimental research, yet be considerably unfit to assume any of these roles if the focus were on historical research.

While relatively few members of any profession take on the above roles on a full-time basis, the research utilizer-practitioner role is a crucial one. Cahoon describes this role as including such aspects as supporting patients who are research subjects, and ensuring that ethical practices are employed.[104]

What kinds of nurse researchers are needed and how many are needed? The answer depends not only on factors *within* nursing (research preparation, the kinds of nursing research being undertaken, and the ways in which the research work is apportioned), but also upon factors *outside* nursing (the priority given to research in health agencies, monetary and honorific rewards for doing research, the atti-

---

[103] Lee J. Cronbach, "The Role of the University in Improving Education," *Phi Delta Kappan* 42 (June 1966), pp. 539 – 45.

[104] Cahoon, "Every Nurse," *op. cit.,* p. 12.

tudes of others [e.g., physicians] toward nursing research, and the availability of research funds and research consultation services).[105]

At whatever level nurses are initially prepared, that is only a mere beginning, for research preparation is a lifelong process. There is no upper limit to the development of knowledge and its application to the improvement of nursing care.

Nursing Research Priorities

What are the priorities in nursing research, and for whom? This double-barrelled question is not only controversial but is itself a priority.

Maximum use of resources requires judicious decision-making. Yet what *does* constitute "maximum use" of nursing research resources?

In one sense, the nature of priorities in nursing research is very similar to that in other fields of research, the above questions being one such example; in other ways, it is not. The case of control of the allocation of funds to a given research area is an example. In Canada, medical researchers have almost exclusive control of the allocation of over $48 million of research funds per year;[106] there is no funding equivalent to the United States' Division of Nursing.[107]

A *comprehensive* current analysis of nursing research priorities does not exist, but themes which would seem to be dominant include the following: research as a priority in itself; phases and types, content, and methodological priorities; and, infrastructure priorities.

RESEARCH AS A PRIORITY

Poole and Stinson, in their discussion on the low value placed on nursing research in Canada, state:

Research has been seen as a 'luxury item,' an intellectual exercise one can go through if one wants, but there is very little appreciation of what nursing research can mean for nursing practice. One of the fundamental

---

[105] For a wider exploration of factors influencing the development of nursing research, see Poole and Stinson, *op. cit.*, pp. 187 – 8.

[106] For more specific figures, see Science Council of Canada, *op. cit.*, p. 82.

[107] For a nursing research analyst's view of the impact of the Division of Nursing funds in the United States, see Marjorie V. Batey, in "Reflections—and the Way Ahead," *Communicating Nursing Research: Collaboration and Competition, op. cit.*, pp. 217 – 9.

reasons for this attitude may lie in the fact that much of nursing research is quite useless, either because the ideas examined or the methods used have been weak, and/or that the topics studied have been irrelevant to nursing practice.[108]

In Canada, if one takes into account the few nurses actually employed to do research; the few health agency budgets which provide for nursing research; the considerable paucity of nursing research literature; the inadequate organization of nurse researchers; the minimal curriculum provision for research; and the comparative lack of reward for doing research, one must conclude that, at this point in time, research is not a priority. This state of affairs is not peculiar to Canada. An American nurse states, "Although the nursing literature stresses research as a very important activity for the nursing profession, many professional nurses even among those who have pursued graduate study, do not give a very high priority to research".[109]

The author remembers her mother describing what a novelty it was for their family to have oranges in the early 1900s. Due to the conditions of the times, oranges were seen only rarely. Now they have become a daily part of most families' diets. It would seem that nursing research, even if valued considerably in principle, is as yet far from being a priority in practical terms, much less part of nursing's "daily diet."

CONTENT, PHASES AND TYPES, AND METHODOLOGICAL PRIORITIES

"What would be worthwhile to study?" As Marc Roberts, an economist, says, it is "disconcertingly difficult to make such decisions."[110] The topics on which nursing research has focused vary widely, vary between countries, and vary over time.

The nursing literature up to the 1950s suggests that national descriptive surveys about nurses and nursing education, very often sponsored by national groups, were the top priority.

Fidler's 1952 overview of Canadian nursing research cites the "Weir Report" (1932) as "The first actual research in this country...." Fidler states that at that time, research "in professional and public relations in nursing education and nursing service" were the shared priorities in both the American Master Plan of the American Nurses'

---

[108] Poole and Stinson, *op. cit.*, p. 188.
[109] Loretta E. Heidgerken, "The Research Process," in *Proceedings of The National Conference on Research in Nursing Practice, op. cit.*, p. 136.
[110] *Op. cit.*, p. 59.

Association, and the Canadian plan, but that the latter also contained a third stated priority, research on the organized profession.[111] A gross analysis of the literature up to the 60s would suggest that both internationally[112] and in Canada[113], surveys (particularly national surveys dealing with standards of education and/or working conditions of nurses) were given the highest research priority by organized nursing. Poole's 1965 – 70 overview of government or service agency sponsored research in Canada indicates particular content emphasis on the analysis of roles and functions of nursing personnel and on patient classification systems, and relatively few citations of direct patient care research,[114] whereas Griffin's analysis[115] of "Nursing Research in Canadian Universities," for the period 1960 – 70 indicates a predominant emphasis on the "patient care" category, with about half of the remaining research on nursing education and nursing service, with minimal (less than 15%) attention to the latter.[116] In contrast, in her analysis of nursing research in Alberta, 1949 – 73, Simms reports that almost half of the projects focused on nursing administration, approximately one third on nursing education, and the remainder on nursing practice.[117]

The author's analysis of Abdellah's 1955 – 68 overview[118] indicates relatively low emphasis on clinical nursing research, model and theory development, and health economic systems as they pertain to nursing, and roughly twenty-five projects reported in each of the areas of measurement and impact of patient care systems, organization of these systems, nursing roles, and health manpower in nursing. Abdellah emphasizes the importance of clinical nursing research as a current priority.

Simpson's analysis of twenty-five years of nursing research in Britain indicates a considerable number of studies in nursing educa-

---

[111] Fidler, *op. cit.*, pp. 114 – 5.

[112] E.g., see Reimann, *op. cit.*, pp. 323 – 8; Simpson, "The First Step," *op. cit.*, pp. 231 – 47; and Johns, *op. cit.*, pp. 11 – 13.

[113] Rose Imai, "Professional Associations and Research Activities in Nursing in Canada," *Proceedings of the 1971 Ottawa Conference, op. cit.*, pp. 89 – 93.

[114] Poole, "Research Activities in Nursing Conducted or Sponsored by Government or Service Agencies, 1965 – 70," *ibid.*, pp. 81 – 8.

[115] Griffin, *ibid.*, pp. 94 – 122, especially pp. 103 – 6.

[116] Simms, *op. cit.*, p. 26, notes that Poole reported some thirty-eight studies from her population over a five-year period, whereas Griffin reported one hundred and ninety-three studies over a ten-year period.

[117] *Ibid*, p. 54.

[118] "Overview of Nursing Research," *op. cit.*

tion and manpower, and a growing emphasis upon research in nursing practice.[119]

On the basis of the contemporary international and Canadian literature,[120] and a gross analysis of research conference[121] and committee themes, it appears that nursing practice is the most talked about current research priority, especially experimental evaluative nursing care research.

A priority which is all but ignored is research on *nursing research*.[122] In the author's view, this is likely to be a most productive area of enquiry.

In the nursing literature, only occasional attempts have been made to rationalize content priorities in nursing research explicitly in terms of content priorities within the *larger* framework of health services research.[123]

Implementation of findings is a much talked about nursing research priority. Caution about this thrust must be exercised, for unless research findings are safe to apply, implementing them is a foolhardy and dangerous business. To date, findings from the vast

---

[119] Simpson, A., "The First Step," *op. cit.*, pp. 235 – 41.

[120] E.g., "C.N.A. Special Committee on Research Report to the Board," Ottawa: The Canadian Nurses' Association, April 1973; "A.N.A. Blueprint for Research in Nursing," *American Journal of Nursing* 62 (August 1962), 69 – 71; Lucille E. Notter, "Twelve Years and Sixty Editorials Later," *Nursing Research* 22 (September – October 1973), p. 387; Lucille E. Notter, *Essentials of Nursing Research* (New York: Springer Publishing Co., Inc., 1974), pp. 6 – 10; Reimann, *op. cit.*, pp. 323 – 8; Simpson, "Nursing Research," *op. cit.*, pp. 110 – 34; Faye G. Abdellah in Abdellah, *et al.*, *New Directions in Patient-Centered Nursing* (New York: The Macmillan Co., 1973), pp. 526 – 36, 546; WICHE and the WICHEN Regional Program for Nursing Education, *Delphi Survey of Clinical Nursing Research Priorities*, Carol A. Lindeman, Project Director (Boulder, Colorado: WICHE, August 1974). See also Fredericke Dittrich, "Perspectives for Nursing in Austria," *International Nursing Review* 20 (November – December 1973), pp. 171 – 3, for differences and similarities.

[121] E.g., *Proceedings of the Colloquium on Nursing Research, March 28 – 30 1973*(Montreal, Quebec: School of Nursing, McGill University, 1973).

[122] One such exception is Vida Jane Swartzentruber, "Research Relative to the Process of Nursing done by Faculty of Baccalaureate and Masters Nursing Programs." Unpublished Ed.D. dissertation, Columbia University, New York, 1970.

[123] E.g., within such frameworks as described by Marc Lalonde, *A New Perspective on the Health of Canadians* (Ottawa: Department of National Health and Welfare, April 1974); and The Economic Council of Canada, *Proceedings of the National Economic Conference: Priorities in Transition Montreal, December 1, 2 and 3, 1974* (Ottawa: Information Canada, 1975). And on the United States scene, Robert Van Hoek, "Bureau of Health Services Research and Evaluation Statement of Program Priorities" (Rockville, Maryland: Public Health Service Resources Administration, Department of HEW, September 28, 1973). See also Evelyn Flook, "Health Services R and D in Perspective," *American Journal of Public Health* 63 (August 1973), 681 – 6.

majority of nursing research are basically invalid and/or not generalizable to a substantial range of nursing situations.[124] This restriction pertains also to the wider field of health services research.

There is great controversy about the extent to which meaningful research can be done in absence of definitive nursing theory;[125] and much debate about the relative merits of and need for descriptive, experimental, and historical[126] approaches to problems significant to nursing.

METHODOLOGY

The issue of nursing research methodology would seem to be a search for improved validity in the strict research sense, yet it would also seem to constitute a symptom of a quest for a research, if not nursing, identity. In the author's opinion, neither of these motivations is inconsequential—or neurotic.

Within the debate as to the relative merits of deductive versus inductive approaches, there are nurse researchers, and indeed institutions, which seem to align themselves heavily with one or another.[127]

Regarding the point that research methods must be consonant with the nature of the phenomenon in question, the dangers of imposing existing social and physical science methods on the study of nursing is highly analogous to the situation social scientists faced in the early 1900s.

In 1929, Mannheim stated:

For it is not to be denied that the carrying over of the methods of natural science to the social sciences gradually leads to a situation where one no longer asks what one would like to know and what will be of decisive significance for the next step in social development, but attempts only to deal

---

[124] Simpson, "The First Step," *op. cit.*, p. 239 writes, "Many of the studies are small scale and in themselves inconclusive." In the author's opinion, this statement is applicable to the majority of nursing research, Canada included. See also Donald O. Anderson, "The Double Standard of R and D," Canadian *Journal of Public Health* 63 (July – August 1972), 317 – 26, regarding implementation issues.

[125] E.g., Rozella M. Schlotfeldt, "The Significance of Empirical Research for Nursing," *Nursing Research* 20 (March – April 1971), 140 – 2; Florence S. Downs "Some Critical Issues in Nursing Research," *Nursing Forum* 8 (No. 4, 1969), pp. 392—404; and Ada Jacox, "Theory Construction in Nursing: An Overview," *Nursing Research* 23 (January – February 1974), pp. 4 – 13. Jacox also emphasizes the "practical," in "Nursing Research and the Clinician," *Nursing Outlook* 22 (June 1974), pp. 382 – 5.

[126] E.g., see Mildred E. Newton, "The Case for Historical Research," *Nursing Research* 14 (Winter 1965), pp. 20 – 6.

[127] E.g., the McGill Unit would seem to favor the inductive.

with those complexes of facts which are measurable according to a certain
already existent method. Instead of attempting to discover what is most
significant with the highest degree of precision possible under the existing
circumstances, one tends to be content to attribute importance to what is
measurable merely because it happens to be measurable.[128]

This concern still exists within the social sciences.[129] While many
nursing researchers seem to merrily apply methods, techniques and
instruments from other fields of enquiries, there is deep concern on
the parts of some about the necessity of evolving ways and means of
enquiry unique to the special measurement problems in nursing. So
far as identity is concerned one wonders if some syllogistic thinking is
going on in the minds of some, to the effect that if only we did have
distinctive research approaches, surely then nursing would be given its
proper accord. Yet to the extent that nursing having its "own" methodology is not only a correlate of, but a condition for, fraternal,
financial, and policy recognition in the larger research and health
services fields, identity is by no means an inconsequential factor.

INFRASTRUCTURE PRIORITIES

It is one thing to view research as a product, as a design and set of
findings and conclusions available in printed form; it is quite another
to see it as a complex process dependent upon masses of different
types of inputs at different times. Within the latter context, some of
the most controversial issues of the day surround the priorities of
communication, ethics, rewards, education, consultation, and leadership.

The resources upon which sound research communication depend
are complex—and crucial. For example, Virginia Henderson's scholarly
and internationally important work in directing the Yale University
School of Nursing's *Nursing Studies Index* is, in this author's opinion,
the most significant single contribution to modern nursing research.

Publication is another crucial priority. Currently, the *Canadian*
Nurse devotes little space to nursing research. While some nurses see
this as deplorable, others argue that most of the 100 000 subscribers
are not interested in such content. A few years ago the editors experi-

---

[128] Karl Mannheim, *Ideology and Utopia.* Translation by Louis Wirth and Edward
Shills [Originally published in German in 1929] (New York: Atarcourt, Brace and
World, Inc., n.d.), pp. 51 – 2.

[129] E.g., Steven Weinberg states his distrust of those " . . . who too confidently apply
the methods of the natural sciences to human affairs." See "Reflections of a
Working Scientist," *Daedalus* 103 (Summer 1974), pp. 33 – 45.

mented with a "Research Corner," and it failed. Would such a technique work today? The McGill *Nursing Papers* is a prime outlet for research pertaining to nursing educators.

The nursing world owes much to *Nursing Research* and to such groups as the ANA and WICHE for their leadership in the publication area. The *Journal of Nursing Service Administration* would seem to be giving increasing priority to nursing research, and the newly established British *Journal of Advanced Nursing* is clearly giving a high priority to nursing research.

What kinds of nursing research outlets does Canada need? Should publication be restricted only to exemplary research? Should as much emphasis be placed on research critiques as on reports? Given that so few nurses are interested in research, how should publications be funded? Should a combined health research journal be initiated?

Publication is one thing, development and maintenance of adequate libraries another. Largely to the credit of CNA's Librarian, Margaret Parkin,[130] there is at least one substantial nursing library in Canada, but, by and large, fine nursing libraries are still a rarity not only within health agencies, but also in universities.

It is widely acknowledged that research conferences are a crucial element in communication, yet in Canada such conferences directly affect only a small number of nurses, and the impact upon related health groups is unknown. Should the CNA be taking more leadership? Should nurse researchers aggressively seek entrance to other health research groups?

As pressing a priority, and perhaps an even more complex communications problem, is the articulation of nursing research with the "outside," for example with medical groups, government policy makers, consumer associations. An interesting project in itself would be to identify others' perceptions and misconceptions about nursing research.

There is little debate about the theme that nursing research should be ethically sound.[131] But there are those who contest that nurses do not have the right to do research on patients except with the approval of physicians.[132] Who "owns" the patient? The patient, perhaps? Pro-

---

[130] Parkin's "Information Resources for Nursing Research," the *Canadian Nurse* 68 (March 1972), pp. 40 – 3 is instructive.

[131] See "Ethics of Nursing Research," the *Canadian Nurse* 68 (September 1972), pp. 23 – 5.

[132] For some interesting discussion on this point, see "Nurse Researchers Second Class No More," *WICHE Report on Higher Education* 20 (June 1974), p. 3; and Leslie Degner, "Decisions Influencing Access to Data," *Decision-Making in Nursing Research*, John D. Godden and Margaret C. Cahoon eds. (Don Mills, Ontario: Thistle Printing, n.d. [©1975], pp. 60 – 2. Also, *Communicating Nursing Research*, *Vol. 7* M. V. Batey, ed. (Boulder, Colorado: WICHE, ©1974), in which this issue is discussed.

tection of human rights is a crucial issue in nursing research today.

In the Skinnerian sense it can be argued that the kinds and amounts of nursing research produced are a function of the reward systems that exist. While such factors as recognition of ideas, specific honors and awards, financial recognition, and increased status constitute important dimensions of any research reward system, having the *time* to do research can also be thought of as a "reward."

Mary M. Roberts writes, "I have often wondered how Ehrlich, doing those 600 experiments [on evolving a drug to combat syphilis], would have felt before he found 606 [the drug salvarsan], if he had been constantly besought, as he worked in his laboratory, to go out and take care of people who were actually suffering from syphilis at the time."[133] Unless there is provision for time for research, whether it is in designing projects responding to questionnaires,[134] or whatever, those involved are not likely to see research as a worthy cause. A great proportion of nursing research has been accomplished in the absence of, or even in spite of, the reward "system," rather than because of it. Perhaps the intrinsic benefit of research is the greatest motivating factor.

Education for nursing research is a much talked about priority, but what are the specific needs and priorities? Should education *about* nursing research permeate the curricula of all health sciences programs? If yes, how many educators are equipped to handle such a task?

There is widespread agreement regarding the need for improved nursing research consultation services in Canada. But how can such services best be provided? Should the CNA and/or provincial associations provide for research consultants? should government? Would active nurse researchers be prepared to travel back and forth across the country consulting on others' projects? Are the consultation needs so diverse that we need consultation teams? What kinds of consultation services could be more adequately developed at local levels? Even with sound consultation services, having competent project directors is still a crucial factor, and the supply is grossly inadequate. Is the idea of national consultation services therefore premature—or is it all the more important?

Within the above priorities, where is the leadership for action to come from? In analyzing the past 25 years of nursing research, Simpson maintains, "There has been no charismatic leader but a slow

---

[133] Roberts, M. M., "Private Duty Nurses," *American Journal of Nursing* 34 (July 1934), pp. 657 – 65.

[134] Johns, *op. cit.*, pp. 12 – 13 underlines the time it takes to respond to survey questionnaires and collect data of other kinds.

growth springing from a variety of sources."[135] She says:

Despite many detractors, nurses have been fortunate to find help and encouragement from experienced research workers from a wide range of disciplines and from some nurses in senior positions far sighted enough to recognize that research in nursing and nurse research workers have an important contribution to make to the development of professional practice and patient care.[136]

All of the six issues outlined in this chapter can be thought of as arguments surrounding better ways and means of achieving the goals of explanation, prediction and control. These goals and issues are fundamental to the larger issue, "What is nursing?"

Summary

The issues in Canadian nursing research fall into six interrelated areas:

1. What Is It?

Nursing research is both that systematic enquiry which requires the expertise of nurses to generate, formulate, carry out, interpret, and/or implement; and it is an attitude, a habit of asking, "I wonder what would happen if ... ?" in relation to all aspects of nursing.

2. Why Nursing Research?

On the one hand nursing research can be viewed as a necessary basis for making decisions about nursing practice; on the other, the emergence of nursing research can be viewed as a normal stage in the development of a profession in any society that places value on rational enquiry.

3. Organization

The issues underlying organization for nursing research and nursing researchers center upon research as a professional organizational priority, funding for research organization, and a multitude

---

135 Simpson, "The First Step," *op. cit.*, p. 242.
136 *Ibid.*, p. 243.

of questions as to what should be the roles of nursing associations at various levels, other associations and governments (especially federal governments), in relation to providing mechanisms for the furtherance of nursing research and the development and association of nurse researchers.

4. *Funding*

The funding of nursing research and the training of nurse researchers continues to be highly varied in the amounts and sources, both internationally and nationally; there seems to be a definitive trend in Canada toward federal funding (and thus federal control); there is a nascent international trend toward organized nursing research units, as yet only barely reflected in Canada; and while it would seem vastly apparent that funding is a key factor in the growth and development of nursing research, it is by no means the sole determinant. The main issues seem to revolve around control, amounts, and funding priorities, and the extent to which nursing research is the responsibility of nursing as such—or of society as a whole.

5. *Preparation*

Preparation for nursing research is both a highly controversial matter, and an extremely difficult practical question in terms of educational planning and resources. As in other fields of research training, really very little is known about what kinds of preparation make a nurse researcher tick. Put another way, there has been little research on the education of nurse researchers. As such, educational preparation is, as yet, based largely not only on tradition, but on tradition from non-nursing fields. Even with all these "unknowns," it would seem reasonable to maintain that Canada does need more nurses prepared at more advanced levels, and prepared to take on a variety of research roles.

6. *Priorities*

While there is much lip-service paid to the importance of research in nursing, in Canada and elsewhere, it would not, as yet, seem to be a top priority in terms of the talent, time, money, and energy allotted. Much of the earlier nursing research focused upon national surveys. Until the 60s, at least, nursing education was the predominant research focus. More recently, the top priority being advocated is clinical nursing practice. The need for research on nursing research is practically ignored. There is wide controversy surrounding the questions of methodology for nursing research, and lack of agreement as to the relative need for historical, descriptive, and experimental research. Within the issue of structure for research support and development, communications, ethics, rewards, education, consultation, and leadership are seen to be prime issues.

These several issues would seem to constitute varying opinions about the degree to which nursing should commit itself to research, and within that question, how nursing can better approach the goals of explanation, prediction, and control. These goals and issues are fundamental to the larger issue, "What is nursing?"

2

Nursing and Interdisciplinary Practice

M. RUTH ELLIOTT, R.N., M.S.

- Nursing and medicine, as the two major health professions have the greatest potential to improve, through collaborative efforts, the quality and quantity of health care. . . . Collaboration between the professions and collegial relationships between its members are advanced by innovative, idealistic educators, administrators, and organizers in nursing. But there are precious few supporters of this line of thinking in medicine or, indeed, among the rank and file of nurses. Why?

- Does Canadian nursing recruit individuals who tend to reflect the same attitudes and values already possessed by practising nurses or, are we inviting prospective nurses with ideas and values quite different from the established norm and, are we willing to listen, to learn, and even to change?

- One of the greatest hurdles that has prevented nurses and doctors from communicating effectively as team members is organization.

- A part of being a member of a highly interdependent team is the need to develop new loyalties and learn some new skills not anticipated or covered during individual training.

- Nursing has the potential to lead the way in educating for teamwork, utilizing as models those team structures that have developed at the community, or "grass roots," level and building upon them.

Introduction

Nursing and medicine, as the two major health professions, have the greatest potential to improve, through collaborative efforts, the quality and quantity of health care.... Collaboration between the professions and collegial relationships between its members are advanced by innovative, idealistic educators, administrators, and organizers in nursing. But there are precious few supporters of this line of thinking in medicine or, indeed, among the rank and file of nurses. Why?[1]

It is broadly recognized that the health of Canadians is dependent upon (1) the quality of research in the fields of physical, mental, and emotional health, and (2) the effectiveness of the health care delivery system based upon an enlightened research program. It is axiomatic that in both these facets of health care, the health professions should play complementary and mutually supportive roles. The focus of this paper will be upon the role of the nurse, particularly as it pertains to the health care delivery system, with some reference to consequent implications for nursing education. In order that the health professionals, workers, psychologists, medical doctors, *et al.*, may function effectively in a collegial manner, certain role changes seem inevitable. In the case of the nurse, this would appear to mean an expanded role with more independence, interdependence, and freedom to apply her professional expertise.

---

[1] Robert A. Hoekelman, "Nurse-Physician Relationships," *American Journal of Nursing*, July 1975, p. 1150.

The Expanded Role of the Nurse:
Independent Practitioner or Physician's Assistant?

Ingeborg Mauksch maintains that:

The emergence of the role called "nurse practitioner" may well be the most significant event in nursing during the last 30 years.[2]

To distinguish the role of the nurse practitioner from that of the physician's assistant, Mauksch describes a number of distinguishing characteristics of the former. The nurse practitioner is accountable to herself and to her clients. She applies to the nursing process a broad background of nursing theory and research, behaves as a decision-maker and risk-taker, and delivers health care interdependently with other health professions. In contrast, the physician's assistant is one who anticipates the physician's needs, carries out his orders and implements, usually without question, the rules and regulations of the hospital or clinic. She is not normally a decision-maker.

One project, designed to test the viability of the concept of the expanded role of the nurse as independent practitioner, was undertaken at the University of British Columbia's Health Sciences Centre Hospital. The project, known as "The Primary Therapist Project,"[3] was conducted in the hospital's in-patient psychiatric unit. In this project, nurses functioned at three levels: the associate nurse level, in which the nurse was responsible to the primary nurse; the primary nurse level, in which the nurse took 24-hour responsibility for planning nursing care; and, the nurse primary therapist level, in which a nurse had the total responsibility for all components of the patient's care. Thus, the nurse primary therapist could be considered in most respects as an "independent practitioner." At the conclusion of the primary therapist project, both nurses who served as primary therapists were asked to respond to the central hypothesis of the study, namely: Can nurses do independent therapy, and can nurses be accountable for therapy? Their responses, as reported by Anderson, *et al.*, were:

Both nurses said that they had been allowed to test this [hypothesis] and they found themselves stimulated, and they were satisfied that they

---

[2] Ingeborg Mauksch, "Nursing is Coming of Age Through the Practitioner Movement," *American Journal of Nursing*, October 1975, p. 1835.

[3] A. M. Marcus, J. Anderson, H. Gemeroy, F. Perry and A. Camfferman, "Primary Therapist Project on an In-Patient Psychiatric Unit," the *Canadian Nurse*, September 1975, p. 30.

could be accountable and could do therapy with patients. The primary therapists said that the program had rounded out their professional lives as nurses and their personal lives as women.[4]

The primary therapist project raised a number of basic questions which relate to role definition;

However, the question has arisen about who has final responsibility for the patients' care. Because of the medical framework within which hospitals operate, there is emphasis on medical responsibility and medical supervision. This implies that the nurse is accountable to the physician, as she is now moving into an area that has previously been defined as medical care. She carries out functions delegated by the physician and must be supervised by him. This maintains the physician as the authority figure, and reinforces dependence on him and accountability to him.[5]

A certain level of role uncertainty also appears to have arisen in the relationship between the nurse therapist and the resident:

The issue raises questions such as: Should nurse therapists and residents work on the same unit? If the independent nurse practitioner is to be a reality of the future, and this appears to be the case, physicians will have to learn to accept the competent nurse and communicate with her as a responsible colleague. Both parties must learn to work together and to develop an environment conducive to patient care.[6]

Another issue closely related to role uncertainty is the question of role overlap. One select committee, commissioned to study this question made this emphatic statement:

It is most important that the physician does not take upon himself those problems that the nurse is competent to handle, nor does she dump on him the problem people she does not like to work with.[7]

This statement is a commentary upon things as they are and suggests that there is too much usurpation of duties on the part of the doctor

---

[4] *Ibid.*, p. 33.

[5] J. Anderson, A. M. Marcus, H. Gemeroy, F. Perry, and A. Camfferman, "The Expanded Role of the Nurse: Independent Practitioner or Physician's Assistant?", the *Canadian Nurse*, September 1975, p. 34.

[6] *Ibid.*, p. 35.

[7] Department of Health Education and Welfare, *Extending the Scope of Nursing Practice*. A report of the Secretary's Committee to Study Extended Roles for Nurses, 1971.

and too great an acceptance of chores on the part of the nurse. One situation where the above arises is when the doctor feels he is more skilled in the handling of anxiety in patients' relatives or in making explanations to persons deeply concerned about their own health or illness. Through interdisciplinary education and interdisciplinary communication these problems related to physicians' and nurses' roles may be resolved.

Factors Related to the Implementation of Interdisciplinary Practice

CHARACTERISTICS OF STUDENTS ENTERING THE HEALTH PROFESSIONS

Nurses and nursing have been the subjects of much careful scrutiny by eager researchers in the social sciences and related disciplines. Much interesting and useful data has been collected which has, more often than not, led to the need for more research. We know a great deal already about certain characteristics of nursing students, such as academic performance, social and demographic background factors; but less information is available which examines nurses in relation to characteristics of persons in other health disciplines. Goodwin has stated that:

New candidates for the profession are selected by established members, and in general tend to mirror the attributes of the latter. A perpetuation of like-minded members is a natural occurrence in the history of any system which continues over time, and possesses distinct advantages for survival. As long as the cycle of stabilization-change-stabilization is gradual and imperceptible, disadvantages of this kind of reproduction are not obvious. But as the cycle accelerates, the perpetuation of exactly the same characteristics over time can at times become dysfunctional for the system.[8]

Goodwin adds that:

The changing and expanding roles and tasks which occur as technology creates new possibilities provide yet another reason for taking a look at the practice of replicating without variation.[9]

Does Canadian nursing recruit individuals who tend to reflect the

---

[8] Marjorie Goodwin, "Correlates of Career Choice," unpublished Master's Research Project, University of British Columbia, 1972, p. 7.

[9] *Ibid.*, p. 7.

same attitudes and values already possessed by practising nurses or are we inviting prospective nurses with ideas and values quite different from the established norm and are we willing to listen, learn and even change? What are the characteristics possessed by the nursing recruit that should be considered in discussing his/her functioning effectively in an interdisciplinary role?

Recruits in the health sciences, as a group, were found to be more people-oriented and more service-motivated than other students (considered as a whole). On the other hand, health recruits showed less interest in bringing about changes, working with ideas, exerting leadership or influence, fostering freedom or equality, or having aesthetic satisfactions. Males were more likely to stress working independently and gaining financial security than were other non-health professional males; females emphasized friendships, a comfortable life, and adventure more than other non-health professional females.

It is difficult to settle upon an "optimum mix" of personality characteristics, values and other attributes for a well-functioning interdisciplinary team. Some trends emerge, however, out of data obtained from other studies. The health professions appear to possess a relatively weak motivation for change, or, in other words, the health professions seem to be recruiting a corps of new members likely to perpetuate the characteristics already possessed by the incumbents of the profession.

The nursing students who participated in Goodwin's study presented a rather distinctive profile of the humanitarian, people-oriented type with indications of interest in teamwork. A high percentage (80%) of the nursing students attached great value to sharing in ideas and knowledge of other fields, and three out of five also considered very important the opportunity to work closely with colleagues in other fields. On these two values, nurses were outstanding among the health sciences and health service persons.

In comparison with other students, nursing students appear to be more outgoing, accommodating, conscientious, trusting, group-dependent, and relaxed. Compared to other females in the survey, nursing students appear more stable, more persevering, less self-sufficient, and less driven.[10]

Analysis of this leads to the observation that nursing students not only have an interest in teamwork and all that teamwork implies, such as working closely together with members of other disciplines, but they possess qualities that, indeed, are needed by a team member, viz.,

---

[10] *Ibid.*, p. 9.

stability, perseverance, accommodation, trust, conscientiousness.

Why, then, is there hesitation in developing interdisciplinary educational experiences in the nursing curricula and interdisciplinary teamwork in health care delivery systems?

SOME DETERRENTS TO INTERDISCIPLINARY PRACTICE IN HEALTH DELIVERY SYSTEMS

One of the greatest hurdles that has prevented nurses and doctors from communicating effectively as team members is organization. The doctor, in most instances, operates as "an individual entrepreneur, with a quasi-contractual relationship with the hospital."[11] The nurse, on the other hand, is usually an employee of the hospital, subject to directives from those higher up the bureaucratic ladder, as well as from other health care workers, including doctors. Ideas or complaints that the nurse has must go through bureaucratic channels, "which takes time and which runs the risk of the message becoming distorted."[12] Few opportunities arise for the nurse and the doctor to exchange thoughts and ideas in an effort to help each other arrive at mutual decisions. Exceptions to this are beginning to receive recognition in certain government health care agencies, but progress is slow.

Other factors to be recognized are power and influence. While the doctor is able to move relatively freely through the institution, discussing suggestions and/or complaints with department heads, usually colleagues, who have direct input to the board of directors, nurses do not enjoy this manoeuverability, or freedom. Thus, the political power, or influence, of the nurse is limited.

The nurse's status remains relatively low, as evidenced by salary levels and benefits. Although gains are being made through the efforts of professional organizations, it is all too common for a nurse to have his/her "dedication" questioned when she applies for a position for which she is qualified, and asks for a wage commensurate with duties and professional responsibilities involved.

The fact that most nurses are women and most doctors, men, has undoubtedly influenced the position of power in the decision-making process. Emotionally and socially, women are used to playing a dependent role in relationship to men, thus tipping the "power scales" even further in favor of the doctor.

Baumgart[13] identifies deterrent conditions prevailing in many

---

[11] Jean Raisler. "A Better Nurse-Doctor Relationship," *Nursing '74*, Vol. 4, No. 9 (September). p. 23.

[12] *Ibid.*, p. 23.

[13] Alice J. Baumgart. "Are Nurses Ready for Teamwork?", the *Canadian Nurse*, July 1972. p. 19.

nursing programs as: (1) anti-nursing-theory bias—the difficulty of many nurses in articulating the nursing needs of patients; (2) the over-emphasis on appealing to outside authority when making decisions— "don't use your head too much, but defer to others"—is a message that is all too frequently given to nurses, both as students and as practising professionals; (3) the careful cultivation of the doctor stereotype. Nursing culture is dominated by a stereotype of the doctor, cultivated in nursing schools, that builds up strong feelings of suspicion and mistrust toward the medical practitioner. These problems, along with the comparatively low reward for clinical competence, effectively slow down the nurse's progress toward full team participation.

Underpinning this whole idea is the concept of democratic functioning and the ability to be "other-person-centered." The team members must be deeply committed to these concepts by showing a genuine concern for the other person, his ideas and feelings, and to acknowledge each person's unique contribution of knowledge and skills to the health team. Leadership should be based on the ability to operate within the bounds of these requirements, on team consensus, not on the basis of prestige and authority.

HISTORICAL ROLE OF NURSING

Let us examine, briefly, the historical influences that have helped to shape the development of nursing through the ages. What nursing is today, to a large extent, has been determined by its past.

Uprichard has identified heritages from the past that have tended to inhibit progress in nursing as a profession.

These are: the folk image of the nurse brought forward from primitive times, the religious image of the nurse inherited from the mediaeval period, and the servant image of the nurse created by the Protestant-capitalist ethic of the 16th to 19th centuries.[14]

These images, while appealing to the humanistic side of man's nature, show nursing in a subordinate position to other professions, omnipresent and uncomplainingly dedicated, with little thought of personal gain. The doctor, on the other hand, has enjoyed an elevated status, offered to him by his grateful patients, their families, and society at large. His image has been one of superior knowledge, intellect, powers and skills which he has carried out within an aura of mysterious language and rites.

---

[14] Muriel Uprichard, "Ferment in Nursing," *International Nursing Review*, Vol. 16, No. 1 (1969).

How different the evolution of these two important health team components! As nursing has developed through the ages, it has been involved in the "growth of scientific knowledge and technology."[15] Alterations in disease, health, and population patterns have affected the role of nursing in relation to its patients. Changes in the social structure saw many women requiring remunerative work in society other than that of wife, mother, or housekeeper. Society needed their skills and talents as the industrial revolution opened up many more jobs for people. Women, too, began to feel the need of a broader choice of occupation than that which previously had been available to them. The development of a humanitarian philosophy, with greater awareness of the sufferings of others, helped nursing become a more viable entity. Still, nursing was very much organized, directed, and chastised by others, and nurses did what they were told.

ROLE OF WOMEN IN SOCIETY

Because the nursing profession is made up largely of women, it seems prudent to examine some of the recent trends relating to woman's role in society.

Roles are, by definition, assignable, and reassignable, at the discretion of society.

It is a historic fact that there is no social role that has not, at some time, somewhere, been played by a woman. Women have been absolute monarchs and heads of states. They have also been (outside of the west) priests. Tinker, tailor, soldier, sailor—women in one culture or another have played every masculine role. And vice versa. Women were once the vintners, the farmers, the weavers, the animal breeders of society. Now men are. Is cooking today a male or a female role? The cook who cooks for nothing is a female—or a housewife. The cook who cooks for $25 000 is a male—or a chef.[16]

Over the past 50 years in North America very little change has occurred in the number or percentage of women who occupy leadership positions in the great institutions: religious, political, judicial, economic, military, educational, professional, cultural and, informational (media). In the past, the policy-making or high supervisory positions were held by men; this remains true today. Women remain predominantly clustered at the bottom of society's organizations, with a smattering in the middle.

---

[15] *Ibid.,* p. 224.
[16] Clare Boothe Luce. "The 21st Century Woman—Free at Last?" *Saturday Review/ World,* August 24, 1974, p. 61.

But out of a female population of about 107 million, there are not today 100 women perched in posts of command or in high supervisory or policy-making positions in its upper branches.[17]

What does this tell us about social and economic equality of women? And since women make up such a large percentage of the nursing force, what effect, if any, does this have on the profession as it relates to and interacts with the other health professions?

Of the 118,897 nurses employed in nursing, males constituted less than 2%, numbering 1,884. Male nurses were employed in all fields of nursing and 87% were working in hospitals or other institutions.

Comparing male nurses and female nurses according to position shows that 5% of male nurses were directors and assistants, compared to less than 3% of female nurses; 12% of male nurses were supervisors and assistants, in contrast to 6% of female nurses; 21% of male nurses were head nurses and assistants, while 11% of female nurses held this position, and 55% of male nurses were general duty or staff, whereas 75% of female nurses were employed in this position.[18]

It would appear that competence and skill alone are not enough to assure women in nursing equal opportunities to step up the administrative ladder to higher salaries, higher status, and more comfortable working conditions. Perhaps women are used to being led by men and perhaps they prefer this. Might our cry for "more men in nursing" tend to aggravate the existing disproportionate situation regarding women in leadership positions in nursing? On the other hand, will nursing require more men in its ranks to provide the leadership so needed in nursing? This is a moot question.

Three major factors have enhanced women's ability to perform a wider variety of roles than was the case in the past:

- thanks to contraception, women are able to assign themselves the role of motherhood or not, as they wish, which leaves them free to accept other societal roles if they choose,
- higher education is much more readily available to women now, thus opening doors for employment that were once closed,
- in the legal area, well-organized women's groups are taking advantage of civil rights legislation and applying this legislation in a constructive effort to end discriminatory practices against women.[19]

---

[17] *Ibid.*, p. 58.

[18] *Countdown* 1974, Canadian Nursing Statistics, Canadian Nurses Association (Ottawa, 1975), p. 10.

[19] Clare Boothe Luce, *op. cit.*, p. 61.

But the question remains: Are these achievements enough to secure for women a firm and equal status with their colleagues in other disciplines, and to assure female nurses positions of recognizable equality on the inter-professional team?

Some Guidelines to Successful Development of Interdisciplinary Health Teams

At present, most nurses have very little opportunity to participate on a health team. For the most part, nurses operate in a "nursing team." Many of these "teams" function by "meeting more or less regularly to pass on information about patients, or to discuss particular patient problems, read administrative directives or distribute assignments."[20] While these may be important administrative duties, they hardly constitute the requirements for a professional health team.

Since the entire concept of health team functioning is an unfamiliar one to health professionals, it may be prudent to look to theories of group behavior as an initial guideline in the development of health teams.

KEY VARIABLES IN THE THEORY OF GROUP BEHAVIOR*

This section will present and briefly define seven selected variables known to be of importance in the functioning of groups.

Goals or Missions. Perhaps the most important aspect of effective team functioning is a clear understanding, by everyone, of the team goals. This is broader than each team member's specific contribution to the goal. The health team inevitably will be confronted with issues such as:

1. How clearly defined are the goals? Who sets the goals?

2. How much agreement is there among members concerning the goals? how much commitment?

3. How clearly measurable is goal achievement?

---

[20] Charlotte Epstein, *Effective Interaction in Contemporary Nursing*, Englewood Cliffs, N.J.: Prentice-Hall, Inc., 1974), p. 128.

* Some helpful references in the field of group behavior are:
E. H. Schein, *Process Consultation*, (Reading, Mass.: Addison-Wesley Publishing Co., Inc., 1969).
W. Bennis, *et al.*, *The Planning of Change*, second edition, (New York: Holt, Rinehart & Winston, Inc., 1969).
I. Rubin and R. Bechehard, "Factors Influencing the Effectiveness of Health Teams," *Milbank Memorial Fund Quarterly*, Vol. 50, July 1972.

4. How do group goals relate to broader organizational goals? to personal goals?

Since a group's very existence is to achieve some goal or mission, these issues are of central importance.

Role Expectations. In working to achieve their goals, team members will play a variety of roles. Among the members of a group, a set of multiple expectations exists concerning role behavior. Each person, in effect, has a set of expectations of how each of the other members should behave as the group works to achieve its goals. In any group, therefore, questions exist about: (1) the extent to which such expectations are clearly defined and communicated (role ambiguity); (2) the extent to which such expectations are compatible or in conflict (role conflict); (3) the extent to which any individual is capable of meeting these multiple expectations (role overload).

These role expectations are messages "sent" between the members of a group. Generally, the more uncertain and complex the task, the more salient are issues of role expectations.

Decision-Making Although decision-making is an essential function of any group, this does not mean that the entire group must be involved in all decisions. The key question here is that of relevance and appropriateness; who has the relevant information, who will implement the decision, and who will be responsible for its consequences? A group may choose from a range of decision-making mechanisms including decision by default (lack of group response), unilateral decision (authority rule), majority vote, consensus, or unanimity. Each form is appropriate under certain conditions. Each will have different consequences, both in terms of the amount of information available for use in making the decision, and the subsequent commitment of members to implement the decision.

Similarly, when a group faces a conflict it can choose to ignore it, smooth it over, allow one person to force a decision, create a compromise, or confront all the realities of the conflict (facts and feelings) and attempt to develop an innovative solution. The choices it makes in both of these areas will significantly influence group functioning.

Communication Patterns. It is insufficient for a group to function as a decision-making, problem-solving unit; the communication of these decisions, solutions, and related information is central to group viability. Anything that acts to inhibit the flow of information will detract from the group effectiveness. A range of factors affects information flow. At a very simple level are the architectural and geographic issues. Meeting space can be designed to facilitate or hinder the flow of communication. Geographically separated facilities may be a barrier to rapid information exchange. Numerous subtler factors also must be considered. Participation—frequency, order, and content—may follow formal lines of authority or status. The best sources of information needed to solve a problem will, however, vary with the problem. Patterns of communication based exclusively on formal lines of status will not meet many of the group's information needs. People's feelings of freedom to participate, to challenge, to express opinions also significantly affect information flow.

Leadership. To operate effectively, a team requires many acts of leadership that are not necessarily performed by one leader, but by many leaders. Group members often misinterpret such a statement as saying "good groups are leaderless." This is not the intent. Depending on the situation and the problem to be solved, different people can, and should, assume leadership. The formal leader of a group may be in the best position to reflect the "organization's" position on a particular problem. Someone else may be a resource in helping the formal leader and another member clarify a point of disagreement. All are examples of necessary acts of leadership. It is highly unlikely that in any group one person will be capable of meeting all of a group's leadership needs.

Norms. Norms are implicit, unwritten rules governing the behavior of people in groups. They define what behavior is "good or bad," "acceptable or unacceptable," if one is to be a functioning member of this group. As such, they become very powerful determinants of group behavior and take on the quality of laws—"it's the way we do things around here!" The existence of norms is most clear when they are violated; quiet uneasiness, shifting in one's seat, joking reminders. Repeated violation of norms often leads to expulsion—psychological, or physical.

Norms take on particular potency because they influence all of the other areas previously discussed. Groups develop norms governing leadership, influence, communication patterns, decision-making, conflict resolution, and the like. Inherently, norms are neither good nor bad. The issue is one of appropriateness—does a particular norm help, or hinder, a group's ability to work?

GROUP DYNAMICS VARIABLES AND THE HEALTH TEAM

Each of the previous six factors describe specific characteristics of any group situation. Let us look briefly now at how these factors have application in the functioning of the health team.

Goals of a health team providing comprehensive patient care are difficult to define. The word "comprehensive" means that the team cannot ignore social and personality problems and emphasize the "relative security and certainty" of medical problems. Considerable anxiety is generated because the team does not really know when, and if, it is succeeding. The questions of priorities and time allocations become complicated; how does one decide between competing activities in the absence of clearly defined goals? A team member wonders whether to spend a half day trying to arrange a school transfer for a child, or to see the other patients scheduled for visits.

No one member of the team has been trained to be knowledgeable in all the areas required. Yet, the complexity of the task demands that doctors become involved in social problems; that nurses become the supervisors of paraprofessional health teams.

Role expectations in health team members are highly diverse because "comprehensive patient care" requires a wide range of skills, knowledge, personal attributes, and background. In the creation of a team, many professional "subcultures" have been brought together and are expected to work in harmony toward a common goal.

As a result of educational background and training, the doctors are accustomed to being primary (if not sole) authority and more expert in medical issues. The specialist role for which they have been so well trained and that is so appropriate in other settings comes under pressure. As a team member, in addition to his specialist skills, the doctor is asked to become more of a generalist. He needs to teach other health workers some of his medical knowledge. He also needs to learn from them more about the social problems facing the community and the character, mores, and values of the particular patient population.

Health professionals tend to maintain strong psychologic ties with their professional specialty groups. The stronger these ties for an individual, the more difficult it will be for that individual to develop needed team loyalty. His sense of professionalism stems from these external reference groups. The careful procedures he/she has been so well trained to do may be neither feasible nor appropriate. Indeed, group conflict within the health team well may center upon "professional standards." Comprehensive group practice may require a redefinition of these standards, and perhaps even the redefinition of a professional.

Nurses and family health workers tend to bring a history of submissiveness. Nurses have been trained to be submissive to doctors. In the team setting, nurses find themselves as coordinators of the work of a team including doctors—a complete role reversal.

A part of being a member of a highly interdependent team is the need to develop new loyalties and learn some new skills not anticipated or covered during individual training. In fact, it is unlikely that, in the face of the mission of providing comprehensive family-centered health care, clearly defined, complete job descriptions will ever be feasible. This reality puts great stress on a team's ability to learn and adapt by itself. In response to a particular problem, the question cannot be "Whose job is it?" but may instead have to be "Who on the team is capable?" or "Who needs to learn how to handle this situation?"

Decision-making, communication and leadership in health teams tend to be problematical. One perplexing problem for the health team is the need to differentiate a variety of decision-making situations. In an attempt to be "democratic and participative" a team might try to make all decisions by consensus. This represents a failure to distinguish, for example, (a) who has the information necessary to make a decision; (b) who needs to be consulted before certain decisions get made; and, (c) who needs to be informed of a decision after it has been made. Under certain circumstances the team may need to strive for unanimity, or consensus; in other cases majority vote may be appropriate.

Perhaps the greatest barrier to effective decision-making in highly interdependent health teams stems again from the "cultural" backgrounds of team members. Doctors are used to making decisions by themselves, or in collaboration with peers of equal status—other doctors, or highly educated professionals. At the other extreme, the community residents who work on the team are used to being passive dependent recipients of others' decisions. Yet many times, on a health team, the doctor and the community workers are, and must behave as, peers, neither one possessing all the information needed to solve a particular problem or make a particular decision. Furthermore, many times the doctor is the one who needs information held by another health worker. When a conflict develops, the required discussion that will lead to consensus is difficult to achieve; forcing, compromise, or decision by default may result. Commitment to decisions is low, the result being that many decisions have to be remade several times—"I thought we decided that last week!"

In respect to communication, a group as diverse in membership as a health team must deliberately strive to maintain an open system. This includes the breaking down of status barriers which separate members so that communication is between persons and not between roles. There also must be a feeling of trust so that each individual will feel free to "tell it like it is," or, better, "tell it like he sees it."

As for leadership, one obvious trend in the health team is to rely on the model best known to all members, viz., "defer to the doctor." This model is indeed quite appropriate in certain medical and surgical procedures. However, continued reliance on that model will result in an overemphasis on medical, instead of social, issues, a lack of shared commitment to decisions (which doctors sometimes interpret as "lack of professional attitude") and less than complete sharing of information, all of which directly affect the task performance.

Norms are implicit, unwritten rules governing behavior. Some of the norms observed in health teams are:

1. "In making a decision, silence means consent";

2. "Doctors are more important than other team members"; "we don't disagree with them"; "we wait for them to lead";

3. Conflict is dangerous, both task conflicts and interpersonal disagreements; "it's best to let sleeping dogs lie";

4. Positive feelings, praise, support are not to be shared; "we're all 'professionals' here to do a job."

5. The precision and exactness demanded by our task negate the opportunity to be flexible with respect to our own internal group processes.

The effect of these norms, and others like them, is to guarantee that a team gets caught in a negative spiral. The norms are those of rigidity, but the complexity of the environment and the task to be done demand flexibility. The frustrating, anxiety-provoking quality of the task places great demands for some place to recharge one's emotional battery. The team is potentially such a place.

In addition to these specific norms of flexibility, support, and openness of communication, a set of higher-order norms is essential. Task uncertainty and environmental changes require that a team develop a capacity to become self-renewing—become a learning organism. Learning requires a climate that legitimizes controlled experimentation, risk taking, failure, and evaluation of outcomes. In the absence of norms that support and reinforce these kinds of behaviors, a team will end up fighting two enemies—its tasks and itself.

INTERDISCIPLINARY EDUCATION OF HEALTH PROFESSIONALS

It is extremely unlikely that a high degree of collaboration among health professionals will occur until a similarly high degree of collaboration occurs in their professional education. It is for this reason that many nurses, doctors, and other health professionals are proposing that a greater portion of professional education, both in the classroom and in the clinical setting, be interdisciplinary in nature, that classes be made up of students from the several professions, and that curricula be focussed upon the health care of the patient as opposed to any one specific professional approach.

The Search for a Model. Dr. John F. McCreary, Coordinator of Health Sciences at the University of British Columbia, has this to say as a result of his experiences on the "Interprofessional Curriculum Committee":

> *Perhaps the greatest single problem associated with the development of interprofessional education in the health sciences is the lack of a model. There is no place that one can turn to examine a complete scheme already in operation, to select, to discard, and to emerge with a modified pattern suitable to one's local requirements.*[21]

Dr. George Szasz, also reporting on the work of the Committee on Interprofessional Education in Health Sciences at the University of British Columbia, has proposed a tentative, four-level model for an interprofessional health sciences curriculum:

First Level *The first level provides the "professional foundation." During a three-month period all new students of the health science center make home and institutional visits, observe the work of health professionals, and focus their attention upon the interaction between the patient and the helper. They explore, through meeting people, the living conditions and the social and health problems in urban and rural communities. Returning from these experiences, the students attend lecture courses, take part in discussions and read recommended books and articles in the relevant fields of sociology, anthropology, epidemiology, statistics and biology. Assisted by small class discussions and by tutorials, the students have opportunities to gain an insight into the historic, philosophic and psychologic background of the client-helper relation. They have numerous opportunities at this level to become experienced in the techniques of interviewing, observing and reporting. Prior to entering the next level the students are given a good chance to understand how the subject matter of the following levels might best enable them to become competent practitioners of their chosen professions.*

Second Level *The second level of the curriculum is the "foundation of medicine," "foundation of nursing," and the "foundation" of other professions. This level consists of a survey of the special knowledge and skills of each profession, and sharing of learning experiences between groups occurs if it is economically worthwhile or otherwise justified.*

---

[21] John F. McCreary, "The Health Team Approach to Medical Education," *Journal of the American Medical Association,* November 11, 1968, p. 1557.

Courses within this level are oriented toward the needs of medical, nursing, or other practices. Within medicine, for example, the learning experiences in the basic medical and clinical subjects are fused. The students may start at the bedside studying the symptoms, signs and the physiologic and biochemical changes brought about by stress; then study the various physical, social and psychologic agents producing stress; the pathologic changes brought about by these, as seen in the laboratory and on the wards of hospitals and in the community. The time duration of this level necessarily varies with each faculty.

Third Level *The detailed study of specific subjects is shifted to the third level: "health sciences in depth." In this level a large number of courses is offered by various schools. The subject matter of these courses may involve anatomy, interalia, behavioral sciences, the history of medical or health sciences, internal medicine, nursing practice, hospital administration and drug distribution systems. The students of the various schools select subjects for intensive study according to their interests, ability and needs after consulting with advisers.*

Fourth Level *Emerging after the completion of three or four units of three monthly periods in the third level, the student enters the last level: "health sciences in practice." In this level, the students become responsibly involved in the team care of patients and they also assume responsibilities for the teaching of lower-year students of the other professions. The time duration of this level is flexible and, to some extent, depends on the student's qualifications to assume his professional responsibilities. The current practice of internship in medicine, and field work in other professions is included in this level. In addition, throughout each of these levels, the student also has responsibilities within community and treatment institutions, and in various models of traditional and experimental systems of primary health care services.*[22]

In regard to the implementation of such a model, Dr. Szasz has expressed a somewhat cautious optimism:

Several of the educational experiments conducted by the Committee demonstrate the feasibility of certain parts of the model in terms of course presentations or arrangements for problem-solving types of learning experiences in mixed student groups. No evidence has been obtained yet, however, to demonstrate that any of these experiences really leads to a lowering of the barriers between professions. Nor is any answer ready to suggest how new types of educational programs can be introduced to a

---

[22] George Szasz, "Interprofessional Education in the Health Sciences," *Milbank Memorial Fund Quarterly*, Vol. 47, October 1969, pp. 469–70.

number of health professional schools, or how the future graduates might be able to utilize their new knowledge in the traditional hospital and community health care structure.

The problems encountered in the introduction of new programs are those that confront any major innovation. A critical mass of the total faculty must eventually be in favor of the project, and this can perhaps best be achieved by the constant application of test situations in which more and more faculty members and members of the practicing professions, and the public, have an opportunity of seeing the advantages and appreciating the problems of interprofessional collaboration.[23]

Nurses, doctors, and other health professionals agree on the need for interdisciplinary models, but these have been slow in developing, both in the training institutions and in the field of health practice. Madeleine Leininger proposes what she refers to as an

... interdisciplinary oval model of team functioning, which facilitates interdisciplinary group sharing and participation by recognizing the value of many disciplines and their contributions to patient care. With this model, the disciplines are expected to actually contribute their ideas and skills to interdisciplinary health planning, implementation and evaluation with a spirit of equal rights and opportunities.[24]

This is in contrast to the stratified pyramid model (or hierarchical model) found in our society and, indeed, in a large number of organizations devoted to health care, including some university faculties and schools.

In the absence of field-tested models of interdisciplinary health education and health practice, it appears that the problem might well be approached through what the innovation theorist refers to as "incrementalism," or "successive approximations." This involves the development of pilot projects and other modest alterations in the structure of health education that can be developed, implemented and evaluated, then modified in the light of that evaluation. It is to some of the recent trends in this direction that we now turn.

Education for the Health Team: University of Toronto. This pilot project, undertaken first in 1972, involved joint planning by interested members of the Faculties of Medicine and Nursing at the University of Toronto. It was decided that a shared experience on the part of nursing and medical students would provide enriched learning oppor-

---

[23] *Ibid.*, p. 473.

[24] Madeleine Leininger, "This I Believe about Interdisciplinary Health Education for the Future," *Nursing Outlook*, Vol. 19, No. 12, 1971, p. 789.

tunities for both. Consequently, it was arranged jointly by the Department of Family and Community Medicine and the Faculty of Nursing that some fourth-year nursing students and final year medical students should practice together in a clinical setting. The implementation of the project is described as follows:

In 1972 – 73, this project was initiated in three Family Practice Units. In each unit one physician and one nurse were designated as the faculty members to guide this experience; a doctor and a nurse therefore constituted the basic health care team, drawing in other health professionals as indicated by the needs of the patient.

At least one Period III final year medical student was assigned to each of the three units for an eight-week Ambulatory Care Block experience in the fall term and the spring term; one nursing student was assigned to each unit in the fall term (10 weeks) and in the spring term (8 weeks). With the guidance of the designated staff from Medical and Nursing faculties, students were expected to provide care to a number of selected families and individuals who required both medical and nursing care. Case conferences involving students, supervising faculty members and others as appropriate were arranged; these were designed to share assessment data, evaluate patient progress and arrive at individual and mutual goals for care. In addition, nursing students shared in the weekly seminars arranged for medical students as part of their Family Community Medicine experience.[25]

As part of the evaluation of this project, both the nursing and medical students were asked to assess the level of achievement of the several objectives for students involved in the project. Table I summarizes the responses of nursing and medical students.

It may be observed in Table I that, in the opinion of a majority of participating students, objectives were met to a moderate or high degree. It also may be observed that the modal response for medical students was "moderate," while the modal response for nursing students was "high." Some anecdotal comments by the students also may be helpful.

Medical students' comments: *"I have much greater awareness of the value of 'teaming,' both from learning point of view and from the patients . . . regarding types of therapy with which I was unfamiliar; They (other disciplines) can be useful in cases of chronic diseases in elderly or*

---

[25] Phyllis E. Jones and Earl V. Dunn, "Education for a Health Team: a Pilot Project," *International Journal of Nursing Studies*, Vol. 11, 1974, p. 62.

Table I[26]

LEVEL OF ACHIEVEMENT OF OBJECTIVES AS ASSESSED BY STUDENTS
(EDUCATION FOR THE HEALTH TEAM: A PILOT PROJECT, UNIVERSITY OF
TORONTO)

MEDICAL STUDENT OBJECTIVES (4 responses)	Level of Achievement High	Moderate	Low
(a) Collaboration with allied health workers	1	2	1
(b) Knowledge of the roles of allied health personnel	1	3	
(c) Knowledge of the interrelationships with nurses		4	
(d) The team as a problem solver	1	2	1
(e) Coordination of care	1	3	
(f) Interpretation of services to the patient	1	1	2
NURSING STUDENT OBJECTIVES (6 responses)			
(a) Collaborate with appropriate disciplines	4	1	1
(b) Identify areas where patients' needs have and have not, been met	5		1
(c) Review and discuss needs with appropriate disciplines	4	1	1
(d) Assume or share leadership role among the nurses	2	3	1
(e) Assume a leadership role among members of the health team	1	5	
TOTAL	21	25	8

debilitated patients and to very broadly screen patients in a general practice; I became aware of the training, capabilities and functions of the nurse practitioner."

Nursing students' comments: "*Collaboration is more easily accomplished outside of an acute care setting where workers are more community and family oriented; I learned about problems of roles, functions, responsibilities and the limitations, unique contributions of each discipline and the economic facets of the team approach; communications must exist among all members of team; conflicting ideas can be used constructively to improve care; collaboration improves communication with patient.*"[27]

[26] *Ibid.*, p. 64.
[27] *Ibid.*, p. 65.

In regard to overall strengths and weaknesses of the project, the most frequently mentioned strength was the interdisciplinary nature of the entire experience. This positive feature was emphasized by the staff participants (doctors and nurses), as well as by the students. Problems most frequently identified by both staff and students were the limited understanding by participants of the project objectives and the limited availability of medical students for practice in the clinical setting. Over all, the staff participants saw the project as worthy, since seven of eight staff respondents felt that the project should continue.

Although this project was limited in scope, it can be used, indeed, to provide guidance for those responsible for interdisciplinary health education in other settings. The following quote from Dana and Sheps seems appropriate:

What matters, in the context of interprofessional education, is not the size or scope of the program in process—but the fact that it is in process rather than fixed, that it addresses itself to a problem or problems for which no one profession has the answer, that it provides an opportunity for students and teachers together to establish meaningful new relationships with one another as they work toward meaningful new relationships with those whom they serve.[28]

A Nursing Course for Medical Students: University of California.[29] A course that has altered the traditional physician-dominated teaching pattern and allowed nurses to help teach physicians was taught by nurses from various agencies and the faculty of the School of Nursing, University of California, San Francisco. It is interesting that the course, entitled "Introduction to Nursing," and offered to first-year medical students, was the result of a petition by eleven medical students to the medical faculty for permission to observe nurses at work and learn about patient care from the perspective of the nurse. This request was granted and, as a consequence, an interdisciplinary course for both nursing and medical students was offered. Course credit was granted to both the nursing and medical students through their respective faculties; the course was organized on the basis of one seminar per week along with one three-hour observational experience, with content relative to patient care and the nurse. Course goals and operational setting are described as follows:

---

[28] B. Dana and C. G. Sheps, "Trends and Issues in Interprofessional Education: Pride, Prejudice and Progress." *Ed. Social Work* 4 (1968): pp. 35–41.

[29] Elizabeth Harding, *et al.*, "A Nursing Course for Medical Students," *Nursing Outlook*, April 1975, pp. 240–2.

The course goals were to alter medical students' attitudes toward nursing, enabling them to work cooperatively with nurses; to provide medical students with an understanding of the potential, breadth, and depth of nursing practice; and to encourage free expression of perceptions and observations about nursing, medicine, and patient care in a group of both nursing and medical students.

The course gave medical students the opportunity to observe a practising registered nurse for a half day a week in a clinical setting. Nurses, who were contacted through their agencies, volunteered to have medical students tag after them for the weekly half day. The nurse was given the goals of the course, topics for seminar and skills lab, and the medical students' rotation schedule, and she worked out with the student how best to make use of their time together. The clinical experience thus varied for each student. Some of the students, for instance, helped the nurses give care while others mainly observed.

The Hospital Setting

Since failure of communication between doctors and nurses is most evident in hospitals, that setting was chosen for the longest observation. Four consecutive weeks were spent on a hospital ward (pediatric, medicine, surgery, and cancer units). When possible, the medical student observed the same nurse each week.

Two consecutive weeks were then spent in a public health agency or in an outpatient clinic and another two weeks with a nurse practitioner. During the last two weeks of the course, the medical students gave direct nursing care under the supervision of a nursing faculty member. The one required skills lab included lecture, demonstration, and practice of range of motion exercise, body mechanics, positioning and transferring patients, and the administration of injections.

The weekly interdisciplinary seminar was used to discuss "nontechnical" nursing skills and the observation experience. Seminar content was presented and discussed with about equal numbers of medical and nursing students taking part, so that one group would not dominate or overpower the other.

The nursing students participated in the seminars in a dual role of teacher and learner. They were there to teach the medical students their own perspective on patient care and also to learn from dealing with the medical students how to communicate more effectively with them.[30]

Included in the course were the following topics: (1) the nursing assessment process; (2) interviewing the patient; (3) "Why I went into nursing;" (4) the doctor-nurse game; (5) teaching and learning theory

---

[30] *Ibid.*, p. 241.

and skills; (6) the nurse's role in discharge planning; (7) the nurse's role in health care delivery; (8) the dying patient, and (9) psychiatric nursing.[31]

For all students, the outcome of the course included a keener interest in, and a clearer perception of, the distinguishing features between the role of the nurse and the role of the doctor. Tangible evidence of this was demonstrated through requests by medical students for additional "skills" labs in their free time, including such skills as: measuring vital signs, drawing blood, administering intravenous fluids and numerous other skills not specifically taught in medical school. For their part, nursing students were motivated to analyze their own clinical experiences, and then to clearly define (and defend) these for the medical students.

Has this interprofessional course been perceived as valuable by the participants? One very encouraging sign is that when the course was offered for the second year, over twenty medical students enrolled, which represented a course oversubscription of nine medical students. The perception of one student nurse was:

The class served to reinforce the positive aspects of nursing and "feminism." As we learned more, we could become more confident in ourselves as nurses. It was a positive, hopeful experience, which left us alternately frustrated and glad, and angry at the system which pits the doctor and the nurse against each other and forgets the patient altogether.[32]

What has been offered at the University of California Medical Center is another attempt to emphasize the need for mutual understanding and collaboration in the educational experiences of nurse and doctor. It has also demonstrated that there are distinct areas of nursing expertise, including but not limited to health assessment, health care, needs of patients, patient education, and patient counseling. Moreover, medical students perceive their need to learn about these from the professional nurse in the interdisciplinary setting.

Interdisciplinary Education for Medical Students: University of British Columbia. Since 1973, all first-year medical students at the University of British Columbia have participated in the course "Family and Community Practice,"[33] designed to focus on the patient as a member

---

[31] *Ibid.,* p. 241.
[32] *Ibid.,* p. 242.
[33] See UBC Medical School Calendar re: the Course "INDE 401."

of a family, living in a community, both factors shaping his life style and his response to health care. Serving as clinical tutors for the students are a variety of health professionals, including nurses, social workers, and general practitioners, from a variety of settings. All are involved in bringing to the students a broad and varied perspective. The students spend part of their time in carefully planned seminars designed to help them develop skills in interviewing and history-taking, as well as to broaden their knowledge of human development and its relation to the health-illness continuum. The rest of their time is spent in a wide variety of community agencies, including extended care units, crisis centers, and doctors' offices, for the purpose of learning to interact with patients, familiarizing themselves with real patient problems, and then working with tutors to arrive at a workable goal. This type of course could serve as a model to include students and tutors from other health professions. The utmost consideration should be given to the appropriate level of students from each profession, the content areas for applicability and the placement of students for supervision. Having had involvement in the project, this writer believes that highly qualified practicing role models, who demonstrate an ability to work well with other professionals, are mandatory. It also has been observed that well-meant attempts at interdisciplinary learning experiences are predictably doomed to failure because of inadequate program planning, badly matched students, and/or faculty who are unable to operate and interrelate by cooperation and compromise. Such educational attempts, of course, are futile and retard the development of genuine interdisciplinary experiences.

The Canadian Scene

It is encouraging to see the mushrooming development of interdisciplinary programs across Canada in which nursing is very much involved. From Newfoundland to British Columbia, concerted efforts are being made by nursing to cooperate with the various health disciplines in an integrated way in order to provide patients or consumers with the best in knowledge, skills, and approaches.

The nurse, acting as a vital functioning member of the health care team, with a sound theoretical framework coupled with highly developed skills, is proving to be a highly competent colleague on the interdisciplinary health team. While it is not a new experience for nurses to be working interdependently with physicians and others, education for this role often has been given low priority and, indeed, often has been absent in the curricula of many schools of nursing. Perhaps, in focusing inward, as a profession, rather than outward to the broader perspective of the health care of the nation, nursing has tended, at times, to become ingrown, narrow, and isolated.

Now, the professional organizations, along with educational institutions, are beginning to take some strides in the promotion and the preparation of members. Responses from the provinces have shown numerous activities of an interdisciplinary nature. The Association of Registered Nurses of Newfoundland has participated in a Royal Commission Report[34] which discusses nursing as it relates to the health care scene in Newfoundland. Concern for the definition and preparation of the Primary Care Nurse, Family Practice Nurse, and Expanded Role Nurse is evident in almost all university schools of nursing across Canada.[35] As well, professional organizations are dealing with legislative aspects of this question.

At McMaster University, an interdisciplinary educational program in health administration has been conducted. The nurse practitioner program of this university is well-established and known across Canada. At Laval University, in Quebec, the course "Problématique de la Santé" (6 credits) offers students in medicine and Nursing Sciences an opportunity to work together for their clinical experience. At the University of Alberta, the Master of Health Services Administration program provides nursing candidates the chance to study and work in concert with the other health professionals with whom they will interact most often.

At the District and Chapter levels of the professional nursing organizations, program planning by interdisciplinary committees is a common practice across Canada.

Clarke, a WHO Fellow, contends that the educational experience must provide professional expertise and prepare the professional to function in an interdisciplinary team.

To be a colleague one must have access to a unique and valued resource —a resource that other members of the team are able to recognize as essential to the overall goal of the team. When individuals engage in new or expanded functions they must demonstrate their capabilities and gain the confidence and trust of colleagues and other professionals.[36]

---

[34] Leonard A. Miller, Royal Commission on Nursing Education, February 1974 (Appendices, p. 30).

[35] Nursing Papers, McGill University School of Nursing, Summer 1974, Vol. 6, No. 2, *passim*.

[36] Heather F. Clarke, "The Team Approach Works!," *RNABC News*, Vol. 6, No. 6, 1974.

In British Columbia the health professionals are provided a unique opportunity to explore and utilize team functioning. The community mental health centers located throughout British Columbia, where the nurse is an integral part of the mental health team—enjoying professional independence, collegial and consumer respect, as well as professional and financial rewards—is a natural modelling experience for aspiring nurses. The community human resource and health centers, developing in British Columbia, as well as several pilot projects in which the nurse works interdependently with the other health professionals, are examples of the health team very much in action. The hierarchical administrative model in nursing is being replaced by the collegial model, and nurses are responding positively to the change.

With the health team now an actuality in many settings, what is needed is for nursing curricula to provide the theory and knowledge to prepare the students for optimum utilization of the existing health care team experiences. Nursing has the potential to lead the way in educating for teamwork, utilizing as models those team structures that have developed at the community, or "grass roots," level and building upon them. There is a tremendous need for research activities in this area, initiated by nursing faculties and schools and supported by the professional organizations. Only by developing in this way can a systematic evaluation of nursing activities, as they relate to the optimum delivery of health care in Canada, be achieved.

Summary

Nursing, in its progressive development toward professionalization, is making significant advancements in theory, practice, research, and communication. Nursing theory may well be one of the major contributions to encouraging effectiveness of health team functioning, and nursing education may be the "cornerstone." In the pursuit of these objectives, experiences of those pioneers in interdisciplinary practice and interdisciplinary education will provide the guidelines. One emerging guideline is that learning should take place within a framework common to the various health professionals. In health care, this can be the patient (client) and/or his family, with a real or potential health problem. The advantages of using this model are:

1. The students of all the health care disciplines can relate to the patient (client) and his family;

2. The patient (client) and his family usually have health needs that can benefit from a variety of health care skills;

3. A systematic evaluation of the results of the interventions suggested or provided by the health team can be done best in a setting that utilizes the vision and expertise of different health professionals.

Once the focus of the health team has been established, team members need to be concerned with the dynamics of their group, i.e., the group process. This will involve some knowledge of the establishment of team goals; roles and role expectations; modes of decision-making; communication patterns; and, leadership and group norms (those implicit, unwritten rules which govern the behavior of people in groups).

In addition to their attention to group focus and group dynamics, each health team member must perceive clearly his or her individual contribution to the group's achievement. In the case of the nurse, this involves application of her special areas of professional expertise, including health assessment, health care, needs of patients, patient education, patient and family counseling. It is becoming more widely recognized that these areas of professional expertise are fundamental to an enlightened health program. Moreover, other professionals are recognizing the essential nature of the nurse's contribution to health care. Perhaps this point was made best by the student nurse who said, "The [interdisciplinary] class served to reinforce the positive aspects of nursing and feminism. As we learned more, we could become more confident in ourselves as nurses."[37]

Nurses are indeed moving toward a higher level of confidence in their expertise. In doing this they must recognize their responsibility to work and educate for cooperation and teamwork, and to continue to build upon past successes, to learn from failures, and to risk closer involvement with colleagues in other professions while maintaining, even expanding, their own professional identity.

[37] Harding, *et al.*, op. cit., p. 242.

Bibliography

ANDERSON, J., A. M. MARCUS, H. GEMEROY, F. PERRY, AND A. CAMFFER-MANN. "The Expanded Role of the Nurse," the *Canadian Nurse*, September 1975.

BAUMGART, ALICE J. "Are Nurses Ready for Teamwork?" the *Canadian Nurse*, July 1972.

BENNIS, W., K. BENNE, AND R. CHIN. *The Planning of Change*, 2nd ed. (New York: Holt, Rinehart & Winston, Inc.), 1969.

CLARKE, HEATHER F. "The Team Approach Works!" *RNABC News*, Vol. 6, No. 6, 1974.

COUNTDOWN 1974. Canadian Nursing Statistics, Canadian Nurses' Association. Ottawa, 1975.

DANA, B. AND C. G. SHEPS. "Trends and Issues in Interprofessional Education: Pride, Prejudice and Progress," *Ed. Social Work* 4: pp. 35–41, 1968.

DEPARTMENT OF HEALTH, EDUCATION AND WELFARE. *Extending the Scope of Nursing Practice*. A report of the Secretary's Committee to Study Extended Roles for Nurses. USA, 1971.

EPSTEIN, CHARLOTTE. *Effective Interaction in Contemporary Nursing*. (Englewood Cliffs, N.J.: Prentice-Hall, Inc.), 1974.

GOODWIN, MARJORIE. "Correlates of Career Choice," Unpublished Master's Research Project. University of British Columbia, August 1972.

HARDING, MARSHA FOWLER, AND NANCY GORDON. "A Nursing Course for Medical Students," *Nursing Outlook*, April 1975.

HOEKELMAN, ROBERT A. "Nurse-Physician Relationships," *American Journal of Nursing*, July 1975.

JONES, PHYLLIS E., AND EARL V. DUNN. "Education for a Health Team: a Pilot Project," *International Journal of Nursing Studies*, Vol. 11, 1974.

KING, M. KATHLEEN. "The Development of University Nursing Education," in *Nursing Education in a Changing Society*, ed. Mary Q. Innis. (Toronto: University of Toronto Press, 1970).

LALONDE, MARC. *A New Perspective on the Health of Canadians*. (Ottawa: Federal Government Publication, 1974).

LEININGER, MADELEINE. "This I Believe About Interdisciplinary Health Education for the Future," *Nursing Outlook*, Vol. 19, No. 12, 1971.

LUCE, CLARE BOOTHE. "The 21st Century Woman—Free at Last?" *Saturday Review/World*, August 24, 1974.

MARCUS, A. M., J. ANDERSON, H. GEMEROY, F. PERRY, AND A. CAMFFER-MAN. "Primary Therapist Project on an In-Patient Psychiatric Unit," *the Canadian Nurse*, September 1975.

MAUKSCH, INGEBORG. "Nursing is Coming of Age Through the Practitioner Movement," *American Journal of Nursing*, October 1975.

MCCREARY, JOHN F. "The Health Team Approach to Medical Education," *Journal of the American Medical Association*, Nov. 11, 1968.

MILLER, LEONARD A. Royal Commission on Nursing Education, February 1974.

NURSING PAPERS. McGill University School of Nursing. Summer 1974, Vol. 6, No. 2.

RAISLER, JEAN. "A Better Nurse-Doctor Relationship," *Nursing '74*, Vol. 4, No. 9, September 1974.

ROBINSON, H. ROCKE. "Health Care in Canada, a Commentary: Background Study for the Science Council of Canada, No. 29." Ottawa: The Council, 1973.

RUBIN, I., AND R. BECHEHARD. "Factors Influencing the Effectiveness of Health Teams," *Milbank Memorial Fund Quarterly*, Vol. 50, July 1972.

SCHEIN, E. H. *Process Consultation*. (Reading, Mass.: Addison-Wesley Publishing Co., Inc.), 1969.

SCIENCE COUNCIL OF CANADA. "Sciences for Health Services: Report 22." (Ottawa: The Council, October 1974).

SZASZ, GEORGE. "Interprofessional Education in the Health Sciences," *Milbank Memorial Fund Quarterly*, Vol. 47, October 1969.

UPRICHARD, MURIEL. "Ferment in Nursing," *International Nursing Review*, Vol. 16, No. 1, 1969.

YEAWORTH, R., AND F. MIMS. "Interdisciplinary Education as an Influence System," *Nursing Outlook*, Vol. 21, No. 11, November 1973.

3

Technical and Professional — What's In a Name?*

MARGUERITE E. SCHUMACHER, B.Sc.N., M.A., Ed.M.

- "The antithesis between a technical and a liberal education is fallacious.

    "There can be no adequate technical education which is not liberal, and no liberal education which is not technical...."

    WHITEHEAD (1929)

- ... it is interesting to note that in nursing education, the development of manual skills and manual dexterity seems to have fallen to ill repute. It is left primarily to the student to learn through self-learning packages, accompanied by audiovisual resources of trainex films, single concept loops, programed learning books, and so forth.... How is the student motivated to emulate her instructor, or the practising nurse who *is* able and *does give* a high quality of care?

- In a WHO Report on Higher Education in Nursing (1973)... nursing was seen not as technical in nature but

---

* The author acknowledges the assistance of Dr. S. Stinson and Miss Glennis Zilm.

rather as an applied science in which the doctor-patient/ family-nurse team remained the fundamental central component in the delivery of health services.

● It is the findings within research which will nourish the profession and the minds of the learners.

Library shelves are lined with reference books on professional and technical education. Papers are written and debates are held not only on these two aspects of education but also on their relation to an occupation. Nursing practice, and particularly nursing education, are very much caught up in some of these perplexities. Some viewpoints presented are that initial programs of nursing education at the auxiliary level and diploma level of preparation are confined to the technical aspects of nursing and that professional nursing begins with the baccalaureate preparation. Studies have been conducted in an attempt to identify distinct differences between the two. (Montag, 1951; Anderson, 1966; Johnson, 1966; Waters, 1972.)

Waters identified differences in the areas of problem-solving and decision-making, in the scope of practice, and in attitudes toward practice. Baccalaureate graduates were found to be more self-directed and willing to risk. They were more likely to consider the psychosocial needs of patients. In contrast, the diploma graduates were found to be involved with nursing problems and interventions that were more likely to be physiological and physical rather than psychological or social. Interestingly enough, though, some of the head nurses cited examples not entirely supportive of the differences. It is noted that generalizations from this study should not be made. The data came from a particular geographical setting and from a limited number of observations and interviews.

Professional v Technical Education

Professional education emphasizes the need for a liberal education. Writers over the ages have debated the issue. Whitehead (1929) states that "a liberal education is an education for thought and for aesthetic appreciation." But, interestingly enough, he does not restrict the need for a liberal education to professional education. In fact, quite the contrary is true.

"The antithesis between a technical and a liberal education is fallacious," he states. "There can be no adequate technical education which is not liberal, and no liberal education which is not technical..." He refers to three avenues of education, namely: the literary culture, the scientific culture, and the technical culture. One method must not be chosen exclusive of the other two. The goal of education must be to identify a dominant emphasis, together with coordinating and infusing some of the other two.

With those comments in mind, it is interesting to note that in nursing education, the development of manual skills and manual dexterity seems to have fallen to ill repute. The demonstration, teaching, and practice of nursing skills or procedures are sometimes not acknowledged as a legitimate integral part of the curriculum. It is left primarily to the student to learn through self-learning packages, accompanied by audiovisual resources of trainex films, single concept loops, programed learning books, and so forth. Yet, where does the student see this procedure and these skills in the overall context of nursing? How is the student motivated to emulate her instructor, or that practising nurse who *is* able and *does give* a high quality of care?

Jourard (1971) states that "we have not had education in this nation. We have had institutions which indoctrinate an ideology, a way to experience and a way to behave." He is critical of the approach of curriculum designs which have not considered the growth of man, but instead, emphasize the training of technicians and functionaries, people who serve the system. Nurses and nursing educators, take heed.

Christman (1972) would seem to support the criticism of curriculum design when he states that nursing curricula have been static and ritualistic, due in part to the fact that education has been given in simple-purpose schools and that students often were recruited from the local population, which resulted in inbreeding.

In a WHO Report on Higher Education in Nursing (1973) participants fully agreed that the skills required of the nurse were the habit of independent life-long learning, analytical thinking, and systematic investigation basic to nursing process, human relations, and communication skills. Nursing was seen not as technical in nature but, rather, as an applied science in which the doctor-patient/family-nurse team remained the fundamental central component in the delivery of health services.

Nursing as a Profession

In examining quality in nursing practice, Stinson, (1970) points out that from a "strictly technical standpoint, today's nurse has more valid factual knowledge at her disposal than nurses, and in many ways doctors, in the twenties. But her over-all ability to make the patient feel secure and cared about may be another matter."

In the writer's opinion the discovery and utilization of knowledge is of prime concern and importance in the development of nursing as a profession. In Stinson's (1970) view, the two conditions that are associated with the degree of professionalization of an occupation are (1) that of supplying high-valued services to society and, (2) regulating these services. She goes on to point out that the attainment of these conditions are dependent on the ongoing socialization of practitioners; the development of the knowledge-skill component; the formulation and implementation of viable standards of practice; adequate systems for articulation and distribution of services; and, ensuring that rewards are such that these several conditions are met.

The professional group must assume the responsibility for inquiry to extend and discover new knowledge. Nurses may see themselves as facilitators of patient care. They may see an increasing need to establish themselves with other health disciplines in interdisciplinary groups. But foremost is the need to establish that core of knowledge and skills peculiar to nursing. This will be done best by the profession through systematic research. The search for knowledge, the discovery of truths, will assist in forming the identity of the nursing profession. However, the accumulation of knowledge is of little avail unless it encompasses a means for the transmission of this knowledge to the practitioner and to the student. Knowledge is used in its broadest sense, which may refer to abstract theoretical constructs and technological advances in the form of skill techniques. Theory must become a part of the practice or we are left in the condition Perkins (1965) has aptly described: "He who knows the theory but not the practice does not know the whole theory."

This transmission of knowledge should be done through the socialization process of the member and through teaching in organized educational programs.

What is the reward system in nursing? This is not clearly identified in the practice field of the profession. On one hand promotional rewards are evident on the administrative ladder as the nurse moves from head nurse, to supervisor, to administrator. A similar opportunity is available within the teaching field. On the other hand no such framework exists at the general staff level. Standards for nursing practice are fuzzy. How is the practising nurse rewarded for her expertise, standards and service ideal? Faculty members in a university setting are cognizant of the fact that rewards are linked with teaching effectiveness, community involvement, and research activity. The nurse in the community or institutional agency lacks such guidelines. Indeed, it would seem that her effectiveness factor in many situations will be judged in relation to her conformity to agency regulations, the speed with which she can complete her assignment, and her dexterity in carrying out manual skills. An unsatisfactory report can be expected for faltering in these areas. There seems to be no recognizable rewards for comforting, caring, or meeting psycho-social needs of clients. Yet, an exploratory study conducted at the Health Sciences Centre, Winnipeg (1974) leaves one with many unanswered questions in relation to the interpersonal milieu and the process of healing. Research needs to be pursued in order to find the answers.

A full debate on whether or not nursing meets the criteria of a profession is not the purpose of this paper. However, it is pertinent that the nature of the practices in the profession be highlighted to give a perspective to the issue at hand. Accepting the fact that there is a technical component in nursing, the writer would like to present the idea of the "wholeness" of nursing. It is not a question of technical v. professional, but rather that these are parts, or components, of the whole. One component does not exist without the other. There may be differences in degree, amount or quality of each component, but at no time is there an absence of one or the other. In this view nursing is an open system with a wholistic approach to practice. The sum total is greater than its parts. The following figures, which were conceived by S. M. Stinson, illustrate the point.

Figure 1.

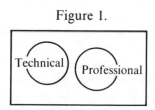

Figure. 1.　*Identifies two separate components. This is not nursing.*

Figure 2.

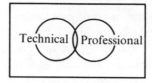

Figure 2. *Indicates an overlapping of these components. This too is unsatisfactory, inasmuch as they signify separate entities but lack a wholeness.*

Figure 3.

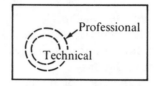

Figure 3. *The dotted line signifies the ever-changing nature of the profession and encompasses the technical aspects that also change. Nursing then is reflected in its wholeness.*

Nursing Education

The question today must not be, where should nursing education programs be located in colleges, technical institutes, or universities; the question to be raised must be, what should constitute the program to prepare the individual for nursing? Where the program should be located will then fall into place.

Nursing education at the diploma level in Canada has moved rapidly from being hospital based to going into educational settings. Although the nursing profession has supported such a move for several decades the sudden change has not necessarily meant a change in the approach to teaching and learning how to nurse. A second point to consider is to distinguish between what is and what ought to be.

Nursing education in Canada is taking various routes. In some areas it begins at the auxiliary level. The learner qualifies to become a certified nursing aide or assistant. The practice of the nursing aide is based on the application of knowledge in the execution of recurring nursing functions, having clearly defined limits. From that level the learner may go into a diploma program to qualify to become a registered nurse.

The Alberta Task Force Report on Nursing Education (1975) proposes that the auxiliary level of nursing practice be separate from that of the professional level. Baccalaureate preparation is being recommended for all who practice nursing. This stand is being taken "in view of the geometric expansion of knowledge, the complexities of modern man's health problems, the development of radical new medical technologies, the increased expectations of consumers for quality health care, the increased role of government within the health-care system and the development of various health-care delivery patterns, it becomes apparent that future professional health-care providers need a broad educational base." The Task Force envisions an increasing role for nurses in areas other than the traditional field of patient care. It sees them increasingly involved in such areas as health education in the school system, in industry, in health agencies, and in the community at large; in promoting and maintaining the health of the community in a variety of ways; and in carrying out observations in the health field that will permit them to advise health agencies and governments on the necessary steps to be taken in order to provide a healthier environment and better health practices throughout the whole of the province.

The writer concurs that the future role of the nurse must include the ability to counsel people on health matters; to teach individuals or families on matters related to the maintenance of health and the prevention of illness; to supervise the health care of well children and older people; to monitor patients with stabilized long-term or chronic illness; to coordinate the health care of people through referral to appropriate agencies; to intervene in crisis situations. (Boudreau, 1972). Some nurses will seek to have additional knowledge and skills to function in a primary health care setting, while others will go on to function in specialized areas in the community or hospital setting. Irrespective of the setting, according to the Alberta Task Force Report (1975), as a professional she will be expected to conceptualize at a high level of abstraction; be able "to use the theory and content of science in imaginative ways while caring for patients and utilize extensive knowledge and skills in order to make sound judgments concerning the overall, continuous management of patient care."

If this is to be the future role of the nurse, it behooves us to continue to teach nursing based on traditional notions. The need for a liberal education is evident. Man is a social being. Nursing acts are performed within a social milieu. This needs to be a dominant emphasis. If behavioral research findings indicate that changes in clients' progress occur because of interpersonal relationships, how is this research being incorporated into the educational program and transmitted into the practice setting? What would happen if the introduc-tory courses in nursing focused in depth on the meaning of health and the meaning of illness, related to the internal frame of reference of both the client and the nurse? The writer is of the opinion that a wide gap exists between the findings of research and its application to both the practice of nursing and nursing education.

At some point in a student's educational career there needs to be time spent at a university. The functions of a university are in the areas of research as well as education. The student in the university setting should be challenged by the zeal and competence of the faculty involved in both of these areas. Research needs to become an integral part of nursing faculties. The need to outline research frameworks is as great as the need to develop theoretical frameworks for curricula. Research for practice and research for education. It is the findings within research that will nourish the profession and the minds of the learners.

Preparation for professional or for technical practice? Which is it to be? Can it be one or the other? The writer is of the opinion that the preparation of the nurse must be professional in nature. There is a technical component that must be recognized and given its due emphasis. However, the technical component does not consist of the total act of nursing. It is not too difficult to learn how to stick a needle into a human being, take a blood pressure, attach wires for electronic pick-ups from a person's organic disturbances. Machines and technical procedures cannot provide human warmth, love and responsive care. According to Jourard (1971) "one of the events which we believe inspires faith and hope in a patient is the conviction that somebody cares about him." If this proves true, it implies that the quality of the nurse-patient relationship is a factor in the patient's recovery. "Direct contact with a patient somehow increases his sense of being a worth-while individual person, and this experience inspires him—it does something to the body which helps it throw off illness."

Professional or technical—which label is it to be? A group of first-year students in a college setting handed in a written assignment. One of them reads as follows:

In the previous paper we attempted to identify areas in which we felt the family has a need for health care. Here we intend to define those areas more clearly, to establish related health goals and criteria by which their successful meeting could be evaluated, and to suggest a plan of care designed to meet those goals. Within this framework we will also attempt to show the role of the nurse in helping the family to identify their health needs and to meet them.

As graduates, will these students be labelled professional or technical?

Summary

Technical and professional—what's in a name? The writer has attempted to outline the need to differentiate between what is nursing practice and what is involved in the preparation of nursing practice. There is a component of technical education and there is a component of professional education. In the clinical setting where the nurse offers her specialized services, technical nursing is but one part of the larger body of knowledge and skills known, or classified, as nursing.

Education in nursing needs to be examined as a whole. Liberal education, scientific education, and technical education are part and parcel of the whole. One theme may dominate at certain points, but there must always be some melding of the other two themes.

Although diploma education has been transferred into a new educational setting, there is no assurance that a change of approach has taken place. A technical setting does not necessarily make nursing education technical in nature. A university setting does not necessarily make nursing education professional and liberal in nature. There is a need to accept nursing as a profession encompassing areas that include technical skills. However, this area is but one aspect of a much greater whole—nursing.

Bibliography

ANDERSON, BERNICE. *Nursing Education in Community Junior Colleges.* (Philadelphia: J. B. Lippincott, 1966).

BOUDREAU, THOMAS J. *Report of the Committee on Nurse Practitioners.* Report to The Department of National Health and Welfare, 1972.

CHRISTMAN, LUTHER, AND RALPH E. KIRKMAN. "A Significant Innovation in Nursing Education," *Peabody Journal of Education*, October 1972.

DeMARSH, G. KATHLEEN. *A Study of the Effects of a Specific Inservice Education Program for Registered Nurses on Patient Welfare and Hospital Operation.* Health Sciences Centre, Winnipeg, Manitoba, 1973.

JOHNS, WALTER H. *The Report of the Alberta Task Force on Nursing Education.* Report to the Department of Advanced Education, Government of Alberta, 1975.

JOHNSON, DOROTHY E. "Competence in Practice; Technical and Professional," *Nursing Outlook*, 13:30–33, October 1966

JOURARD, SIDNEY M. *The Transparent Self*, (Toronto: Van Nostrand Reinhold Co., 1971).

LIVINGSTONE, RICHARD. *On Education*, (New York: The MacMillan Co., 1945).

MONTAG, MILDRED L. *Education of Nursing Technicians*, (New York: John Wiley and Sons, 1951).

PERKINS, JAMES A. "The University and the Arts," *T. C. Record*, 66, May 1965, p. 676.

STINSON, SHIRLEY S. *Deprofessionalization in Nursing* (Ann Arbor, Michigan: University Microfilms, Inc., 1970).

WATERS, VERLE, AND SHIRLEY S. CHATER, *et al.* "Technical and Professional Nursing" *Nursing Research*, Vol. 21, No. 2, March–April 1972, pp. 124-31.

WHO. *Higher Education in Nursing.* Report on a Symposium Convened by the Regional Office for Europe of the World Health Organization. Regional Office for Europe. WHO Copenhagen, 1973.

II NURSING PRACTICE

The practice of nursing is a continual challenge to the imagination. Creative imagination plays a vital part in the development of all professions. It is the sine qua non *of scientific and technological achievement.*

Today the word creativity is "part of a growing resistance to the tyranny of the formula, a new respect for individuality, a dawning recognition of the potentialities of the liberated mind." There is need for freedom of thought and inquiry if this unpredictable, capricious, open, independent, zealous, synthesizing process of creativity is to flourish.

FLORIS E. KING
Nursing Papers, June 1970, "Opening Doors: Creativity in Nursing"

Clinical practice is the essence of nursing. The recipient is a client seeking preventative care or a patient seeking acute care. The setting varies from the institution to the community. *Quality* care is the paramount focus. This section emphasizes two major issues that face the nursing profession in the attempt to maintain quality—expertise and education beyond initial basic preparation. One article presents the nurse who seeks further education in order to assist patients in obtaining optimal care. The other article examines professional issues pertaining to those nurses who are a consistent part of the work force but who are not required specifically by the profession for accountability in their performance by actual demonstration of ongoing competence. It is essential that Canadian nursing continue to address itself to these two critical issues.

Is there a national consensus on nursing practice? Is it a provincial matter, an inconsistent matter, thereby preventing solid growth of the image of professional nursing in Canada? It seems illogical to assist the development of some nurses who possess skills of an exceptional quality, while ignoring the skills of the majority of care-givers. Can it be that the few who have outstanding competence are expected to make up for those who are unmotivated or unable to become experts? Are we, as a profession, relieving the majority of their responsibility for continued self-development?

Nursing is not alone in pondering this question. Many other professions are seeking to develop membership guidelines and regulation.

"Quality of life" is a term applied to every aspect of human existence from deciding on a domicile, to health care, to political issues: these include such essentials as housing, environment and human rights. "Quality of life" is a major emphasis in nursing. The development of expert abilities is as essential to the profession as the ongoing performance of those who are the consistent providers of twenty-four hour care. We, as a profession, cannot continue our daily involvement in nursing without holding definite beliefs about these major issues.

4

Maintaining Competence: Realities and Myths

ISOBEL KAY, R.N., B.N., M.Ed.
DOROTHY KERGIN, R.N., B.S.N., M.P.H., Ph.D.

- ...The abilities of health professionals to provide competent and effective care are under increased public scrutiny. As new moves develop among segments of the population and one hears the phrase "Five years ago we. ...," one realizes that social change is also happening in communities where nurses live and work. Have all nurses kept up with the advancements of knowledge and practice? Can we continue to condone irresponsible and blanket re-registration in the 1970s? To maintain competency and to reduce professional obsolescence, nurses, as well as other health professionals, must, therefore, have opportunities to practice learned skills and to acquire additional skills that are necessary because of new knowledge or for entry into a new field of practice. We will continue to learn as long as we live but can nurses be relied upon to learn what is required in order to fulfill their obligation to Canadian society?

"Educate! Educate!! Educate!" This was the cry of the socialist reform movement of the 19th century. Unfortunately, this adult education development was seen as patronizing, dilettantish, puritanical—and boring.[1] It was part of a literary drive, an after-work vocational upgrading for reading clubs and leisure activities.

The slogan is again reverberating in educational halls, conference rooms, and living rooms in this century. The 60s and 70s may well be remembered by future generations as the time when there was a great demand for adult education and continuing education. Education for what?—to fill the extended leisure hours? Education for whom?—anyone and everyone who wants it? Education by whom?—by anyone who decides he has something to teach?

The soft note that began in the 60s is reaching a crescendo in the 70s. Health professionals are caught up in the educational movement. The abilities of health professionals to provide competent and effective care are also under increased public scrutiny.

In this paper, the authors discuss reasons for continuing education; the challenge of the task; responsibilities of nurses and nursing to insure care by competent nurses; and, issues that need to be faced in order to meet the challenge.

Why Continuing Education for Nurses?

Journals, periodicals, reports and newspapers come in ever-increasing stacks across the desk, and libraries require extensions to accommodate the volumes of new writings. As new moves develop within segments of the population, one hears the phrase "Five years ago we ...," and realizes that social change is definitely happening within communities where nurses live and work.

Toffler aptly labels this development the "accelerative thrust." "Doctors and executives alike complain that they cannot keep up with the latest developments in their fields. Hardly a meeting or conference takes place today without some ritualistic oratory about 'the challenge of change'."[2]

Amid this deluge of new information, many nurses can be heard to say, "Once a nurse, always a nurse," or "What's so different about bedside nursing today, compared to nursing 10 years ago?" Can we be

---

[1] Margaret Gillett, *A History of Education: Thought and Practice* (Toronto: McGraw-Hill Ryerson Ltd., 1966), p. 215.

[2] Alvin Toffler, *Future Shock* (Toronto: Bantam Books, 1971), p. 19.

delivering, in agencies across Canada, the same kind of care that was given in the 50s? Have all nurses kept up with the advancements of knowledge and practice? Nurses have been told that they are members of a noble profession, but the majority of them have not continued their education in a formal manner. Yet, annually nurses reapply for registration with their respective provincial bodies, thus entitling each to call herself "Registered Nurse," and to continue to minister to the public.

Can we continue to condone this irresponsible and blanket re-registration in the 1970s? What alternatives do we have?

In the nineteenth century, Florence Nightingale (who strongly opposed proposals for nurse registration and examination) wrote of the need for continual learning. "Indeed, every five or ten years a nurse after leaving the hospital really requires a second training nowadays."[3] In a 1928 issue of the *American Journal of Nursing*, Judd wrote, "I venture to advocate that the nursing profession give up the doctrine that a nurse is forever competent because at one time somebody put on her the stamp of approval as a graduate.... I am willing to assert that some continuation of training in service for nurses would promote the well-being of the nation."[4]

We assume that all nurses are competent when they graduate from approved schools and pass registration examinations, but professional competence cannot be forever assured. "Rustiness" results from the lack of proper use of knowledge and skills. Professional obsolescence occurs when we fail to grow and fail to keep up with changes. Dubin[5] describes the condition of obsolescence as the reverse of the activity of learning. Obsolescence, he says, is a decremental process comprised of the loss of acquired knowledge and the non-acquisition of new learning which occurs unless effort is made constantly to repair the erosion and to stimulate growth and innovation. An obsolescence index can be obtained:

$$\frac{current\ knowledge\ understood\ by\ nurses}{current\ knowlege\ used\ within\ the\ field}$$

To maintain competency and to reduce professional obsolescence, nurses, as well as other health professionals, therefore must have

---

[3] Florence Nightingale, "Nurses, Training of, and Nursing the Sick," in *Selected Writings of Florence Nightingale*, compiled by Lucy R. Seymer (New York: The Macmillan Company, 1954), p. 333.

[4] Charles H. Judd, "Adult Education," *American Journal of Nursing*, XXVIII (July 1928), p. 654.

[5] S. S. Dubin, "Motivational Factors," in *Professional Obsolescence*, edited by S. S. Dubin (Lexington, Mass.: Lexington Books, D. C. Heath and Company, 1971), p. 39.

opportunities to practice acquired skills* and learn additional skills that are necessary because of new knowledge, or, for entry to a new field of practice. As well, the profession as a whole must have mechanisms for dealing with individual members whose skills are obsolete, or who show evidence of lack of competency. Along with those who may be administratively accountable for the actions of nurses, such as directors of nursing and physician-employers, the profession also must decide upon the type and number of practice errors that can be tolerated, with minimal harm to recipients of nursing care.

Everett Hughes has considered the problem of mistakes and failures as a major theme in human work, whether that work be done by physicians or plumbers. Hughes tells us:

The more times per day a man does a given operation, the greater his chance of doing it wrong sometimes. True, his skill may become so great that his percentage of errors is nearly zero.... One who never performs a given action will never do it wrong. But one who has never tried it could not do it right if he were on some occasion compelled to try.... Some skills require more repetition than others for the original learning and for maintenance. In some, even the most proficient make many failures, while in others the top level of skill is close to perfection. Occupations, considered as bundles of skills, are subject to the contingencies contained in all combinations of these factors of learning and of maintaining skill, and, correlatively, subject to variations in the probability that one will sometimes make mistakes.[6]

Nurses, being human, are indeed capable of making mistakes, even though, like physicians and plumbers, they rarely acknowledge this fact. Too often one has the feeling that nurses expect one another to be above error and that each mistake, no matter what its effects might be, should result in self-castigation and public confession.* The myth that nurses are perfect must be destroyed—nurses *do* make mistakes. But mistake-making cannot always be equated with obsolescence.

---

* The word "skills," as used by the authors, is intended to include technical, intellectual, and psychosocial skills, which, although not yet defined clearly and behaviorally, are understood to be those that are expected of a competent nurse.

[6] Everett C. Hughes, "Mistakes at Work," *Canadian Journal of Economics and Political Science* XVII (August 1951), p. 320 Reprinted in *Men and Their Work* (London: The Free Press of Glencoe, Collier-Macmillan Limited, 1958), p. 89.

* For instance, the use of incident or "special" reports as a means to "confess errors," as reported by Virginia H. Walker and Eugene D. Selmanoff, "Functions of the Special Report", *Ritualism in Nursing and its Effect on Patient Care* (Indianapolis, Indiana: Indiana University Medical Centre, 1964), pp. 69-74.

In order to assure the public that services are provided by practitioners who recognize their responsibilities to provide good nursing care and who have the abilities to do this, nurses, like other groups, develop various techniques. Among these are:

1. Adopting codes of ethics that describe standards of behavior that ought to be followed by members in their services to society and in their professional relationships. Not only may codes of ethics be used to describe appropriate behavior under various conditions, they also may be used to develop definitions of deviant behavior, such as behavior that represents professional misconduct.

2. Inculcating in students the routines and methods of performing particular acts. Students are instructed in the importance of performing certain tasks routinely in order to limit risks to patients; for instance, the reading of medicine labels a specified number of times and the sequence of events involved in carrying out an aseptic procedure. (Educators proclaim that principles are taught, but in the application of these principles, certain defined steps are followed.) Furthermore, institutional policies and procedures, or environmental controls, may be established in order to protect patients, staffs and employers. Examples of such policies are: unit dosage systems, isolation procedures, and requirements for physicians' written orders for medications. Nursing staffs of various health agencies acquaint new staff members and students with "the way things are done here."

3. Developing standards that describe the characteristics or environmental conditions that are believed to permit members to provide services effectively. Professional associations, for instance, may develop and publish recommended standards for the organization of nursing services, including optimal staff-patient ratios.

4. Establishing regulations to ensure that all who practice have met minimum standards of either education or practice or both. With the exception of Ontario and Alberta, provincial nurses' associations regulate the admission and curriculum standards of nursing educational programs within their provinces, to guarantee minimum qualifications of those whose names subsequently may be recorded on a register.[7] Provincial Acts also give to the regulatory bodies the responsibility for establishing equivalent criteria to be met by graduates of other jurisdictions who wish to become registered or certified. In Ontario, the responsibility for establishing criteria for initial registra-

---

[7] Helen Sabin, Doris Price and Betty Sellers. "Nursing: What it is and What it is Not," in *Contemporary Issues in Canadian Law for Nurses,* edited by Shirley R. Good and Janet C. Kerr (Toronto: Holt, Rinehart & Winston of Canada Ltd., 1973), pp. 63–82.

tion belongs to the College of Nurses of Ontario.[8] In Alberta, educational standards are set by the Committee on Nursing Education, appointed by the Universities' Coordinating Council.[9]

5. Maintaining mechanisms to deal with members who are alleged to have performed acts that endanger patients, or who are likely to perform such acts. All Provincial Nurses' Acts give the primary responsibility for disciplining members to the organization that has the power to enter names on the registers. That is, for due cause, names also may be "struck off." "Due cause" usually relates to evidence of incompetency, incapacity or professional misconduct. The Acts generally describe the grounds for such actions, the procedures to be followed and the appeal mechanisms. In some provinces, the power to suspend or cancel registration certificates is reserved for the organization's council, or executive. In the most recently promulgated acts, those of Ontario and Quebec, a non-nurse serves as a required member of a discipline panel. In Quebec,[10] a lawyer is appointed as chairman of the discipline committee. In Ontario,[11] one member of each panel that begins a discipline hearing must be a lay member of the College Council. These requirements apply to all the "self-regulating" health professions covered by the Acts of these two provinces and may be regarded as evidence of increased public (government) concern for the quality of health care and for the qualifications of practitioners who provide that care. Both Acts also require lay representation on the governing councils of the professional regulatory bodies.

An increasingly well-informed public has accentuated the need to hasten the spread and use of new knowledge in the delivery of health care. "Higher education and income levels, as well as expanded coverage by health care schemes is shifting the role of the consumer as 'patient' to that of 'buyer' thereby strengthening his position to demand more and better health services."[12]

To maintain adequacy in performance of skills and to prevent professional obsolescence and to assure the public who have trusted

---

[8] Ontario Legislature, "Part IV: Nursing," *Bill 22, The Health Disciplines Act, 1974* (Toronto: J. C. Thatcher, Queen's Printer for Ontario, 1974), pp. 47–60.

[9] Alberta Association of Registered Nurses, *The Registered Nurses Act* (Edmonton: AARN, 1966), p. 5.

[10] National Assembly of Quebec, Chapter IV "Corporations," *Professional Code* (Quebec: Charles-Henri Dube, Quebec Official Publisher, 1973), p. 34.

[11] Ontario, *Health Disciplines Act*, p. 48.

[12] June Nakamoto and Coolie Verner, *Continuing Education in Nursing: A Review of North American Literature 1960–1970* (Vancouver: Adult Education Research Centre and Division of Continuing Education in the Health Sciences, University of British Columbia, 1972), p. 3.

professional groups in self-regulation of adequate standards of care, nurses in Canada can no longer continue with the *status quo*. The *status quo* is voluntary, non-directional, not good enough—continue learning, we must!

What should be learned? We hear the terms: the expanded role of the nurse, blurring of roles, better utilization of professional skills, "nurse practitioners." Education has a critical role to play in future developments within nursing. Increased knowledge and skills are needed by nurses with the potential for leadership in the organization and the practice of nursing care. Included are increased psychosocial skills and articulation, so changes can be made.

What Do We Mean By Continuing Education?

We realize that there is a necessity for additional knowledge and skills, but what is this term, "continuing education"? Many adults have learned by doing, from work experience, from mentors, and from colleagues. These types of incidental learning processes are too haphazard for accomplishing the task of continuing education for nurses. We will continue to learn as long as we live, but can we be relied upon to learn what is required in order to fulfill our professional obligations to Canadian society?

Education is a process of planned, integrated, and goal-directed experiences involving "*modifications* within the individual which are characterized by some kind of *improvement* in the way of skills, habits, understandings, techniques, attitudes and values."[13]

Voluntary v Mandatory

In the author's views, the non-system of voluntary continuing education for nurses has failed, but still we question whether mandatory continuing education will improve competence and/or prevent obso-

---

[13] Peter E. Siegle, *Mountains, Plateaus and Valleys in Adult Learning*, 1953, cited in *Occasional Paper II, The Concept of Lifelong Integrated Learning "Education Permanente" and Some Implications for University Adult Education*, edited by A. A. Liveright. Report of a seminar on Education Permanente convened by the International Congress of University Adult Education, New York University, Washington Square Campus, August 1967. (n.p.: International Congress of University Adult Education, February 1968), p. 5.

lescence. What is needed is a universal commitment to continued learning, rather than continuing education. (The term "continuing education" is used loosely to describe any program which is offered to adults outside of formal compulsory schooling. Because learning is rarely evaluated, one cannot presume that attendance at continuing education programs leads to continued learning. Therefore, the authors place emphasis, in this context, on continued learning.) There have been ample opportunities for continuing education and many nurses have taken advantage of these, but one questions what impact they have had on actual nursing care.

Much of what needs to be learned is available in books and journals, but many nurses do not read them. There are postgraduate courses, lecture courses, credit courses, institutes, workshops, conferences, in-service programs, and correspondence courses. Flaherty found that, although there was apparent interest in continuing education among nurses, the actual number of those who were engaged in continuing education was small.[14] One would conjecture that, if this study were replicated today in other provinces, the findings would be similar. Flaherty reported that nurses who participated most in educational programs were those employed in administration, in teaching, and in public health. Only about 4% of nurses in her sampling reported that employers granted time off with pay to attend professional meetings and conferences. This could account for the high proportion of senior nursing personnel who attended.

No systematic studies have been conducted across Canada to determine how much educating is going on. The proportion of nurses who participate in continuing education offerings, nurse leaders in agencies and institutions tell us, is small. Record-keeping is limited and evaluation is rare.

Continuing education as a series of planned, goal-directed educational experiences is minimally available in Canada, except through formal collegiate or university courses. Therefore, planned programs of study are available only to those who can afford the luxury of leaving the work force for a period of time or to those who are fortunate enough to live near a teaching center where such a work-study program exists.

The only Canada-wide program which has continued for several years is the Nursing Unit Administration course sponsored jointly by the Canadian Nurses' Association and the Canadian Hospital Associa-

---

[14] M. Josephine Flaherty. "An Enquiry into the Needs for Continuing Education for R.N.'s in the Province of Ontario." (unpublished master's thesis. University of Toronto. 1965). p. 108.

tion. This continuing education program fulfills a need for nurses who are in management positions. It does not provide education in practice expertise. Continuing education programs which are available are sporadic and at the whim of someone who feels he/she has something worth teaching. Attendance is usually voluntary, except where an agency "sends" a nurse.

Health professionals in some American states have attempted to remedy the problem of non-participation in educational programs by instituting a system of mandatory continuing education.

Some professional groups in Canada, the College of Family Physicians of Canada and the Canadian Dietetic Association, for example, also have gone the route of mandatory continuing education or are contemplating it. A specific amount of mandatory continuing education is required for continuing licensure and/or membership in the respective organizations. The assumption is that by forcing nurses to attend meetings or conferences and to read professional journals, learning, and therefore continued competence, will be ensured. These professional groups are beginning to identify problems concerning requirements for mandatory continuing education. The medical profession is examining and questioning the difference between continuing instruction, when physicians take advantage of continuing education programs to meet licensing requirements, and continuing self-education following determination of educational goals.[15] If the external motivation of licensing bodies for continuing education is the drive that forces physicians to attend educational sessions, it is doubtful whether it will be possible to come to any conclusion regarding the effect of such an exposure on the care which patients receive.[16] If evaluation of the effect of these programs on patient care is not possible, Brown and Uhl suggest it is foolhardy for busy physicians to participate.[17]

While recognizing the need for continuing education to maintain professional competence, Miller describes present educational programs as being primarily *content oriented*, "which encourages dependence upon teachers."[18] He recommends a shift to a process model,

[15] Hugh T. Carmichael, "Self Assessment Tests," *Journal of the American Medical Association*, CCXIII (September 7, 1970), pp. 1656–7. (specific reference: p. 1657).

[16] Gerald H. Escovitz, "The Continuing Education of Physicians: Its Relationship to Quality of Care Evaluation," *Medical Clinics of North America*, LVII (July 1973), pp. 1135–47. (specific reference: p. 1135).

[17] Clement R. Brown and Henry Uhl, "Mandatory Continuing Education: Sense or Nonsense," *Journal of the American Medical Association*, CCXIII (September 7, 1970), pp. 1660–8. (specific reference: p. 1667).

[18] George E. Miller, "Continuing Education for What?" *Journal of Medical Education*, XLII (April 1967), pp. 320–6. (quote: p. 324).

"toward an augmented concern for educational diagnosis and individualized therapy."[19] This means the identification of discrepancies between optimal and actual performance, which is the beginning of the educational process.

Dubin examines the problems experienced by professional engineers in attempting to prevent obsolescence. He describes a tendency to learn from verbal rather than from written contact with information sources. In a profession where most members are employed in corporations, he believes that it is the immediate supervisor who counts in the development of subordinates. He categorically states that "education comes not by exposure to, but by engagement with the world."[20]

Concern about mandatory continuing education is also being expressed by some American nurses. Stevens questions whether required attendance at educational programs assures that the nurse will absorb and transfer new learning to her work situation. If a nurse does not maintain professional practice through continuing education, will "force-feeding" change his/her attitude toward maintaining competency? The only way one can judge whether a continuing education experience really benefits and protects the client is to evolve a valid testing system. While some states have laws for mandatory continuing education, no proposed law requires an evaluative process in the nurse-client situation.[21] Canadian nurses' associations are proceeding slowly, undoubtedly recognizing the problems of mandatory continuing education. For example, the RNABC has taken the position that "participation in continuing education by registered nurses should be on a voluntary basis and that criteria for re-registration should focus on the competence of the individual."[22]

Few continuing education programs have originated from a careful identification of health care problems. Canter suggests that "we tend to dabble in the various popular topics of the day"[23] based on important names of resource people and current fads without identifying practice needs of individual nurses.

---

[19] *Ibid.*

[20] Dubin, *Professional Obsolescence*, p. 54.

[21] Barbara J. Stevens, "Mandatory Continuing Education for Professional Nurse Relicensure: What Are the Issues?" *Journal of Nursing Administration,* IV (September-October 1973), pp. 25 – 8. (specific reference: p. 25).

[22] Registered Nurses Association of British Columbia, "Position Statement on Continuing Education for Re-registration," (Vancouver: RNABC, September 1974), p. 1. (Mimeographed.)

[23] Marjorie Moore Cantor, "Staff Development: What About the C.E.U.?" *Journal of Nursing Administration,* IV (September-October 1974), pp. 8 – 9. (quote: p. 8).

The importance of continuing education is not refuted intellectually by Canadian nurses. Flaherty found that the majority of nurses in her sampling recognized the need for continuing education.[24] Hospital accreditation protocols specify a criterion of continuing education for nurses. Most hospitals and agencies appoint a person who is given the responsibility for continuing education although the appointee may not be prepared for this function. Professional associations conduct programs for their members. Independent groups of consultants and pharmaceutical companies stage workshops and seminars. The list is endless, but to what end? Has the means become the end?

With the present state of affairs in Canadian nursing, we are at the crossroads. Shall we bow to external pressures and institute mandatory continuing education? The alternative is to plan meaningful and productive continuing educational programs designed to prevent obsolescence. The question is, who is responsible for ensuring that all nurses maintain at the very least a minimum level of competence? Responsibility for this rests with employers and with the individual nurse herself, as well as with professional associations.

Myths and Realities

Professional associations have recognized their obligations to encourage educational programs that may ensure that changes in responsibilities and tasks are understood by those who will perform them and that a minimum level of competence is established. This may include a requirement for retraining after a period of inactivity. Through the powers accorded them under their acts, the Newfoundland,[25] British Columbia, and Saskatchewan[26] associations require that nurses who have been inactive in nursing for five years or more must complete a refresher course before re-registering; Alberta requires a reference from an employer under such circumstances, before a nurse is readmitted to the register;[27] and both Ontario[28] and Quebec,[29] under their

---

[24] Flaherty, "Enquiry," p. 108.

[25] *Newfoundland Registered Nurses Act, 1953*, Bylaws: Section 7. (St. John's: Association of Registered Nurses of Newfoundland, 1953). n.p.

[26] *The Registered Nurses Act and Bylaws of the Saskatchewan Registered Nurses' Association*, Bylaw XIII, Section 6 (Regina: SRNA 1973), p. 19. (Bylaws as amended 1974).

[27] Alberta Association of Registered Nurses, *Bylaws* (Edmonton: AARN, 1966), p. 3.

[28] Ontario, *Health Disciplines Act*, p. 48.

[29] Quebec, *Professional Code*, p. 20.

new acts, clearly have the power to control the re-employment of registrants. In fact, these two acts encourage the establishment of conditions for assessing the competence of all those personnel who are "registered."

Collectively, nurses regulate their practice, as well as exercise some control over those who use the title "registered nurse," or in Quebec, "nurse." But how well is this collective responsibility handled? As discussed later, studies that evaluate the effect on practice of educational programs are few and rarely report anything except the personal satisfactions of participants. Data regarding disciplinary functions also can be misleading. Ontario 1973 statistics report the following:[30]

Number of annual renewals (R.N.):   *66 900*

Number of complaints (R.N.)

    Incompetence   *15*
    Incapacity (alcohol, drugs)   *4*
    Malpractice   *7*

Discipline Charges and Decisions (R.N.):

Incompetence:	*Cancel: 3*	*Reprimand: 2*	*Dismiss: 2*
Incapacity:	*Cancel: 2*		
Malpractice:	*Cancel: 2*	*Reprimand: 1*	

Total hearings for registrants charged under the Act: 12

A proportion of the 66 900 registered nurses who renewed their registration very likely were not employed in nursing during that year. We can assume that a substantial number of those employed in 1973, either full-time or part-time,* participated in situations in which they were subject, formally or informally, to peer and/or employer appraisal of work performance. It is hard to believe that the small number of nurses about whom complaints were made or who were seen by the Discipline Committee, were incompetent, incapable, or guilty of malpractice. While it might be comforting to assume that the

---

[30] College of Nurses of Ontario, *The Annual Report 1973* (Toronto: C.N.O., 1974), pp. 4, 10, 17.

* *Countdown 1973* reports that registered nurses employed full-time or part-time in nursing in 1972 in Ontario totalled 43,285. See "Table 1: Professional Nurses Registered in Canada, by Employment Status and Geographical Location, 1972," *Countdown 1973* (Ottawa: Canadian Nurses' Association), p. 9.

majority of the Ontario registered nurse population is practising safely, with due acknowledgement to the right to make mistakes, this assumption is unsubstantiated. Chance alone dictates that complaints will be made about 0.04% of the re-registering population (26 nurses). Is current competence a fact or a myth? What is the price of protection— of nurse by nurse, in patient comfort, and in public dollars?

Employers of nurses are finding that they must direct more and more resources toward the educational development of their staffs in order to ensure that the employer's responsibility to provide safe and humane care is met. Employing organizations mount "in house" programs to increase the skills of nursing personnel in coronary care, intensive care, critical care, parent education, family therapy, physical assessment, and personnel management. Not only may nurses regard provision of educational programs during working hours as an employer responsibility, they also may expect to receive higher salaries when they begin to function at a level that was really an agency expectation of employment or transfer.

For years nurses have argued that the costs of basic education should be borne by the educational system rather than by the health system. Given the accelerating costs of health services, a concerned public may attempt to shift at least some of the costs of continuing education to the recipient, that is, the individual nurse. Programs may need to be offered by educational institutions rather than by service agencies. This may relate to refresher courses for nurses who wish to return to the nurse work force after a certain period of absence. Lacking the availability of such courses, the returning nurse may find herself being offered employment other than that of professional nurse; nursing assistant for instance, or equivalent, or a position in a category of restricted practice.

In order to place continuing education programs in educational institutions it is necessary to have a method or methods for defining the needs of individual nurses and of grouping these in a cost/effective way. To achieve this, more rigid and thorough evaluation tools are needed to evaluate each nurse in the nurse/patient situation. The very general evaluation of performance presently in use in most employing agencies gives inadequate data. Nursing audits tend to focus on what is recorded rather than what is done. Peer and supervisor evaluations generally look at the "good" and the "bland," and couch negative comments in phrases that begin with "showing improvement in ... ," or "occasionally has a problem with ... but on the whole ... ," or just "satisfactory." Employers, having defined the expectations and educational needs of prospective employees, have a responsibility to express these needs explicitly in operational or behavioral terms. With the collaboration of educators, educational "prescriptions" or components that then can be utilized by the practitioner to fulfill her/his own learning needs, should result.

At present, competency evaluation is idealistic and voluntary. Nursing organizations have not stated criteria for competence, evaluation tools have not been developed, employers have not been convinced of the need for extensive evaluations, and educational institutions lack the resources to meet all the needs. Lastly, the majority of nurses who are left with an option to participate or not in continuing education offerings remain uncommitted. No one has told them that their performance needs upgrading. Under the voluntary system, those nurses who appear to need continuing education the most are those who are the least motivated to participate.

While the authors agree with the stance taken by the RNABC in continued promotion of the concept of individual responsibility and accountability for practice, they argue that professional associations lack the necessary punch. The employing agency, on the other hand, can use pressure to motivate individuals. "The degree of individual initiative is usually closely related to the encouragement and stimulation of more senior colleagues."[31] Dubin cites a research study (Landis 1969) which asks, "How does your immediate supervisor feel about further job-directed education and training?" The results: 15% of supervisors were very encouraging, 47% somewhat encouraging, and 37% not encouraging at all. Landis concluded that it is "the immediate supervisor that counts in the development of subordinates."[32] This applies to formal continuing education as well as on-the-job problem-solving.

The concept of individual responsibility for competency is a noble one. Without peer review and without evaluation against acceptable minimal criteria how does the individual know whether performance improvement is necessary? Like a mariner in the ocean, the nurse is sailing well but without a chart, coping with storms and sharks, but going nowhere.

The concept of restricted or limited registration is one that all registration jurisdictions undoubtedly will have to explore in the next decade. Should a nurse who initially meets basic registration requirements but who has been continuously employed in a specialized environment, such as intensive care, psychiatry, or public health, or whose energies have been directed almost exclusively to administration

---

[31] Dubin, *Professional Obsolescence*, p. 7.
[32] Dubin, *op. cit.*, p. 32.

or teaching, continue to be recognized as having general practice qualifications through registration? Alternatively, should that nurse be recognized as having developed a specialized area of competence that represents expertise in one field but not in others? These are critical issues that must be dealt with by the nursing profession in the immediate future.

The current situation is at best piecemeal and at worst nonexistent; the many approaches to maintenance of competence by nurses constitute independent, rather than integrated, approaches to development and learning. Continuing education for nurses is necessary. However, nurses are so busy at present with piecemeal approaches to the problem that few are taking time out to plan a concerted course of action.

Before an integrated system for the continuing education of individual nurses can emerge, the answers to many questions must be provided. Among these questions are the following:

- What do educators and nursing service personnel agree is the level of skill required of new graduates?
- Can educational programs continue to have as a major goal the preparation of generalists who can begin practise in *any* setting?
- Can organizations employing nurses identify accurately the strengths and weaknesses of staff, so that the former are enhanced and the latter overcome through continuing education?
- Are individual nurses prepared to identify their own learning requirements and needs and engage in programs of self-development activities that may require the investment of their own resources in terms of time and money?
- Can colleges and universities offering nursing educational programs really abandon their lock-step approaches to learning?
- Provincial associations have invested much energy toward improving conditions of employment by collective bargaining for nurses. Will they direct similar attention toward the development of objective measures of safe practice, thereby reassuring society (represented by government) that employment of nurses is good value?
- Because we lack the objective measures of competence, must we fall back upon the mechanism of mandatory continuing education, with equally imprecise measures of learning?
- Can nurse researchers direct their energies toward developing measures of basic nursing competence rather than justifying clinical nurse specialists and other highly specialized practitioners?
- Is the profession willing to recognize the need for evaluation and research in continuing education programs with respect to the impact on professional competence?

In this essay, the authors have attempted to look at the issue of maintaining competency of nurses in Canada. At this stage in history, we agree that continuing education is necessary to prevent professional obsolescence and more specifically, to provide optimal health service to Canadians. But again—are nurses individually and/or collectively willing to accept this fact, or will the myth of "once a nurse, always a nurse" persist?

5

The Clinical Nurse Specialist

MARGARET BOONE, B.Sc.N., M.S.
JUNE KIKUCHI, R.N., B.Sc.N., M.N.

- There is a need for a person who can give in-depth nursing care, demonstrate the potentials of the expanded role of the nurse and both foster and participate in research. There have been many changes since the original concept of "clinical specialist" in the 30s and the 40s. There will be many more changes in the future. It is impossible to predict the future, but it is possible to speculate on trends. It would appear that the need for master's education has been accepted by nursing; however, many still feel that the person with this preparation will have maximum input when utilized in the teaching and administrative areas. Will more and more clinical nurse specialists enter these areas until once again the clinical component is lost? Is the primary function of the clinical nurse specialist to assist the patient in coping with hospitalization and illness, or is it to function as a role model in assisting nurses to give individualized care? If the prime function is to assist the nurse to give better patient care through acting as a role model, then the care which is given to the patient becomes the by-product of the main goal.

Nursing in Canada today is exciting, frustrating, and confusing because of the rapidity of change. The proliferation of knowledge in the biological, behavioral, and social sciences, plus the advancement of technology, has expanded the realm of nursing and has resulted in a greater degree of sophistication in the delivery of patient care. The accessibility of information by various forms of mass media has increased the public's awareness of the changes and potentials within the health care system resulting in a demand for a high level of health care.

As increased demands are placed on the health care system, Canada is entering into a time of monetary restraint. These two factors force a careful examination of the effective utilization of manpower. New and emerging roles within nursing must, therefore, be understood so that their potentials can be maximized. One such role is that of the nurse clinician.*

Reiter has defined the nurse clinician as follows:

...a generic title, not a functional one. It describes a "state of being"—an accumulation of a depth of knowledge and experience that might be put to work in any number of positions—provided, of course, that the holder of these qualifications remains actively engaged in nursing practice.[1]

Nurses functioning in this role are, therefore, in hospitals, schools, communities, and a variety of other health care settings. Job descriptions may vary considerably with each agency and with each clinical nurse specialist. Teaching, patient care, consultation, or research are included in this role.[2] The multiplicity of functions adds to the confusion and creates controversy for those within and outside of the role.

Clinical nurse specialists seem to agree that their primary responsibility is one of patient care. The other functions, while important, may be peripheral. Agencies utilizing such a person, however, may expect each aspect of the role to be of equal importance. During the developmental stages it is difficult to be restricted to one primary function since this may decrease the creative potential of the practitioners. Yet, clearer guidelines would assist others to understand and to utilize this person more effectively. Because of the ambiguity in the definition,

---

* For the purposes of this paper, the terms Clinical Nurse Specialist and Nurse Clinician will be used interchangeably except in reference to the study by Coombs.

[1] F. Reiter, "The Nurse Clinician," *American Journal of Nursing*, February 1966, Vol. 66, No. 2 p. 273.

[2] E. Lewis, *The Clinical Nurse Specialist*, (New York: The American Journal of Nursing Co., 1970).

there is still controversy concerning the necessity, the expectations, and the potential of the clinical nurse specialist.

Is There a Need for the Clinical Nurse Specialist?

Although nurses think of this as a relatively new role in the field of nursing, the concept was discussed by nursing leaders in the 1930s and 1940s. In 1933, Stewart recognized the need for "experts in the nursing art and specialists in the clinical branches they represent."[3] She envisioned the preparation of these specialists being conducted in a university setting closely tied-in with the clinical areas. A study of universities and colleges in 1938 showed that curricula were developed to prepare specialists in "nursing school administration, teaching and supervision, public health, hospital administration, and clinical nursing."[4] The researchers stated that of the ten schools offering programs in clinical specialties, it was difficult to discern whether these were separate programs or components of the teaching and administration programs.

In the early 40s, it was recognized that more emphasis should be placed on the clinical component of nursing programs. Both Canadian and American writers pointed out that head nurses were well prepared with teaching methods but were lacking in advanced clinical knowledge; they knew how to teach but not what to teach.[5] Nurses became increasingly aware of this gap and by 1946 universities in the United States initiated programs with more clinical content in order to satisfy this need.[6]

Canadian writers[7] most frequently cite the Second World War as a

---

[3] I. Stewart, "Post-graduate Education—New and Old" *American Journal of Nursing*, April 1933, Vol. 33, No. 4, p. 363.

[4] L. Oates, "Advanced Professional Curricula: A Survey of Advanced Professional Curricula in Nursing Offered by Universities and Colleges in the United States," *American Journal of Nursing*, August 1938, Vol. 38, No. 8, pp. 909–16.

[5] A. Mayo, "Advanced Courses in Clinical Nursing: A Discussion of Basic Assumptions and Guiding Principles" *American Journal of Nursing*, June 1944, Vol. 44, No. 6, p. 579. Committee on Nursing Education of the Canadian Nurses' Association, "Post-graduate Courses in Clinical Supervision," the *Canadian Nurse*, June 1945, Vol. 41, No. 6, p. 466.

[6] _____ "Teaching at the Bedsides," *American Journal of Nursing*, May 1946, Vol. 46, No. 5, p. 281.

[7] Postwar Planning Committee of the Canadian Nurses' Association, "Nursing Sisters Return to Civilian Life," the *Canadian Nurse*, December 1945, Vol. 41, No. 12, pp. 975–77.

prime factor in the development of advanced preparation in clinical specialties.[8] The depletion of experienced nurses on the home front during the war necessitated the preparation of other nurses to fill this gap. Nurses returning from overseas were required to enter clinical areas unfamiliar to them such as tuberculosis and psychiatric nursing. Funds provided for the education of veterans encouraged many nurses to return to school for postgraduate programs. Nurses with advanced psychiatric preparation were needed to assist individuals in readjusting to civilian life. The concept of the clinical nurse specialist thus began to develop with courses in a clinical component designed to augment the existing programs in teaching and supervision, spurred on by the needs of a postwar society.

In 1944, the following definition emerged to describe the clinical nurse specialist:

A clinical nurse specialist is a graduate professional nurse who is an expert practitioner because she has broader knowledge, deeper insight and appreciations, and greater skills than those that can be acquired in a basic nursing course of generally accepted standards. She is therefore better able to analyze, explore and cope with nursing situations in a specific clinical field and, in addition, to cooperate with other specialists in the improvement of service to the patients.[9]

This definition is similar to the ones developed by such current nursing leaders as Simms,[10] Watson,[11] McPhail,[12] and Barrett.[13]

It would appear then that there has been little change in the past 30 years. This is not so. The increase in knowledge in the physical, behavioral and social sciences and the advancements in technology have increased the nurse's awareness of the patient's needs. This new awareness of the physical and emotional needs can pose a dilemma for nursing unless an adequate solution is found.

The term "in-depth care" has been frequently cited to describe

[8] M. Blanche Anderson, "Postgraduate Clinical Experience," the *Canadian Nurse*, September 1942. Vol. 38. No. 9. pp. 659 – 60.

[9] A. Mayo. "Advanced Courses in Clinical Nursing: A Discussion of Basic Assumptions and Guiding Principles," *American Journal of Nursing*, June 1944. Vol. 44. No. 6, p. 580.

[10] L. Simms. "The Clinical Nurse Specialist: An Approach to Nursing Practice in the Hospital," *Journal of American Medicine*, June 1966. Vol. 198. No. 6, pp. 207 – 9.

[11] J. Watson, "The Clinical Nurse Specialist," *Ontario Medical Review*, May 1973, pp. 326 – 7.

[12] J. McPhail, "Reasonable Expectations for the Nurse Clinician," *Journal of Nursing Administration*, September – October 1971. pp. 16 – 18.

[13] J. Barrett. "Administrative Factors in Development of New Nursing Practice Roles," *Journal of Nursing Administration*, July – August 1971. pp. 25 – 9.

that care which can encompass all the needs of the patient. But what does this term mean? Does "in-depth care" mean a higher degree of involvement with the family in order to provide more individualized nursing care? does it mean a greater degree of technical knowledge and skills in terms of procedures and equipment? does it mean a greater liaison with all members of the health team in order to provide an easier, smoother hospitalization for the patient? Is it in fact a combination of these three concerns? The totality of nursing care must include continuous contact with the family; the nurse must have sophisticated knowledge about growth and development and crisis intervention. The nurse must provide for liaison with all members of the health team. How feasible is this? Does this require a person with advanced knowledge and skills?

Awareness of needs inevitably leads to a search for improved methods of care. Research is necessary to find the best possible methods of delivering high level nursing care. Where are the nurses who are prepared with an understanding of research methodology in order to meet this need?

Nurses are becoming cognizant of their potential role within the health care team. Many non-nursing tasks are being assigned to other workers and new nursing tasks are being acquired. This can be both challenging and frightening. Role models are needed to assist nurses in meeting this challenge, to allay fears and to demonstrate their contribution to health care.

There is, therefore, a need for a person who can give in-depth nursing care, demonstrate the potentials of the expanded role of the nurse and both foster and participate in research.

McPhail describes such a person in the following manner:

A nurse clinician is a graduate of a master's programme in nursing, with a major in a clinical specialty, who is responsible for increasing his own clinical knowledge and competence and for enhancing the quality of nursing care and the quality of the organizational climate for learning and research.[14]

At the present time, some agencies see the clinical nurse specialist as a panacea—a person who can alleviate all of the problems. If this thinking persists, will the agencies and the clinical nurse specialists become disillusioned? Is nursing prepared to understand the role enough to utilize it effectively?

---

[14] J. McPhail, "Reasonable Expectations for the Nurse Clinician," *Journal of Nursing Administration*, September – October 1971, pp. 16 – 18.

What Are Reasonable Expectations for the Clinical Nurse Specialists?

In the 1960s, three leaders in clinical nursing, Erickson,[15] Simms,[16] and Reiter[17] saw patient care as the main expectation of the role of the clinical nurse specialist. This was patient care given on a one-to-one basis to facilitate the accomplishment of individualized nursing care. The increased fragmentation of care was seen by these writers as the main reason for needing a person who could care for the patient through all aspects of his hospitalization, collaborate with other health team members and provide continuity of care within the community.[18] The belief in the way in which this person would function led to a heavy emphasis on patient care and courses relating to clinical expertise in the graduate programs in nursing. This was a change from the former programs in teaching and administration in which the clinical component was an adjunct. The role, however, is still developing.

The emphasis seems to have changed of late from a direct caregiver to the more diffuse approach of teacher, consultant and researcher. This changing emphasis may have resulted as nurses have begun to examine the role from an administrative point of view.[19] Ways are considered in which an agency can attain maximum utilization of a person prepared at the master's level.

There have been many changes since the original concept in the 30s and 40s. There will be many more changes in the future. It is impossible to predict the future but it is possible to speculate on trends.

In the 30s and 40s the emphasis on the role of the clinical specialist became less and less important until eventually the specialists functioned primarily in the fields of education and administration. Today, many clinical specialists continue to enter the areas of teaching and administration, where the demand seems the greatest. It would appear that the need for master's education has been accepted by nursing; however, many still feel that the person with this preparation will have maximum input when utilized in the teaching and adminis-

---

[15] F. Erickson, "Nurse Specialist for Children," *Nursing Outlook*, November 1968, Vol. 16, No. 11, pp. 34 – 36.

[16] L. Simms, ' "The Clinical Nurse Specialist: An Approach to Nursing Practice in the Hospital," *Journal of American Medicine*, November 7, 1966, Vol. 198, No. 6, pp. 207 – 9.

[17] F. Reiter, "The Nurse Clinician," *American Journal of Nursing*, February 1966, Vol. 66, No. 2, pp. 274 – 80.

[18] *Ibid.*

[19] J. Barrett, "Administrative Factors in Development of New Nursing Practice Roles," *Journal of Nursing Administration*, July – August 1971, pp. 25 – 9.

trative areas. Will more and more clinical nurse specialists enter these areas until once again the clinical component is lost?

It is interesting to ponder the reason for a change in emphasis from the original expectations of the clinical nurse specialist functioning primarily in patient care and on a "one-to-one" basis. Highly specialized care administered to a select group of patients can be both costly and limited in influence. While the "one-to-one" approach to care may seem to be ideal, it is difficult to prove its effectiveness and therefore difficult to convince others of the need for such an approach. The size of the caseload may, however, diminish these problems if it is sufficiently large to appropriately utilize these services. It must, at the same time, remain selective so that the depth of care is not diluted. The clinical nurse specialist, in giving care, influences improved nursing care primarily through role modelling. While this is perhaps one of the most effective means of teaching, it requires a great deal of time, patience, and manpower.

Administrators recognize the advantages of this service but also must concern themselves with improving patient care throughout the entire agency. At the present time there are few people prepared at the master's level to meet the demands of service. The concept of "in-depth care" makes administrators and nurses impatient to meet the challenge and to provide this level of care to all patients.

In order to have a more widespread influence and to have greater input in improving patient care, some clinical nurse specialists may base the selection of patients on the learning needs of the staff. This poses the question—is the primary function of the clinical nurse specialist to assist the patient in coping with hospitalization and illness? or, is it to function as a role model in assisting nurses to give individualized patient care? This leads to a consideration of the by-product. If the clinical nurse specialist's prime goal is to assist the patient and family to cope with the illness, this may be accomplished in several ways. The clinical nurse specialist may do this by involvement with all aspects of care, that is, physical and emotional. She or he may accomplish this goal through conferences with nursing staff or by acting as an advocate for the patient and the family on an in-and-out patient basis. In all cases the by-product should be increased learning by all the health team members with whom the clinical nurse specialist works. If, however, the prime function is to assist the nurses to give better patient care through acting as a role model, then the care that is given to the patient becomes the by-product of the main goal. Cases then must be highly selective to not only provide in-depth care for the patient, but also to provide maximum learning experiences for the staff.

The selection of patients to benefit from this care must be decided by the agency and the clinical nurse specialist. It should be kept in mind that the clinical nurse specialist brings additional knowledge and clinical expertise to the planning and giving of nursing care.

In 1971, McPhail developed her expectations of the clinical nurse specialist to cover a broad range of functions. Her basic expectation for the nurse clinician was to serve as a role model while giving nursing care. She also envisioned this person assisting staff in the implementation of the nursing process, teaching patients and person-nel, demonstrating interpersonal skills, fostering a spirit of inquiry and participating in research.[20] A selection of articles compiled by Lewis in 1970 again indicates the variety of approaches currently being used by clinical nurse specialists in their attempts to meet the common goal of improving patient care.[21] Some may work within the in-service depart-ments giving more formal teaching sessions; others may function as consultants, assisting staff to assess patient needs and find new approaches to nursing care.

It is impossible at this time to determine the expectations of the role as it exists in Canada since there has been a dearth of literature in this area.

It seems impossible, then, to decide at this time which approach is most effective. During this period of exploration into the role of the clinical nurse specialist, it is most beneficial that nursing consider and try a variety of approaches. No matter which approach is used, success is dependent on the mutual agreement of both the agency and the clinical nurse specialist on the role that will be carried out.

How Is the Clinical Nurse Specialist Best Prepared?

The greatest controversy surrounding this role, at the present time, seems to be the educational preparation of this person. Watson believes that preparation must be attained at the master's level. She sees the trend toward specialization necessitating that the nurse have a depth of understanding in a specific clinical area, "beyond what is possible to attain in basic preparation."[22]

---

[20] J. McPhail, "Reasonable Expectations for the Nurse Clinician," *Journal of Nursing Administration*, September – October, 1971, pp. 16 – 18.

[21] E. Lewis, *The Clinical Nurse Specialist*, New York: The American Journal of Nursing Co., 1970.

[22] J. Watson, "The Clinical Nurse Specialist," *Ontario Medical Review*, May 1973, pp. 326 – 7.

Advanced courses offered at the graduate level of education prepare the nurse with the additional theory necessary to function in this role. The courses in the behavioral sciences enable the nurse to understand the dynamics of interpersonal relationships. These may be staff relationships, family relationships or nurse-patient relationships. Advanced courses in the biological and the physical sciences increase the nurse's ability to make judgments in both the planning and the giving of nursing care. The ability to examine approaches in order to improve nursing care is fostered through advanced programs in research.

These programs may appear to be rather general and to encompass all areas of nursing. Each program is geared toward the specialty chosen by the student. The paediatric program may concentrate on the child's growth and development and ways of assisting the child and the family to cope with illness. The rehabilitation program, on the other hand, studies more closely the growth and development of the adult and the aged and ways of assisting people to cope with a chronic or debilitating illness.

Theory alone does not suffice in preparing the clinical nurse specialist. A major portion of the program includes closely supervised clinical experience. This experience affords the graduate ample opportunity to apply theories and to test skills. These programs with both theory and clinical practice are the most appropriate means of preparing the clinical nurse specialist. At the present time, few programs exist and graduates are limited.

As with any change, a lag exists between the recognition of the need and the appropriate means to meet the need. In Canada, in 1968, Marossi realized that:

A nurse with advanced preparation and depth of clinical experience, with particular awareness of the physical and psychological needs of patients, and with facility in applying nursing knowledge and skills, would bring insight, vision, and breadth to the nursing care of our patients.[23]

Jenny agreed with the need for such a person.[24] Both also agreed that a nurse with a master's degree was the most appropriate person to function in this role. In 1968, however, there were few nurses prepared with this level of education and consequently both authors sought other means to meet this need. As a result, they suggested the use of

[23] N. Marossi. "The Nurse Clinician in a Community Hospital," the *Canadian Nurse*, April 1968, pp. 32 – 3.

[24] J. Jenny. "The Nurse Clinician in Canada," the *Canadian Nurse*, April 1968, pp. 30 – 1.

nurses with a broad experience. Barrett questions whether a nurse less prepared academically, but with extensive experience, can fulfill the expectations of this role. She recommended that this supposition be tested.[25]

It would appear that the role itself is becoming established. More hospitals and agencies are asking for this type of service. In an effort to meet the demand, many persons not prepared at the master's level are entering this role to fill the need. This may be happening for a number of reasons. In some cases, agencies simply cannot find people prepared with master's education, or budget restrictions may prevent the hiring of such a person. However, in some instances the role has been accepted, but not the educational preparation needed to attain the full potential of the role. If there are more people prepared, and if studies prove the effectiveness of the master's prepared person, will this trend be lessened?

Georgopoulis and others tested this hypothesis through the use of the nursing kardex and the intershift report. Three experimental units were used with the clinical nurse specialist functioning as a team leader on each of the units. Three control units were used, two of which were placed under a traditional head nurse and the third was assigned, as team leader, a competent nurse who attempted to simulate the role of the clinical nurse specialist. The results showed that the experimental units out-performed the control units in every major respect of the evaluative nurse reporting.[26]

The supposition also was tested by Coombs in her attempt, "to determine whether or not it was feasible for one clinical nurse specialist to demonstrate her role so that four nurses (without a clinical Master's degree but with clinical, administrative and teaching experience) could learn and assume many of the role activities in an integrated and comprehensive manner".[27]

This project was conducted over a two-year period. In the first year, the clinical nurse specialist acted as a role model for the four nurses. During the second year, the role modelling was not present,

[25] J. Barrett, "Administrative Factors in Development of New Nursing Practice Roles," *Journals of Nursing Administration*, July – August 1971, pp. 25 – 9.

[26] B. Georgopoulis and L. Christman, "The Clinical Nurse Specialist: A Role Model," *American Journal of Nursing*, May 1970, Vol. 70, No. 5, pp. 1030 – 9.
B. Georgopoulis and M. Jackson, "The Nursing Kardex Behaviour in an Experimental Study of Patient Units With and Without Clinical Nurse Specialists," *Nursing Research*, May – June 1970, 19: 196 – 218. B. Georgopoulis and J. Sana, "Clinical Nursing Specialization and Intershift Report Behavior." *American Journal of Nursing*, March 1971, Vol. 71, No. 3, pp. 538 – 45.

[27] R. Coombs, *Development and Implementation of the Nurse Clinician Role*, DM16, Ontario Department of Health, 1973.

rather, the nurses attended classes in physiology, interviewing, teaching methods, and nursing care planning. The results of this study showed that this type of "on-the-job" training conducted by one clinical nurse specialist did not produce the anticipated results. The four nurses participating in the study recommended formal courses in the specialty and in the sciences conducted outside of the job situation and followed by field work with the clinical nurse specialist.

The outside nurse observers participating in the project noted the following differences between the clinical nurse specialist and the nurse clinicians:

Two major differences emerged when the job descriptions of the clinical nurse specialist and the nurse clinicians in the project were compared. Clinical nurse specialist nursing activities were based on pre-role acquisition of scientific and in-depth knowledge and were written so that they focused directly on the patient: nurse clinician nursing activities frequently implied on-the-job learning and focused more on nursing personnel than on the patient.

The observers, when asked to compare the two roles, felt that the nurse clinician differed from the clinical nurse specialist in that the specialist demonstrated more (1) specialized skills, (2) commitment to giving direct patient care, (3) knowledge from advanced study of nursing care, (4) concern with improving existing care by nursing research, (5) confidence in definition of dependent and independent functions, (6) concern for preventive health care, (7) freedom from ward administrative responsibilities, (8) flexibility in hours of work, (9) time spent in direct consultation with other health team members, (10) time spent in interpreting the role and learning about community resources, and (11) skill in assessment of how the patient experiences illness, hospitalization and treatment.[28]

These studies give some indication that depth of understanding in a clinical specialty is necessary to function in the role of the clinical nurse specialist and that this may, perhaps, only be attainable through graduate education. If this is so, will nursing education be able to meet this demand?

Can Nursing Utilize this Person Effectively?

There is little use in understanding the need, developing role expectations, or preparing persons for this role if nursing cannot learn

---

[28] *Ibid.* p. 342 – 343.

to utilize these people effectively. We have found that often some other non-nurse members of the health team can utilize us more effectively than members of our own profession. Other professions may be more willing to try out the services of the clinical nurse specialist since this person does not infringe on their area of functioning.

Nursing must change in order to accommodate the entrance of new roles. This means that careful consideration must be given to the factors effecting change if we are to integrate successfully the role of the clinical nurse specialist into the nursing profession. Richards outlines the methods that she, as an administrator, used to facilitate the effective integration of the role of the clinical nurse specialist into the hospital setting.[29] One important step in introducing this new role is to include staff members in the planning. According to Barrett, the involvement of staff comes well before the initial planning of the job description.[30] Supervisory and Head Nurse staff must be involved first, in order to determine the need for the clinical nurse specialist within the specific agency.

If nurses are allowed the opportunity to determine the need for themselves, they more readily accept the clinical nurse specialist as an agent to assist them in meeting these needs. Along with this involvement, there also must be support from the administrators, as "a Clinical Nurse Specialist, regardless of her preparation and level of competence, can do very little to improve patient care without the endorsement and active support of administrative and professional staff in the hospital."[31] This support can be attained through the mutual defining of goals and methods of achievement.[32] The responsibility of the Director of Nursing does not end here. Baker and Kramer found that this support must be on-going.[33] The guidance provided for the evolvement of the clinical nurse specialist must, at the same time, allow for creativity and flexibility in order to reach the maximum

---

[29] J. Richards, "Integrating a Clinical Nurse Specialist Into a Hospital Nursing Service," *Nursing Outlook*, Vol. 17, No. 3, March 1969, pp. 23 – 5.

[30] J. Barrett, "Administrative Factors in Development of New Nursing Practice Roles," *Journal of Nursing Administration*, July – August 1971, p. 27.

[31] L. Simms, "The Clinical Nurse Specialist: An Approach to Nursing Practice in the Hospital," the *American Medical Association Journal*, November 7, 1966, Vol. 198, No. 6, p. 209.

[32] M. Woodrow and J. Bell, "Clinical Specialization: Conflict Between Reality and Theory," *Journal of Nursing Administration*, November – December 1971, pp. 23 – 8.

[33] C. Baker and M. Kramer, "To Define or Not to Define: The Role of the Clinical Nurse Specialist," *Nursing Forum*, Vol. LX, No. 1, 1970, pp. 41 – 55.

potential of both the role and the person in the role.[34]

To date, little has been written on the role as it is practised in Canada. Very little has been written about the actual pressures placed on the clinical nurse specialist as he/she attempts implementation. We have, therefore, chosen to discuss the factors impeding or facilitating the development of the clinical nurse specialist within our own health care system.

Forces Affecting the Implementation of the Role of the Clinical Nurse Specialist

In the preceding pages, the effectiveness and the potentials of the role have been discussed based on the thoughts and findings of other authors. As experienced clinical nurse specialists, we have found external and internal forces, both inhibiting and enhancing, which determine success or failure of the role.

EXTERNAL FORCES

The external forces (environmental) are authority structure, time scheduling, stability, staff acceptance, the role of the Head Nurse, and communication.

There seems to be little agreement to date concerning the position of the clinical nurse specialist within the authority structure of an agency. Baker and Kramer found that line positions actually decreased the mobility of the person, but did give a definite area of control and a positional source of authority. A staff position, on the other hand, allows for the self-selection of patients. A third authority structure also was found in which the line of authority was determined by the functions.[35]

Kirkman and Miller suggest a staff position for the clinical nurse specialist since his/her authority is derived from both knowledge and skills. They further suggest that the line position "dilutes the ability of the clinical nurse to fully explore and develop her role as a professional."[36]

Woodrow and Bell found that authority was not inherent with

---

[34] J. McPhail, "Reasonable Expectations for the Nurse Clinician," *Journal of Nursing Administration*, September – October 1971, p. 16.

[35] C. Baker and M. Kramer, "To Define or Not to Define: The Role of the Clinical Nurse Specialist," *Nursing Forum*, Vol. IX, No. 1, 1970, pp. 48 – 9.

[36] R. Kirkman and M. Miller, "The Clinical Nurse Specialist . . . a Community Hospital," *Journal of Nursing Administration*, February 1972, p. 32.

knowledge and skills, since staff did not follow through with suggestions and implement change. They saw, therefore, that without the needed authority, their potential for effectiveness was diminished.[37] If the clinical nurse specialist is to be in a line position as a Head Nurse or a supervisor, many of the non-nursing tasks must be removed since "the objectives established for the role will not be met if the clinical nurse specialist's time must be spent in providing institutional services."[38]

In our particular agency, we have always functioned in a staff position. Although there have been disadvantages to this, the advantages seem to make this a preferred approach. Without the authority inherent in a line position, the relationships with staff are, perhaps, easier to establish and to maintain. Staff members feel free to discuss problems and to explore ideas. Perhaps a person in a staff position is less threatening. Teaching may be facilitated by this lack of authority. The advice or plans given to the staff may be accepted or rejected since we have no power to enforce implementation. This then means that the staff must consider the advantages and disadvantages of each suggestion before deciding to use it. Because of the "thinking-through process," the learning that takes place becomes an integral part of nursing care.

A staff position allows one to work in a colleague relationship with each member of the nursing hierarchy in order to explore new approaches to nursing care.

Because we are not staff members of any particular area of the hospital, we have more freedom to follow patients through all aspects of hospitalization. The ability to give care to the patient whether he be in the Outpatient Department or transferred to another ward facilitates the greatest continuity of care.

There are, however, disadvantages to this mobility as well. It is more difficult to effect change without the aid of authority. Although suggestions may be accepted and put into practice, they also may be rejected or modified. Unless the staff is sufficiently motivated to see the need or to want to try out new approaches, many suggestions may go either unused or may remain dormant.

We have wondered whether our staff position confuses other members of the nursing team. The overlapping of many roles within the nursing profession makes it difficult to delineate functions clearly.

[37] M. Woodrow and M. Bell, "Clinical Specialization: Conflict Between Reality and Theory," *Journal of Nursing Administration*, November–December 1971, p. 27.

[38] J. Barrett, "Administrative Factors in Development of New Nursing Practice Roles," *Journal of Nursing Administration*, July–August 1971, p. 29.

Nursing colleagues often wonder who is the most appropriate person to utilize in a specific situation. If a staff nurse wishes to gain more understanding of a patient's needs, does he/she approach the head nurse, the supervisor, or the clinical nurse specialist? All of these people set teaching as a priority. If there is a problem with a patient does the head nurse call the clinical nurse specialist or the supervisor? The situation also may cause confusion for the clinical nurse specialist. If we wish to know how the patient is progressing, do we ask the nurse caring for the patient, the team leader, or the head nurse? If we have suggestions for change, do we bring these to the team leader, the head nurse, or to the supervisor?

An agency, in order to utilize the services of the clinical nurse specialist effectively, must consider the advantages and disadvantages of a staff position or of a line position. The persons in the agency should choose the authority structure most appropriate to their needs and to the needs of the clinical nurse specialist.

Another external factor in determining the effectiveness of the role is the utilization of time. It is important that the clinical nurse specialist be allowed the flexibility to determine the most effective use of his/her time. Such flexibility allows the freedom to plan time according to the needs of the patient and those of the staff. Should a crisis arise during the evening or night hours, the clinical nurse specialist may be present to assist. This twenty-four hour availability is accepted by the clinical nurse specialist and by the staff as part of the role. Self-determined time scheduling affords the maximum in continuity of care as well as a great degree of job satisfaction for the care giver.

While patient and staff needs may be met best in this manner, there is a real danger that the clinical nurse specialist's personal needs will go unmet. Priorities must be set, although initially this is very difficult. To allow this person time to rest and to recharge, compensatory time should be given at the discretion of the clinical nurse specialist. The appropriate utilization of time will allow the clinical nurse specialist to attain the greatest potential of the role.

The shift rotation of general staff nurses also must be remembered in a discussion of the effective utilization of time. Shift work, the twelve hour tour of duty and several days off in the middle of the week, all lead to difficulty in providing for the continuity of care or for effective teaching. We also belong to a profession wherein rapid turnover of staff creates difficulties in establishing an effective, or stable, program. As clinical nurse specialists, we have a responsibility to assist nurses in improving patient care. Ideally, we should be able to work within an area for a certain period of time, effect change and then withdraw from that area. With a rapid turnover in staff, however, nurses may leave at the point at which teaching is most effective and the entire process must be initiated again with new staff members. Change is, therefore, slow.

The method used in determining the caseload is a factor that must be considered carefully. Approaches used are those of referral, unit-based, or by specialty. There are advantages and disadvantages to both methods.

Under the referral system, the staff nurses are required to request the services of the clinical nurse specialist. This method functions well when the staff nurse has the ability to assess fully the needs of both the patients and the staff. The services offered by the clinical nurse specialist may be readily accepted by the staff since the need has been assessed and assistance sought. If this skill in assessment is lacking, cases are referred late when the crisis is most acute and early intervention is impossible. This lack of skill also may mean that some cases requiring special assistance never may be referred since the needs go undetected. Under the referral system, the staff nurse must recognize that he/she needs assistance and, unfortunately, in many instances this is seen as an admission of failure. We have questioned this sense of failure when nurses seek assistance from other members of the health care team. It, perhaps, becomes difficult for nurses to get help from their own colleagues, since they feel that they, themselves, are expected to give the level of care that this new person demonstrates.

The availability and visibility of the clinical nurse specialist seems to stimulate the staff referral of patients. We have found that under the referral system, additional cases often are referred when we already are present on the ward. We also have found that the nurses think we must be extremely busy in some other part of the hospital and that their case is not serious enough to warrant our assistance. Thus, a very appropriate referral may never be made.

The unit-based approach confines the services of the clinical nurse specialist to a small geographical area such as one ward. The use of a more defined area may overcome some of the problems since the clinical nurse specialist is available and is able to assist staff in the assessment of needs. Early detection of problems is possible and, as a result, appropriate intervention can be planned. The unit-based approach also gives stability in on-going teaching. The presence of the clinical nurse specialist, however, does not solve all of the problems. The staff of that particular ward must be sufficiently motivated to understand the role and to seek to improve patient care.

The caseload also may be chosen with regard to a specific group of patients or needs. The use of the specialty area allows the clinical nurse specialist to be sufficiently prepared with a greater understanding of the patient's needs, both physically and emotionally, in one area. The staff also will use us more as resource persons if we come well-prepared with a greater body of knowledge about a particular aspect of care. This system may be less threatening to the staff, since the services of the clinical nurse specialist are given to all patients within that specialty. This also gives a clearer delineation of the role and gives stability so that staff more readily can understand the services that are being offered.

If a clinical nurse specialist is to work within one specialty area for a period of time, assist the staff to understand the problems and approaches of that specialty, and then move on to another area, careful consideration must be given to the establishment, maintainance and phasing out of such programs. The first area of concern is whether the nature of the specialty falls within the category of acute or chronic care.

If the problem is acute and the patient is faced with one crisis that can be solved, or aided by, nursing intervention, then it is feasible to work for a period of time in this area, assist the staff nurses and then gradually phase out the involvement. The majority of these patients and families require assistance for one hospitalization. They are not necessarily readmitted, or if they are, they may be able to cope without further intervention.

"Chronic" specialties, however, pose other concerns. If we become involved in the nursing care of these patients in order to assist them and to assist the nurses, and if, in so doing, we establish rapport with the patient, developing a trusting environment that allows for support and assistance, can we then pull out of this program without unnecessary upset to the patient? Can this important "one-to-one" contact be carried out by the ward staff faced with shift rotations?

No matter which method is selected to determine the caseload, the full utilization still is dependent on the staff's understanding and feeling about the role.

We mentioned previously that the staff may see this as a threatening role. This may be the result of the staff nurse's self-image. If the nurses are lacking in confidence, they may find it difficult to seek help or to meet the challenges of the new approaches in patient care presented by the clinical nurse specialist. If, on the other hand, staff nurses are confident in their own abilities, they are eager to accept help whenever the need arises. These nurses are also keen to find ways of expanding their own knowledge and skills. In order to motivate all staff members, the clinical nurse specialist must decrease the element of threat. We have found that this is partially possible by accentuating strengths rather than always dealing with weaknesses.

Diplomacy is required. The clinical nurse specialist must use discretion in deciding when to interject advice. Advice must be given subtly and at the appropriate time so that the needs of the staff are met as well as the needs of the patient. If the clinical nurse specialist is not sensitive to the needs of the staff and allows them to flounder or tries to overrule their attempts, the threat inevitably will be increased.

We have found that the nurses are comfortable working with us when we work together at their pace. Participating in patient care, performing skills and expressing similar frustrations creates a feeling of mutuality between the clinical nurse specialist and the staff nurse. It is most helpful if the clinical nurse specialist can begin to be viewed as a person rather than as a role and thus staff can begin to see that this particular person is neither threatening nor ominous.

How can the clinical nurse specialist become known as a "person"? Although to some this may seem insignificant, following are some of the methods we found most helpful in our own situations: we have coffee with the ward staff, we attend ward parties, we enter into small talk discussions with staff. We assist in care if the time allows. We also let them help and support us. We try to avoid the use of terminology unfamiliar to them, but rather we introduce this slowly and when they are ready to accept it.

Perhaps one method that assists in establishing a mutual bond is our presence during the evening and night shift and on weekends as the need arises. They then see that we, too, must contend with difficult working hours. This accomplishes another purpose as well. Staff nurses, as McPhail[39] points out, often feel envious of the time that the clinical nurse specialist can allow in caring for one patient. They speculate that with the same amount of time, they could achieve the same results. When the nurses become aware of the time pressures actually experienced by the clinical nurse specialist, they begin to realize that more is involved in achieving the results than simply an adequate allotment of time.

Decreasing the element of threat is only one method of facilitating the staff's utilization of the clinical nurse specialist. They must be motivated not only to use this role but also to seek better ways of meeting the patient's needs. By giving the staff feedback on patients who are transferred or discharged, by passing on compliments from patients and families, and by acknowledging care well given, we find the staff nurse's eagerness to learn is greatly enhanced. They become

---

[39] J. McPhail, "Reasonable Expectations of the Nurse Clinician," *Journal of Nursing Administration*, September – October 1971, p. 18.

more willing to seek us out as resource persons, to continue to find new approaches to both the patients for whom they are caring, and for subsequent nursing intervention.

A key person in the hospital structure is the head nurse. In situations where the clinical nurse specialist works in close liaison with this person, the head nurse can either inhibit or enhance the full utilization of this new role.

We have found, in our experience, that we are able to categorize head nurses into three distinct groups according to their ability to utilize the clinical nurse specialist. In the first category, the head nurses are willing to make referrals and to seek assistance; however, these referrals are often inappropriate. These head nurses do not seem to fully understand the potential of their own role.

The most challenging group to work with are head nurses in the second category. These nurses understand the responsibility inherent in their role but lack confidence in the implementation. Even though they may lack the confidence, they feel responsible to carry out all aspects of nursing care by themselves. Inability to do this may be seen by them as failure. Thus it is difficult for them to accept assistance from other members of the health team. When the clinical nurse specialist is called to assist patients or staff, these head nurses may be threatened since they see this as losing part of their role; in this case, staff development.

In the third category, the head nurses understand their roles and have confidence in carrying out their responsibilities. They are able to assess their strengths and weaknesses and are able to accept assistance when it is needed. They generally make appropriate referrals and are able to complement the clinical nurse specialist.

Closely aligned with the confidence of the head nurses are the expectations that they set for their staff. If high expectations are set, the staff will be challenged and motivated to provide care as well as to accept new approaches. If high expectations are not set, the staff nurse will not be motivated and consequently will not seek to improve patient care.

INTERNAL FORCES

Although external forces are paramount in effecting the role of the clinical nurse specialist, internal forces are equally as important. These are the personal forces of the clinical nurse specialist.

Realistic role expectations must be established by the clinical nurse specialist. He/she must keep in mind that it is not possible to effect change all at one time. Expectations must be attainable. They also must be set with consideration for the staff's expectations, not aimed at maintaining a status quo. Rather they must give the clinical nurse specialist and the staff goals to strive for. The clinical nurse specialist does not work in isolation in establishing role expectations. If the expectations are beyond the capacity of the staff nurse's understanding or capability to strive toward, frustration will result for all. If, on the other hand, the expectations continually are set within easily attainable limits for the staff, the clinical nurse specialist will become frustrated because there is no push to strive for the higher level of care which he/she may envision. This will mean that the clinical nurse specialist may lose interest and thus be unable to stimulate others. When this results, the role is not utilized appropriately.

The clinical nurse specialist must recognize that his/her role is always dependent on others. When the patient care is given by the clinical nurse specialist, that care must be carried through by the ward staff when the clinical nurse specialist is not present. If the role is one of teaching or of consultation, the application of the developed plan must be made by the ward staff. Continuous dependence on others can be stimulating, since each person brings a new dimension to care and the opportunities to influence others are many. It also may be frustrating when care is not carried through effectively. As clinical nurse specialists, we recognize that the ward staff may be faced with a lack of time or a clear understanding to carry through the plan as developed. It is easy to adapt to these situations. The frustrations are greatest when suggestions for care are never carried through and the staff seems uninterested even though a referral has been made for assistance. This lack of action on the part of the staff is very discouraging. The clinical nurse specialist must then look for new ways to approach the staff in order to assist them to understand, to implement, or to rework the plan.

It may seem appropriate for the clinical nurse specialist to implement nursing care in many instances. Working through other members of the nursing team, however, affords an excellent opportunity to assist the staff in the application of the knowledge that is shared.

Another factor that the clinical nurse specialist must continually contend with is the possible loss of skills. The clinical nurse specialist, by encouraging others to implement care, runs the risk of having very little opportunity to utilize his/her own skills. This inevitably leads to a dilemma. We must strive for a situation in which the clinical nurse specialist has an opportunity to practice and the staff nurses have an opportunity to try new approaches. Along with maintaining clinical skills, the clinical nurse specialist also must strive to maintain and broaden his/her own body of knowledge. As clinical nurse specialists, we see this self-motivation as an integral part of the role. It is only by increasing our own body of knowledge that we can share new theories and stimulate in others the need to find new ideas and approaches in nursing care.

Nursing can best utilize the clinical nurse specialist by allowing him/her the opportunity for continuous learning. The clinical nurse specialist needs the time to read, to talk to others in the field, to attend conferences and to put to use any other learning opportunities.

Kirkman and Miller[40] ask that the clinical nurse specialist not become discouraged with the slowness of change. Patience is perhaps the clinical nurse specialist's greatest internal force. Without it, frustration and discouragement result for all.

We have found that six months are required to establish the role in a specific area. This is the time necessary to lay the groundwork before any changes are forthcoming. For someone entering the role with many new ideas, it may be difficult initially to be patient and to hold back. Even after the role has been established, patience is still required. The clinical nurse specialist must continuously assess the staff's readiness to accept new ideas, since changes can only take place with their cooperation. The clinical nurse specialist may subtly plant the seeds of an idea along the way, but then must wait until the staff is ready to accept and to implement the change. This may be a long wait, but it is futile to campaign actively until the staff itself is ready.

Along with patience goes diplomacy. The clinical nurse specialist must determine the most effective and diplomatic method by which to make suggestions and to implement changes.

As we have said, working through others may be difficult. In a case in which the staff nurse does not seem to be achieving the level of care planned, we find that it requires more patience to assist the person than to implement the care ourselves.

Continuous staff turnover may also tax one's patience. When staff turnover is rapid, progress is much slower. Staff members may leave at a point when they are capable of working effectively with the clinical nurse specialist and have integrated the shared knowledge. The clinical nurse specialist may then find it necessary to begin again with new staff members. With patience, the clinical nurse specialist is willing to allow nurses time to fully understand the role and thus find the most appropriate way to utilize this time effectively.

It is apparent then that there are many internal and external pressures on the clinical nurse specialist. In an attempt to teach and to assist staff to give care, this person must be constantly aware of

---

[40] R. Kirkman and M. Miller, "The Clinical Nurse Specialist in a Community Hospital," *Journal of Nursing Administration*, January – February 1972, p. 33.

supporting others, of accentuating strengths and of being diplomatic in choosing the approach to be used. This means that the clinical nurse specialist is continuously giving. It can lead to a depletion of strengths and energies without some form of recharging. This may come in the form of gratification from others. Nurses are often reluctant to admit that their needs, too, must be met, yet this is an integral part of job satisfaction.

How can this need for gratification be met? Perhaps the most obvious source is the patient and the family. We have found it most rewarding to see the patients respond to our care, to have them thank us for our contribution and to have them inform us of their progress following discharge.

The staff may also help us to find gratification. Although seemingly insignificant, and perhaps unnecessary, the following actions by staff are important motivators: implementing our suggestions, showing enthusiasm for certain ideas, thanking us for our contributions, and recognizing our strengths in order to utilize us appropriately. Often the staff members fail to see that we, too, have human needs. They sometimes do not recognize that we need support in some instances, that we, too, need to show emotions and need to be dependent. They can help us by allowing us to share emotions with them and by making us feel that we are part of their team and therefore not alone in a particularly trying situation.

In our paediatric experience, we are often in a position of supporting concerned parents for long periods of time. The staff can be most supportive by periodically asking how we are doing and how they can help, by offering to stay with the family while we have coffee or take a break or by coming and sitting in the room with us and the parents, thus showing us *their* support.

To utilize the clinical nurse specialist appropriately there must be a mutual responsibility shared by the clinical nurse specialist and the staff, showing support for each other.

The clinical nurse specialist must be in contact with colleagues in order to refurbish knowledge and to sound out ideas. As Barrett points out, it is difficult for the clinical nurse specialist to function alone in an agency.[41] The sharing of knowledge and experiences can assist in stimulating new ideas and new approaches.

Another internal force for the clinical nurse specialist is the desire or the motivation for self-evaluation. It is imperative that the work of

---

[41] J. Barrett, "Administrative Factors in Developing of New Nursing Practice Role," *Journal of Nursing Administration*, July – August 1971, p. 26.

the clinical nurse specialist be constantly evaluated. This may be done on a short-term basis in a specific situation or on a long-term basis over a specific period of time. The clinical nurse specialist must be able to evaluate his/her strengths and weaknesses.

An evaluation, however, also must be made together with administration and staff. The role expectations established mutually with these people provide excellent criteria for evaluation. This mutual evaluation should indicate whether the needs of the agency and the clinical nurse specialist are being met. If they are not, it then becomes necessary to examine the reasons for this and to plan any appropriate changes.

Evaluating is an on-going process. It is necessary to establish regular intervals to evaluate progress. It is also beneficial if a plan is established whereby conferences are held periodically wherein the Director of Nursing and the clinical nurse specialist are able to discuss his/her work openly. Continuous evaluation by the clinical nurse specialist, by the staff and by administration will indicate whether needs are being met and whether the full potential of the role is being recognized.

Conclusions

Throughout this chapter we have presented questions and concerns that frequently are posed about the role of the clinical nurse specialist. We have presented information from writings and from our own experience in order to assist the reader in examining the role from both a theoretical and a practical view. We also have attempted to draw some conclusions from the material presented.

The increasing complexity of health care and the greater expanse of knowledge have created the need for the clinical nurse specialist.

There are numerous ways in which the clinical nurse specialist may function. It is, however, of prime importance that the role expectations be realistic and that they be developed in a way that best meets the needs of both the agency and the clinical nurse specialist.

In order to fulfill the basic expectations of the role, we feel that graduate education at the master's level in a clinical specialty is a prerequisite. While the controversy over preparation is still apparent, the majority of studies support the need for a graduate education. The person prepared at this level can achieve certain results. Other members of the nursing profession also must accept as a mutual responsibility, their part in developing the full utilization of this role.

Bibliography

ANDERSON, M. BLANCHE. "Postgraduate Clinical Experience," the *Canadian Nurse*, September 1942, Vol. 38, No. 9, pp. 659-60.

ARADINE, CAROLYN, AND MARY JEAN DENYES. "Activities and Pressures of Clinical Nurse Specialists," *Nursing Research*, September-October 1972, Vol. 21, No. 5, pp. 411-8.

——. "Teaching at the Bedside," *American Journal of Nursing*, May 1946, Vol. 46, No. 5, pp. 280-1.

BAKER, C., AND M. KRAMER. "To Define or Not to Define: The Role of the Clinical Nurse Specialist," *Nursing Forum*, Vol. IX, No. 1, 1970, pp. 41-5.

BARRETT, J. "Administrative Factors in Developing of New Nursing Practice Roles," *Journal of Nursing Administration*, July-August 1971, pp. 25-9.

COMMITTEE ON NURSING EDUCATION OF THE CANADIAN NURSES' ASSO-CIATION. "Post-Graduate Courses in Clinical Supervision," the *Canadian Nurse*, June 1945, Vol. 41, No. 6, pp. 466-7.

COOMBS, R. *Development and Implementation of the Nurse Clinician Role*. DM 16, Ontario Department of Health, 1973.

ERICKSON, F. "Nurse Specialist for Children," *Nursing Outlook*, November 1968, Vol. 16, No. 11, pp. 34-6.

GEORGOPOULIS, B., AND L. CHRISTMAN. "The Clinical Nurse Specialist: A Role Model," *American Journal of Nursing*, May 1970, Vol. 70, No. 5, pp. 1030-9.

GEORGOPOULIS, B., AND M. JACKSON. "Nursing Kardex Behaviour in an Experimental Study of Patient Units With and Without Clinical Nurse Specialists," *Nursing Research*, May-June 1970, 19, pp. 196-218.

GEORGOPOULIS, B., AND J. SANA. "Clinical Nursing Specialization and Intershift Report Behavior," *American Journal of Nursing*, March 1971, Vol. 71, No. 3, pp. 538-45.

JENNY, J. "The Nurse Clinician in Canada," the *Canadian Nurse*, April 1968, pp. 30-1.

KIRKMAN, R., AND M. MILLER. "The Clinical Nurse Specialist in a Community Hospital," *Journal of Nursing Administration*, January-February 1972, pp. 30-3.

LEWIS, E. *The Clinical Nurse Specialist*. (New York: The American Journal of Nursing Company, 1970).

MAROSSI, N. "The Nurse Clinician in a Community Hospital," the *Canadian Nurse*, April 1968, pp. 32-3.

MAYO, A. "Advanced Courses in Clinical Nursing: A Discussion of Basic Assumptions and Guiding Principles," *American Journal of Nursing*, 1944, Vol. 44, No. 6, pp. 579-85.

McPHAIL, J. "Reasonable Expectations for the Nurse Clinician," *Journal of Nursing Administration*, September-October 1971, pp. 16-18.

OATES, L. "Advanced Professional Curricula: A Survey of Advanced Professional Curricula in Nursing Offered by Universities and Colleges in the United States," *American Journal of Nursing*, August 1938, Vol. 38, No. 8, pp. 909-916.

POSTWAR PLANNING COMMITTEE OF THE CANADIAN NURSES' ASSOCIATION. "Nursing Sisters Return to Civilian Life," the *Canadian Nurse*, December 1945, Vol. 41, No. 12, pp. 975-7.

REITER, F. "The Nurse Clinician," *American Journal of Nursing*, February 1966, Vol. 66, No. 2, pp. 274-80.

RICHARDS, J. "Integrating a Clinical Specialist into a Hospital Nursing Service," *Nursing Outlook*, March 1969, 17, pp. 23-5.

SIMMS, L. "The Clinical Nurse Specialist: An Experiment," *Nursing Outlook* August 1965, pp. 26-8.

————. "The Clinical Nurse Specialist: An Approach to Nursing Practice in the Hospital," the *American Medical Association Journal*, November 7, 1966, Vol. 198, No. 6, pp. 207-9.

STEWART, I. M. "Postgraduate Education—New and Old," *American Journal of Nursing*, April 1933, Vol. 33, No. 4, pp. 361-9.

WATSON, J. "The Clinical Nurse Specialist," *Ontario Medical Review*, May 1973, pp. 326-7.

WOODROW, M., AND J. BELL. "Clinical Specialization: Conflict Between Reality and Theory," *Journal of Nursing Administration*, November-December 1971, pp. 23-8.

III NURSING IN LEGISLATION AND POLITICAL ISSUES

. . . [let us] look at the nature of nursing within the present and future health care delivery systems since these are related to, and directed by, structural arrangements. These, and perhaps other structural changes, imply a great deal for nursing. They imply a radical change in the definition of nursing as practiced in many of the health care institutions. We need to recognize more than one nursing role. The restructuring of facilities and the redefining of roles will take place in a revolutionary kind of social movement. Our attempts in the past have been to effect change in an evolutionary manner and this has not been very successful.

JOAN M. GILCHRIST
Nursing Papers, December 1973, "The Nature of Nursing in the Health Care Structure"

The metamorphosis in nursing has been amazing in the past two decades. No part of nursing has escaped the implications of change. Behavior that once was seen as inconceivable now is being applauded. Nurses are striking, getting involved in planning change, and are being heard in the political arena. The scope and involvement of health care, the defining of nursing, and the complexity of modern living have necessitated that nurses continue to be active in both the planning and the delivery of health care.

The history of Canada makes us acutely aware of the heritage of our health care and the existing system makes us proud of our efforts. Montgomery has clearly outlined significant historical events that have shaped what we enjoy today in our health resources. Of critical importance to us in our pride is the warning that we need to continue to be involved in the planning and provision of health needs.

Involvement in planning is pinpointed by Labelle. Her key focus is on commitment and accountability. What is said is not new but neither is it a "popular" nursing practice. Actively working for a strong belief is a responsibility as well as a privilege. Nurses are by number the largest force in health care work and therefore should have a strong voice and a highly visible image.

Any profession that is forward moving and rapidly growing needs the support of its members. Mussallem emphasizes the necessity for nurses to learn to use political action in order to bring about advancement in the nursing profession as well as to promote Canadian health care issues. She encourages more active participation through political awareness and involvement as well as through a sound base knowledge of the development and growth of the nursing profession in Canada.

6

The Legislative Healthscape of Canada: 1867 – 1975

MITZI I. R. MONTGOMERY, Ph.D.

- A concise outline of the factors affecting the development of our health services from Confederation to the present is required if we are to understand the growing concern today by all segments of society about inefficiency, ineffectiveness, and the waste of costly health resources. . . . Governmental programs must be rigorously examined in terms of whether the needs of the Canadian people, rather than the needs of our governments, are being met. The healthscape of Canada has changed considerably since Confederation. Perhaps at this point in time in Canadian society, there is a need for all citizens to face squarely the issue of how to preserve the rights of individuals . . . in an era of big business, big labor and big government.

The enjoyment of the highest attainable standard of health is one of the fundamental rights of every human being, without distinction of race, religion, political belief, economic or social condition.

The health of all peoples is fundamental to the attainment of peace and security and is dependent upon the fullest co-operation of individuals and States.[1]

Canada, a signatory of the Constitution of the World Health Organization, subscribes to the foregoing principles enunciated in the preamble to the Charter. The federal government also endorses the 1948 United Nations Universal Declaration of Human Rights in which it is stated that the social security rights for every member of society are considered indispensable.[2] However, these endorsements must be considered, not only in terms of self-interest and international obligations, but from a humanitarian perspective through which philosophical ideals can be translated into action. In this context, it is evident that much still needs to be done in Canada to make these social obligations a reality for all Canadians, including all disadvantaged groups and individuals.

The evolution of organized health services in Canada has been recorded fully elsewhere.[3] However, a concise outline of the factors affecting the development of our health services from Confederation to the present is required if we are to understand the growing concern today by all segments of society about inefficiency, ineffectiveness, and the waste of costly health resources. A chapter such as this can only briefly indicate the scope of the legislative history, the emerging health care roles of governments and the underlying problems in terms of a current patchwork of expensive health care programs.[4] These governmental health programs must be rigorously examined in terms of whether the needs of the Canadian people, rather than the needs of

---

[1] World Health Organization, *Basic Documents*, (Geneva, 1974), p. 1.

[2] The 1948 United Nations Universal Declaration of Human Rights, Part I, Articles 22 and 25, cited in *Everyman's United Nations: A Complete Handbook of the Activities and Evolution of the United Nations During Its First Twenty Years, 1945-1965*, (New York, 1968), p. 588f. Health, education, and welfare are under provincial jurisdiction; consequently, the Canadian government can only support these international declarations in principle.

[3] J. E. F. Hastings and W. Mosley, *Organized Community Health Services*, (Ottawa, 1964), pp. 1-8. In this study, prepared for the 1964 Royal Commission on Health Services, there are numerous other references cited in the introduction pertaining to the development of health services in Canada.

[4] The term "health care" is used in a comprehensive way and includes personal health care. It is the writer's opinion that the WHO definition of health is unrealistic and encourages expectations that cannot be met. The writer contends that it is necessary to redefine health in a more realistic, functional way and to update our outdated attitudes to sickness and health. A functional view of health is examined by Mary Arnold, "A Social System View of Health Action," *Administering Health Systems: Issues and Perspectives*, Mary F. Arnold, L. Vaughn Blankenship and John M. Hess (eds), (Chicago, 1971), pp. 15-34.

our governments, are being met. The purpose of this chapter is to sketch a historical, legislative healthscape[5] from 1867 to 1975 and to highlight some of the social and political factors and their relationships, planned or not, on developing Canadian health policy in the past and in the present.[6]

Confederation to the First World War Period

BNA Act

The British North America Act contained little emphasis on health and welfare for the people of Canada—then 3¼ million in number.[7] Perhaps this lack of emphasis reflected in part the frontier, pioneer spirit where individuals, families, and communities relied on their own initiative and enterprise to survive. The peoples' conception of the role of good government was one which was small, inexpensive, and noninterfering.

At the time of Confederation there were recurring epidemics of cholera, typhus, and smallpox, and although certain public health measures were initiated, it became clear that responsibility for health measures and services had to be delegated to various levels of government.

Under the BNA Act, the federal government was assigned responsibility for "quarantine and the establishment and maintenance of marine hospitals. The establishment, maintenance and management of hospitals, asylums, charities and eleemosynary institutions in and for the provinces, other than marine hospitals"[8] came under the jurisdiction of the provinces, which could, in turn, delegate various responsibilities to municipalities or private organizations.[9]

---

[5] The words landscape, seascape and more recently soundscape are well known in our society. The term 'healthscape' is used here for the first time and in the same sense, only it depicts an expanse of Canada's health scenery with highlights on certain 'healthmarks' (landmarks) that are of interest from a historical and contemporary perspective.

[6] For an interesting discussion of the liberal-democratic, political and economic matrix that shaped health services in three countries see Odin W. Anderson, *Health Care: Can There Be Equity? The United States, Sweden and England*, (New York, 1973), pp. 24-36.

[7] This is an estimate taken from population figures of 1861. See Government of Canada, *Census Canada, 1870-1871*, (Ottawa, 1876).

[8] See R. MacGregor Dawson, *The Government of Canada*, (Toronto, 1970), pp. 20-49. Also Appendix A. The exclusive powers of the provincial legislature are discussed on p. 524.

[9] There was great reliance placed on private charities during this period, and the right of government to assume new social obligations was often challenged. See D. G. Creighton, *British North America at Confederation*, (Ottawa, 1963), p. 70f and p. 82. This book also provides an interesting portrayal of the period leading up to Confederation.

The main pressures leading toward Confederation centered around trade and commerce and national defence. But these forces were not strong enough to overcome the regional, and then provincial, loyalties of those times and those of the years following. However, throughout the ensuing years pressures for national unity[10] increased and the great issues in the parliamentary debates swung back and forth dealing with the national interest and provincial rights, and centralization and decentralization.

Many authors refer to a tendency in Canadians to defer to authority, and be more accepting of economic inequality, social stratification, and hierarchy.[11] They also argue that English-Canadian political and business leaders were and, in fact, still are willing to use government to develop and control the economy, and that the general populace acquiesced, or, at least, appeared to accept this paternalism.[12]

Economic concerns were of prime importance during the early years of Confederation. The governments considered the health and social well-being of the people only in the light of economic costs to the country. This can better be appreciated by the fact that the period from 1871 to 1901 was one of economic hardship and depression for the Canadian people. The federal government consequently placed a low priority on health needs at that time, while concentrating on the economic nation-building enterprises.[13]

The Public Health Act of 1875 in the United Kingdom had a marked impact on provincial health policy in Canada. Under provincial legislation, each province passed a Public Health Act, conforming essentially to the British Act, which required (1) a provincial board of health, and (2) every municipality to appoint, on a permanent basis, a local board of health, a medical officer of health, and a sanitary inspector. Control of communicable diseases, environmental sanitation, and the provision of medical assistance for the poor were to be the major concerns for the new local boards. The provision of facilities for the care of the sick, however, was left to private charity and the church to carry on as they had in the past.

---

[10] See John Porter, *The Vertical Mosaic: An Analysis of Social Class and Power in Canada*, (Toronto, 1965), p. 368f.

[11] This is discussed in greater detail by Seymour Martin Lipset, *The First New Nation: The United States in Historical and Comparative Perspective*, (London, 1963), chapter 7.

[12] J. A. Corry, *The Growth of Government Activities Since Confederation*, (Ottawa, 1939), quoted by Kathleen Herman, "The Emerging Welfare State: Changing Perspectives in Canadian Welfare Policies and Programs, 1867-1960," *Social Space: Canadian Perspectives*, (Toronto, 1971), pp. 131-41.

[13] Porter, *op. cit.*, p. 137.

In 1890, a resolution was presented in parliament to establish a Health Department "for the purpose of preventing the spread of disease, collecting mortuary statistics and educating the people, as far as possible, in all health and sanitary matters" (1890, p. 1659).[14] It was proposed that this new department would be an economic measure as well as a health measure and "that the money spent will be returned to the people tenfold" (1890, p. 1664). When Prime Minister Sir John A. Macdonald entered the debate, he raised the issue with which subsequent governments have been grappling right up to the present time: "One of the difficulties to be encountered in this matter arises from the divided authority of the Federal Parliament and that of the different provinces... that before 1872 there were certain statutory powers given to the Federal Government on this subject [health];[15] but it was found, from the nature of the division of powers, that the officers who could be best utilized,... and who could really aid most effectually in the stopping of the spread of disease, were officers of the Provincial Governments—so much so, that Parliament repealed the clauses giving those special powers to the Federal Government. The same reason which induced Parliament then to throw the responsibility principally upon the Provincial authorities exists at this moment" (1890, p. 1678). The motion was subsequently withdrawn.

The responsibility for health and the administration of the 1867 Quarantine and Health Act was vested in the Department of Agriculture. By 1900, a Director General of Public Health, responsible to the Minister of Agriculture, was appointed to administer the 1899 Public Works (Health) Act. His function was really a policing one to see that all workers involved in public works projects, such as the national railroad development, were covered by hospitalization in cases of communicable disease, and that suitable housing was provided for the workers. The first federal incursion into the provincial health jurisdiction had taken place.

The wheat boom in the decade following the turn of the century, the rapid population and economic growth, and the trend to urbanization resulted in an expanding national economy that produced wealth and increased incomes for many but, at the same time, created social and economic inequities. This increased industrial development, with its concomitant socio-economic dislocations, accelerated the demand by the people for the federal government to assume greater leadership

---

[14] These references, noted in this manner (year, page number), are taken from the *House of Commons Debates: Official Report*, and are often referred to as "Hansard."

[15] These powers were vested in the Department of Agriculture, which was established in 1868.

in the provision of social services rather than focusing primarily on economic expansion. The changing socio-economic views of politicians was becoming more apparent, as noted in the debates in parliament pertaining, for example, to tuberculosis[16]: "private charity has not yet been able to cope with this difficulty to any extent" (1905, p. 1354), and "no greater obligation devolves upon this House than to provide some means of lessening this great evil. If we wait for municipalities and private charities to come to the rescue of these unfortunate people, many of them will die. . . . Besides being so fatal, this disease costs the people of the Dominion millions of dollars every year" (1905, p. 1355).

Some political scientists argue that the two major federal parties shared the same conservative values during the post-Confederation years.[17] Consequently, any reform legislation to bring about social change, or initiate social programs, often was facilitated by external pressures on the federal members "to do something," and their response was to cope with the crisis usually in economic terms rather than adhering to the political philosophy and principles of their respective parties. As an example, the federal government was concerned with the prevalence of tuberculosis in Canada at that time. Their solution was to increase the annual federal grant to the voluntary National Tuberculosis Association. However, it was becoming more evident, as noted in the parliamentary debates, that ways and means had to be found to overcome the constitutional constraints, if Canadians were to receive at least a basic minimum of health care services that they were beginning to demand.

The Period Between the Wars

The issue of physical fitness during the First World War provided the opportunity for the federal government to establish a beachhead on provincial jurisdictional soil. Government officials, military leaders, and the Canadian people were shocked by the alarming recruiting statistics which revealed that over half of all adult males of military

---

[16] In 1905, an estimated 40 000 persons had tuberculosis and at least 8 000 had died from the disease. See Herman, *op. cit.*, p. 134.

[17] An interesting commentary on the characteristics of the two major political federal parties is by Porter, *op. cit.*, pp. 373-7. For a concise overview of the development of Canada's political parties from Confederation to the present see F. H. Underhill, *Canadian Political Parties*, (Ottawa, 1964).

age were physically unfit for active service. This finding, coupled with the information of high rates of morbidity and mortality throughout Canada, in comparison to countries in Europe, developed into major health issues that demanded government attention and action.[18] At the end of the war, there was a gradual build-up of industrial unrest as thousands of returning soldiers poured into the country seeking work or health treatment, along with increased numbers of new immigrants searching for a new life and security from war.

The devastating effects of the influenza epidemic, and the multitude of war widows created further social dislocations requiring national attention. There was a feeling expressed by some of the honorable members in parliament that the country was "politically, socially and economically disorganized" (1919, p. 344). Various interest groups, women's organizations, and labor bodies began to petition government for action on these matters.

In late 1918, a delegation representing the Trades and Labour Congress and the Canadian Manufacturers' Association came together and presented a brief to the federal government urging the creation of a Bureau of Public Welfare "to deal with such matters as health, sanitation, town planning, housing plans, accident prevention, and every other matter pertaining to the physical efficiency of the nation" (1919, p. 1169). For the first time since Confederation, workers and employers had joined in a common cause to pressure government to act responsibly in promoting "the welfare and prosperity of the people."

The result of this pressure was the drafting of a bill in 1919 to establish a *Department of Health* at the federal level. "The powers of the minister administering the department extend to and include all matters and questions relating to the promotion or preservation of the health and social welfare of the people of Canada over which the Parliament of Canada has jurisdiction" (1919, p.843). The new department, in addition to its existing federal health responsibilities, would be authorized to deal with issues relating to child welfare, venereal disease control, establishment of food and drug laboratories, creation of a publicity and statistics division, provision of leadership to the provinces, and coordination of efforts at all levels to preserve and improve the public health. Ontario and Quebec, in particular, vigorously denounced this development on the grounds that it was unconstitutional, but the *Department of Health* was thus established.

A Dominion Council of Health was created at the same time to

---

[18] See the debates in Hansard (1919, pp. 1165-73).

facilitate the exchange of information, to encourage the integration of services, and to develop health policies. The members included the federal deputy health minister, the chief medical officer of each provincial department or board of health, plus five other persons selected by the governor-general-in-council to represent a cross-section of society. A scientific adviser for public health also was appointed.

In parliament, during this period, the question of provincial rights also was discussed but certainly not resolved (1919, p. 1170 ff). The debates at this time focused, as well, on the concept of social welfare, and there were some who would have liked "to see the new department described as the Department of Public Welfare, which term would include not only health but many other things that ought to come within the purview of this Government. There was a time not long ago—and I think the idea persists still with some men in representative positions—that Government ought to deal solely with roads, bridges, and tariffs. That has been the idea largely in the past; but during the last decade, particularly upon this North American continent, an entirely new principle, and one which is going to be recognized more fully in the future, has been adopted by many governmental bodies. That principle is that Government is concerned not only with making roads...and providing other means of transportation, but in looking after the personal welfare of those who are left in such a position that they are unable to take care of themselves. You may call that paternal government..." (1919, p. 156). The frontier thinking was gradually being eroded by the subtle development of the "Daddy Knows Best" syndrome.[19]

It was during this period in 1919 that a committee was appointed by parliament to consider industrial and labor concerns and in their report, unemployment insurance was advocated for the first time as "a system of state social insurance for those who, through no fault of their own, are unable to work, whether the inability arises from lack of opportunity, sickness, invalidity, or old age" (1940, p. 1648). No action was taken at the time, but there was growing recognition on the part of some of the honorable members during the 1919 parliamentary debates that the broader issue of social justice would have to be considered sooner or later.[20]

---

[19] An article using this title by Barbara Wootton in Great Britain expresses concern that professionals [this also could include government officials] are more interested in obtaining job satisfaction and meeting their own needs rather than being concerned with all peoples' needs and rights. See "Daddy Knows Best," *Twentieth Century,* (Winter 1959), p. 256.

[20] There are some interesting quotations taken from Hansard pertaining to the issue of social justice. See Herman, *op. cit.,* p. 135 in particular.

The transition from the old individualism to the new liberal reform that took place in Canada between the two World Wars was brought about by Mackenzie King's Liberal Party in response primarily to a challenge by the socialist CCF party.[21] King, in his matchless "half-radical and half-conservative" style, would champion social reform, extension of public ownership, the welfare state, and increased control of the economy "but not too much." He established the Liberal Party as the center party in Canada with the twin objectives of strengthening national unity and extending social security in a free enterprise economy. Thus, this party would attract votes from the moderates on the left and the right of the political spectrum and maintain a position of power for many years.[22]

In 1927, after 20 years of debate, the Old Age Pension Act, the first of the "shared cost programs," was passed in parliament with the provinces being responsible for initiating and administering the pension schemes and the Federal Government reimbursing 50% of the cost to any participating province. During the early 1930s the federal share was raised to 75% and by then all provinces and territories were involved. The act was also extended to cover the destitute blind who were at least 40 years old.

In 1928, the federal government recognized the need for consolidating certain departments, feeling that they had achieved the purpose for which the *Soldiers' Civil Re-establishment Department* had been created. It merged with the Department of Health to form the *Department of Pensions and National Health*. By this time, under the auspices of the Invalided Soldiers' Commission, 44 new or renovated hospitals had been established to provide comprehensive treatment and rehabilitative services to all veterans. Other provincial facilities were used as well for veterans. This responsibility was then taken over by the newly formed *Department of Veterans Affairs*. There were still some who felt

---

[21] The Co-operative Commonwealth Federation Party merged with labor in the 1950s to become the New Democratic Party (NDP). These two political parties, the writer submits, should be classified more as social democratic rather than in pure socialistic terms, although the CCF had, and the NDP has, a strong radical socialist element in its organization. See also G. Horowitz, "Conservatism, Liberalism and Socialism in Canada: An Interpretation." *Political Science*, 32, no. 2, May 1966, p. 163f.

[22] From 1930 to 1975 the Liberal Party has been in power approximately 34 years. R. B. Bennett, in the early 1930s, and John Diefenbaker, in the late 1950s and early 1960s, have been the only Conservative Prime Ministers during that period. Prime Minister Trudeau has emulated his liberal predecessor as noted in his early writings and then in recent years in the political arena. See P. E. Trudeau, "The Practice and Theory of Federalism," in Vaughan, Frederick, et al. (eds), *Contemporary Issues in Canadian Politics*, (Scarborough, Ontario, 1970), pp. 2-21.

that the Department of Health had done nothing "to justify its creation or existence" over the years. "No department of government... offers such great possibilities of service to this country... But it has been sterile ... " (1928, p. 2011).

It was during this same year that the House of Commons adopted a motion authorizing "the Select Standing Committee on Industrial and International Relations... to investigate and report on insurance against unemployment, sickness and invalidity."[23] For the next two decades resolutions would be debated in the House concerning health insurance and state medicine. The early advocates of these measures in the House were often doctors.[24] For example, in 1931 Dr. J. P. Howden proposed in the House that "a measure of federal state medicine would be in the best interest of the Canadian people" (1931, p. 996), and he recommended a form of health assurance rather than health insurance. Although the majority of the members who took part in that debate supported the resolution in principle, there was strong opposition to several aspects of it. Prime Minister R. B. Bennett asked: "How many honorable members have considered the implications of that resolution? How many have considered its effect upon the existing provincial organizations, medical and otherwise? How many realize it means the entire disbandment of the medical associations of the country of private practitioners, and the substitution therefore of the state as employer of all medical men of Canada?... To ask suddenly, after a few minutes debate in the afternoon, to change the whole theory upon which thus far in this country the medical profession has conducted its business is rather a large order.... If this motion were to pass in the form in which it now is, it is a direction to the government of Canada to proceed to nationalize the medical services of the country. This would be an experiment in socialism... " (1931, p. 1009).

However, the Minister of Pensions and National Health recognized that "the health of the people is a matter of first consideration ... there should be a system of medical treatment in this country for those who need it" (1931, p. 1001f). But he, along with the Prime Minister, asked that the resolution be withdrawn due to the complexity

---

[23] *Health Insurance*, report of the Advisory Committee on Health Insurance appointed by Order in Council, P.C. 836, dated February 5 1942, (Ottawa, 1943), p. 68 cited in *Royal Commission on Health Services*, (Ottawa, 1964) p. 232, hereafter referred to as the Hall Commission.

[24] The medical profession has expressed mixed emotions regarding health insurance over the years. In 1934, the Canadian Medical Association recommended certain measures, but it was not until 1943 that the CMA asserted that health insurance should be introduced. See G. Harvey Agnew, *Canadian Hospitals, 1920 to 1970: A Dramatic Half Century*, (Toronto, 1974), p. 162f.

of the issue, the lack of time to consider it, and their concern regarding provincial rights.

The Depression had a devastating effect on the Canadian economy, affecting people from coast to coast on the farms and in the towns and cities. Individuals and families could no longer be self-sufficient and self-reliant; circumstances were such that hundreds of thousands turned to the government for relief. By 1935, under pressure from the provinces, organized labor, and the Canadian people, the Conservative government presented to the House an Employment and Social Insurance Bill "to establish an employment and social insurance commission; to provide for a national employment service; for insurance against unemployment; for aid to unemployed persons; for other forms of social insurance and security." (1935, p. 13). Prime Minister Bennett, arguing that the bill was constitutional, suggested that there was "a widening conception of the federal authority with respect to many matters" (1935, p. 279), and promised that the people of Canada would eventually receive "not only insurance against unemployment but also health insurance, invalidity insurance, and insurance against old age" (1935, p. 1066).

The Leader of the Opposition, Mackenzie King, challenged the constitutionality of the bill and argued that "those measures of social legislation . . . are beyond the legislative competence of this parliament" (1935, p. 1621). He stated that the Liberal party approved in principle the social legislation, but contended that what was required to make the bill law was an amendment of the BNA Act.[25] However, the bill was passed, only to be declared *ultra vires* (beyond the scope of legal power) by the Privy Council at a later date. It was left to the newly-elected Liberal government, in 1940, to carry out the necessary constitutional requirements in order to pass a new National Unemployment Insurance Bill, which then was supported by the provinces.

For the first time the insurance principle was introduced into the social welfare debates that had taken place during that five-year period. No longer were the 19th century attitudes of poor relief dominant in the thinking of most of the members of parliament, but the resolution of old problems would be replaced in turn by new inequities. For example, coverage was not universal in the Unemployment Bill; those who were self-employed or worked as fishermen, farmers, loggers, nurses, teachers, police, and domestics were excluded.

---

[25] Herman suggests that the Liberal Party supports the principle of a federal state with reasonable powers and autonomy vested in the provincial legislatures. Whereas, the Conservative and CCF parties are firm advocates of a strong central government. See Herman, *op. cit.*, p. 135. See also Porter, *op. cit.*, p. 375; Lipset, *op. cit.*, p. 262f; and Trudeau, *op. cit.*, pp. 2-19.

It was evident also that the higher wage earner paid the same percentage of his wages for a premium as the lower wage earner, thus adding a heavy burden to those who could least afford it. However, the flood gates for social reform were opened. In the seven-year period between 1930 – 1937 government expenditures at all levels for public health and welfare increased from 10.4% to 25.2%.[26]

The political climate during the early 1940s was such that in order to counteract the CCF party's surge toward power, King and his Liberal government recognized the need to adopt an extensive reform program. "A New Social Order for Canada" was the Liberal election slogan in 1945, which appealed to the electorate and resulted in a Liberal victory but, with a reduced majority, an erosion of support from the left to center and a defeat for major party status by the CCF.[27] However, there was some consolation for the socialists: over the years there had developed between the Liberal and CCF parties an "antagonistic symbiosis." This relationship allowed the CCF party to introduce social welfare innovations in parliamentary debates which, in turn, enabled the Liberal party to implement some of them in law.[28] Evidence of this symbiosis is certainly apparent in the 1970s as well.

In 1944, the *Department of National Health and Welfare* was established. During the debate in the House, Prime Minister King reflected that "when the resolution was drafted it was thought that social welfare being a wide term would probably serve to include health as well...," but he had decided that "changing the name might give the impression that the government was not as much concerned with national health as with some other features of the measure, whereas the contrary is the fact" (1944, p. 4256). In Section 5 of the bill the extensive duties, powers and functions of the minister are described and they "include all matters relating to the promotion or preservation of the health, social security and social welfare of the people of Canada over which the parliament of Canada has jurisdiction" (1944, p.4295).

The 1944 Family Allowance Act was the first major piece of social legislation to redistribute part of the national income with benefits payable to all families regardless of income. Though the intent may

---

[26] Herman, *op. cit.*, p. 139. In 1866 the total cost of charitable and social programs, including education, had not amounted to more than 9% of total expenditure in British North America, and was expected to diminish over the years. See Creighton, *op. cit.*, p. 82.

[27] Horowitz, *op. cit.*, p. 168f.

[28] *Ibid.*, pp. 167-9.

have been to effectively reduce, over the years, the "social ills" so prevalent in society, the outcome was not outstanding, due in part to the negligible sum provided to each family.

After years of debate within the House, and outside by all the political parties and various sectors of society, a special Dominion-Provincial Conference was held in 1945 to discuss draft legislation for a Health Insurance Act. The provinces rejected this proposal but their resistance was lessening and was not as vigorous due to federal persuasion and their offer of financial palliatives. The attitude of the federal government had changed their health and welfare course by 180 degrees since Confederation but they knew there was still much more to do following the end of the war.

The Postwar Years

In 1948, as a result of further provincial-federal negotiations, a National Health Grants Program was passed in parliament. Prime Minister King stated that "these measures—represent first stages in the development of a comprehensive health insurance plan for Canada" (1955, p.3404). This was another shared-cost program, whereby the federal government agreed to pay all the provinces, except Quebec, a stated sum of money for construction of hospitals and for health purposes, and the provinces would match the amount given.[29] The total expenditures under this program would total $900 million during the period 1948 – 1970. However, the matching grant principle favored the wealthy provinces and created difficulties for the poorer regions of the country, which could not afford to accept, because they could not match the total grant allocation. Therefore some provincial governments could not provide in full the necessary health services.

Although it was stated in 1955 that "one of the greatest drawbacks to a national health scheme is the fact that we are under a federal system" (1955, p.6242), the Federal Grants Program had a marked impact particularly on the construction of hospitals throughout the country during its fifteen years' duration. Minister of Health Paul Martin elaborated upon this program in 1950 and expressed the Government's future position regarding health insurance. "The new services being developed and the new hospitals being built with these federal grants are hastening the moment when, in every province, it

---

[29] For further details see Hansard (1948, p. 6178f.), and Anne Crichton, *Community Health Centres: Health Care Organization of the Future?* (Montreal, 1973), p. 4-2f.

will be possible to consider further action toward hospital and medical care insurance for which, of course, the federal government stands ready to provide assistance, under satisfactory agreements for dominion-provincial co-operation" (1950, p. 3889).

By 1957, following a year of intensive debate and pressure both from within the House and without from the general public, the federal government introduced a proposal for a federal hospital insurance program. The basic objective of this proposal was "to provide, in co-operation with the provinces, protection for all Canadians against the possibility of heavy or unexpected hospital expenses..." and a beneficial by-product would be "to put the nation's hospitals, again in co-operation with the provinces who will have responsibility of administration, on a much sounder footing" (1957, p.2643).

The question of provincial rights was not overlooked by the federal government. "The Bill will neither require, nor indeed countenance federal interference in provincial affairs. It will fully respect and safeguard provincial autonomy and jurisdiction" (1957, p. 2643). This affirmation enabled the government to opt out of providing coverage to provincial institutions where patients were mentally ill or tubercular as they "are now being taken care of substantially by the provinces, who regard them as their normal charges..." (1957, p. 2677). Other exemptions included custodial care institutions, such as nursing homes and homes for the aged, with the result that over 50% of all patients in Canadian hospitals would not be covered by this plan (1957, p. 2661).

The financing formula was described in the House: "the bill will embody the formula for sharing costs based partly on the actual provincial experience... For all provinces, taken as a whole, the federal contribution will amount to 50% of those costs defined as shareable,[30] while for each province the federal contribution will amount to 25% of the *per capita* shareable costs for the nation as a whole, plus 25% of the *per capita* shareable costs for the province itself, multiplied by the population covered in the province" (1957, p. 2644). Thus, the poorer provinces would receive greater financial benefits *per capita* than their more prosperous counterparts.

The Hospital Insurance and Diagnostic Services Act was finally passed in 1957 and it required that every province wishing federal assistance have legislation that allowed for the licensure, inspection, and supervision of hospitals. However, because it was stipulated by the liberal government that the act would not become operational until a majority of the provinces representing the majority of the people of

---

[30] Shareable costs did not include depreciation or interest charges for which hospitals would be responsible. See Hansard (1957, p. 3103).

Canada came into the plan, it was left to the newly-elected conservative administration in 1958 to remove these restrictive features. The act then became a reality.

The provincial hospital insurance plans are administered by separate commissions in some provinces and by provincial departments of health in others. To finance the plans, the provinces and territories use general tax revenues, hospitalization taxes, and premiums in various combinations.

In recent years, the specter of rising costs in hospital services and the lack of flexibility in the insurance plan, which, over the years, prevented the provinces from attempting innovative, alternative health programs, have resulted in a continuing re-examination of cost-sharing plans by both federal and provincial bodies. This matter will be explored later in this chapter.

Following the recommendations of the Royal Commission on Health Services in 1964, the Health Resources Fund Bill [1966] was passed "to provide for the establishment of a health resources fund to assist provinces in the acquisition, construction and renovation of health training facilities and research institutions" (1966, p.6715). A fund of $500 million was made available over the period 1966–1980 with the federal government contributing 50% for any reasonable provincial project that had at least a five-year duration period. Of the $500 million, $25 million was set aside as an extra bonus to the Atlantic Provinces for joint projects in which they would all participate.

The members of the Royal Commission on Health Services had set as their objective, "the best possible health care for all Canadians," and, in order to achieve this goal, examined "in detail the health status of the nation; the existing health services: present problems, deficiencies and future requirements; the educational potentialities for health personnel; health costs, present and future, and their effect upon the Canadian economy as well as the ability of the Canadian economy to support an extended programme".[31]

It was the view of the Royal Commission that "there is an enormous gap between our scientific knowledge and skills on the one hand and our organizational and financial arrangements to apply them to the needs of men, on the other" (1966, p.7545).

The commission report laid the groundwork for the federal government's next major action in the health care field and in 1966 the Medical Care Bill was proposed in the House. The intent of the

---

[31] The Hall Commission, *op. cit.*, p. 104.

federal government was "to introduce a measure to authorize the payment of contributions by Canada toward the cost of insured medical care services incurred by provinces pursuant to provincial medical care insurance plans... The federal government has for some years been examining ways and means of ensuring that the opportunity for good health, which is now viewed in western democracies as a right possessed by all should be available to every citizen of our country" (1966, p.7544). Thus, the fourth major shared-cost health program in the federal health insurance plan came into being.[32]

The financial contribution by the federal government to the participating provinces and territories would be "half of the *per capita* cost of all insured services furnished under the plans of all participating provinces, multiplied by the number of insured persons in that one province,"[33] provided the plans met the following criteria: comprehensive coverage, portability of benefits, universal availability and non-profit administration.

Needless to say, the response in the House by many honorable members to this proposal was one of jubilation. "We want it [national health insurance] placed on the statute books as quickly as possible" (1966, p.7561). Stanley Knowles, the NDP constitutional expert commented: "It was really a delight this afternoon to hear all the arguments that we [NDP] have used over the years to try to get the Liberals to move, now being used by the minister... social responsibility... economic sense... public scheme... to redistribute the cost of medical care... according to their ability to pay and according to their need" (1966, p.7591). The "antagonistic symbiosis" was still operating.

Concerns, however, were also expressed. Some felt the act did not go far enough—"the plan still leaves a large area of health needs untouched... in terms of essential and prescribed drugs, dental care, optometric care, and all the ancillary health services" (1966, p.7557). The issue of provincial consensus before the federal government could expand its shareable costs to one province was challenged—"why should we have to wait for consensus?... no reason why this legislation should not be sufficiently flexible to provide that when a province has established physicians' care under the plan—it is free to make

---

[32] The three other cost-shared programs are the National Health Grants Program, Hospital Insurance and the Health Resources Program. The Canada Assistance Plan, established in 1966 by the federal government, provides for federal contribution to the provinces for improving and extending welfare services and for comprehensive health services, including drugs, dental, and optical care, to people in need. See Hansard (1966, pp. 6407-10).

[33] Health Programs Branch, Department of National Health and Welfare, *Health Services in Canada 1973*, (Ottawa, 1973), p. 2.

provision for some of the other health services" (1966, p.7557). This honorable member supported his argument by stating that the Hospital Insurance Plan would have been delayed in 1958 if consensus had been required.

There were other members who thought that the welfare state philosophy expressed in the act was questionable. "A government-dominated scheme, whether it is compulsory by direct premium or compulsory by being charged to general taxation leads inevitably to a loss of individual freedom. Nothing is more compulsory than taxation. ...I am convinced that if the public were fully aware of the ultimate cost in relation to the benefits that will be received under the legislation as proposed at the present time, they would be most hesitant to accept such a plan ... I think they would reject it" (1966, p.7564).

The questions of priorities and costs also were examined. "There are priorities within our responsibilities in the area of public welfare which must be established. We cannot afford, the public purse cannot pay for, the over-all cost of public welfare to which we are to-day committing ourselves" for example, education, health care and pensions (1966, p.7565). But others suggested that "the cost of medicare is not a new cost. It is simply a redistribution of the cost, so that instead of the burden being placed on the sick, it is distributed over the entire population on a basis that has some relation to ability to pay" (1966, p.7557).

A conservative health critic in the House warned the members: "Social programs must be or ought to be financed out of increased national productivity. Surely there should be some relation between the quantum of such benefits and the index of our productivity. Unfortunately, Canada has a top-heavy, three level government structure ... and with a tax system frequently operating to stultify incentive, has been dispensing social welfare and wage increases without too much regard to its ability as a nation to pay for them out of increased productivity" (1966, p.7574).

Within two years of the passage of the Medical Care Act, the federal government, concerned with accelerating health costs, established the Committee on Costs of Health Services in Canada, and seven task forces were appointed to examine specific health areas. The reports, completed in November 1969, recommended a variety of approaches to curtail rising costs and to improve the quality of care.[34] Emphasis was placed on "co-ordinated government planning of health services, regionalization for both planning and operational purposes ...

---

[34] Government of Canada, Department of National Health and Welfare, *Task Force Reports on the Cost of Health Services in Canada*, (Ottawa, 1970).

caution in incurring additional capital costs for new hospital beds, including teaching beds... measures to economize within the framework of the hospital system through increased operational efficiency, improved manpower utilization, and a variety of considerations relating to levels, standards and availability of patient care."[35]

It was during this period that the Science Council of Canada appointed a Health Sciences Committee in 1969, to explore the utilization of science and technology in the health care field, and with this as a backdrop, to then examine and report on the overall level and adequacy of research and to develop principles and policies for distributing public research funds and to determine the appropriate organizational mechanisms required to carry this out.[36] In a nutshell, the results of this study revealed the following: the inadequacy of existing research to assist in developing a comprehensive and coordinated system of health care; the lack of adequate funding in the bio-medical field, and a need for increased funding in health care and health related social research; and the need to establish a Health Care Research Council.[37] The central issue of the report centered around what the public was getting for its money. In other words, the services delivered in the health care system should be worth the price paid.

It is difficult to place an economic value on health or health care, but to keep things in perspective it should be noted that although total expenditures on personal health care amounted to 5.5% in 1969, the average Canadian spent a greater proportion of his money on travel and transportation (13.1%); clothing (8.1%); recreation and reading (4.0%); smoking and alcoholic beverages (3.8%), than he did on medical and health care (3.4%) in that year.[38]

The Committee argued that the health system can become more cost effective and efficient; it looked at how management, interhospital co-operation, research, quality control, manpower, rationalization of payments, and organization can help to achieve this objective.[39]

During the period 1970–1974 the Liberal Government, through its Minister of Health and his provincial counterparts, examined the existing hospital and medical insurance legislation for the purpose of developing a new approach to health care financing. Minister of

---

[35] A. P. Ruderman, "Task Force Reports on the Cost of Health Services in Canada: A Review Article," *Canadian Journal of Public Health*, July-August, 1970, Vol. 61, No. 4, p. 322.

[36] See H. Rocke Robertson, *Health Care in Canada: A Commentary*, (Toronto, 1973).

[37] *Ibid.*, pp. 145-56.

[38] *Ibid.*, p. 110.

[39] *Ibid.*, pp. 111-31.

Health Marc Lalonde, in the 1973 Commons' Debates on health care, presented the federal government's position: "A new approach is ... required—a rational and flexible approach which rewards efficient and effective provision of services and discourages inefficiency, ineffectiveness and the waste of costly resources; ... encourage the evolution of the present system into one capable of meeting the needs of the future ..." (1973, p.3668).

He outlined six objectives as a basis for developing a new financial arrangement with the provinces: "One, to reduce the rate of escalation in the cost of health services without impairing the quality of care, but introduce a form of contribution that would provide a greater incentive for control of costs; two, to give the provinces greater flexibility to determine their priorities in the health care field and to pursue the most effective approach in line with these priorities, consistent with the existing national standards; three, to optimize the use of all health resources; four, to permit the development of special programs like the thrust fund to bring about reorganization of the health care delivery system and thereby improve the efficiency of the system. "The fifth objective was to simplify the financial arrangements between the federal and provincial governments, and the final objective was to meet the existing system of comprehensiveness, accessibility, universality and portability in respect of the basic hospital and medical care services and to obtain agreement for the co-operative development of additional standards in the over-all area of health services" (1973, p.3669).

The provincial ministers of health agreed in principle with the need for a new financing formula but could not agree on an acceptable cost-sharing arrangement. Also, they were, and are, concerned that the federal government's proposed financing formula does not include coverage for the provision of denticare and pharmacare or any other new innovative programs.

The Minister of Health bluntly stated to the House that "the federal government is merely using the major instrument at its disposal [fiscal policies] to exert its force for fundamental change and to play the necessary role of the catalyst in expediting such change" (1973, p.3669). He then hit the constitutional ball back into the provincial court "if the provinces decide to reject it (the proposed financing formula) or refuse to consider it any further ... let us not hear any more about federal rigidity and refusal to co-operate. I think the Canadian public and this House should know at whose door any blame should lie" (1973, p. 3672).

The Health Minister's outburst came during a debate in the House that had centered around an NDP motion disapproving of the federal government's proposed health care cost-sharing arrangements, and they wanted clarification of this matter. The Leader of the Opposition, Robert Stanfield, argued against this type of federal cost-sharing arrangement, the acceptance of which, he thought, would be to the detriment of the provinces; he contended that "the whole point of this exercise [federal cost-sharing proposal] is to limit the increase in the financial responsibility of this government" (1973, p.3678).

The debate within the House and outside at the federal-provincial Ministers of Health meetings still is going on and has yet to be resolved to the satisfaction of all parties.

In the 1973 Speech from the Throne, it was stated that the total social security system of the country would be examined, and by April of that year a joint federal-provincial review of Canada's social security system had been established. The Minister of National Health and Welfare indicated the government's intention "to develop a comprehensive, logical, and hopefully imaginative approach in this field" (1973, p. 3403f). During this examination they would look at employment, social insurance and income supplementation. The Minister suggested that the outcome of this review could be a major breakthrough in federal-provincial constitutional arrangements. By spring 1975 all Canadians had learned how far down the welfare state road the country had moved.

The healthscape of Canada has changed considerably since Confederation. Perhaps at this point in time in Canadian society there is a need for all citizens to face squarely the issue of how to preserve the rights of individuals, along with the concomitant responsibilities, in an era of big business, big labor and big government.

Four Provincial Issues

Provincial governments have contributed their share to the volumes of health studies that have proliferated throughout Canada during the last decade.[40] The results of their efforts have helped to speed changes in provincial organizational structures and systems of health care delivery.

---

[40] For example, *Health Security for British Columbians*, (The Foulkes Report, 1973); *Manitoba's White Paper on Health Policy*, (1972); Ontario Ministry of Health, *An Implementation Plan for the New Orientation and Structure of the Ministry of Health*, (1972); Government of Quebec, *Report of the Commission of Inquiry on Health and Social Welfare*, (1967). The Nova Scotia Council of Health in 1972 presented a report to the Government: *Health Care in Nova Scotia. A New Direction for the Seventies*.

At this juncture it may be useful to comment briefly on certain concepts that are being incorporated into the changing provincial health systems.

"Regionalization"[41] of health services was encouraged as far back as 1948 when the Federal Health Grants program required each province to develop and distribute equitably a network of hospital facilities and services.[42] The Hall Commission, The Federal Report of the Task Force on Health Costs, The Ontario Council of Health Report, and numerous other reports published throughout the country since 1948 have recommended the establishment of health regions. The objectives of a regional system would be "to achieve a balanced and integrated system of health care facilities; to improve distribution of services; to identify health needs, set realistic goals and establish priorities in health programs and services within each area; to achieve greater co-operation with other areas of planning; to improve and strengthen needed existing services; to develop new health services and apply new knowledge; to eliminate . . . duplication, and to prevent fragmentation of health services at provincial and local levels."[43]

The proponents of regionalization advocate that health planning should proceed from the grassroots to the larger provincial system, because only the local people know and appreciate the local needs and problems that are unique to that specific area. If access and the other appropriate health objectives are to be achieved, it is postulated that this only can be done on a local and regional basis.

The opponents argue that factors such as lack of efficiency, increased economic costs, and public confusion are bound to result from the creation of another level of government and the people who need the health care will suffer in the transition period while regions are being organized. Concern is also expressed that "entrenched interests and weight of custom," which may develop in regional areas over time, will preclude central governments from introducing necessary changes that will benefit all Canadians.[44]

---

[41] For an in-depth analysis of regionalization, with particular reference to Ontario and Quebec, see J. T. McLeod, *Consumer Participation, Regulation of the Professions, and Decentralization of Health Services,* (Toronto, 1973), pp. 113-49. Also Robertson, *op. cit.,* pp. 100-106; The Foulkes Report, *op. cit.,* chapter 5; Province of Ontario, *The Ontario Committee on Taxation Report* (Smith Report), Vol. II, (Toronto, 1967), chapter 23.

[42] For an interesting historical commentary on Canadian hospitals, see Agnew, *op. cit.*

[43] McLeod, *op. cit.,* p. 132.

[44] This has been one of the concerns of central government in Great Britain regarding National Health Service and in the recent changes in the reorganization of the NHS this regional power would be modified. See Roger M. Battistella, "The 1974 Reorganization of the British National Health Service: Aims and Issues," *The New England Journal of Medicine,* September 1973, p. 610.

Technology is now available to link local areas to the central body so that appropriate, effective, and efficient planning can take place on a local, regional, and provincial basis; thus, a systems approach to change and delivery of health care services can develop to provide the best planning and service possible.

Decisions are being made by provincial governments to establish regional areas. These decisions, based on insufficient data and evidence, suggest that regionalization is the best and most appropriate approach to contain accelerating costs, to improve effectiveness and efficiency, and to involve the local citizens in health planning. Experimental projects, looking at all the aspects of regionalization, need to be carried out to determine if these objectives are being achieved by regionalization or if other alternatives are better. Provinces must learn from one another's mistakes and successes in this area and then come up with their own patterns of health services delivery to meet their own particular needs.

"Consumer involvement"[45] is not a recent phenomenon in a democratic society, but much more is being written about it in those government reports concerned with planning and delivery of health care. It is evident that professional planners and government officials do not know what is best for people in all areas of a province, and if a society is to be democratic then the individual must have more of a say in public problem-solving and decision-making in the health field, as well as in other areas of public concern.

The question of efficiency and cost-effectiveness of individual participation can best be summed up by the following statement: "While conventional wisdom argues that participation slows down decision processes, adds to the overall cost and design of implementation, and introduces a host of irrelevant factors, participation may do precisely the opposite. Most decision-making studies never examine the costs of overcoming consequences not foreseen in advance. There can be no better way of discovering these unforeseen consequences, long a major problem of administration, than by involving in the decision processes those likely to be affected by them. A slower decision can become economical over the long term. Participation in other words may be cost-effective through cost-avoidance, something that may be widely accepted in a few years."[46]

---

[45] McLeod, *op. cit.*, pp. 30-55 is an excellent source to examine regarding this complex issue.

[46] From a paper written by Frederick Thayer for the Ontario Government Committee on Government Productivity, quoted in *Citizen Involvement* (a working paper prepared for the Committee on Government Productivity, April 1972), p. 25.

Such authors as Alvin Toffler in *Future Shock* and Donald Schon in *Beyond the Stable State*, express concern that existing institutions can neither keep up nor cope with the accelerating changes taking place in society. They advocate anticipatory democracy, where the individual has more say in decision-making, becomes more aware and sensitive to the critical issues in society, and is willing to assume conscious control of changes that will affect him. Thus, he learns to anticipate and design the future.[47]

There is a need for all of us to recognize that individuals, government, "ad-hocracy,"[48] and labor must strive to work in concert in the next decade in order to achieve mutually desired objectives in the health care field.

"Regulation of the professions"[49] is another concept receiving increasing attention as provincial governments determine what, if any, changes should occur. For so long this sensitive area has been considered a matter of professional right rather than a right delegated by the state. Arguments for and against professional regulation and control by the state can be documented.[50]

The Royal Commission Inquiry into Civil Rights in Ontario states very bluntly: "The granting of self-government is a delegation of legislative and judicial functions and can only be justified as a safeguard to the public interest. The power is not conferred to give or reinforce a professional or occupational status. The relevant question is not, 'do the practitioners of this occupation desire the power for self-government?' but, 'is self-government necessary for the protection of the public?' No right of self-government should be claimed merely because the term 'profession' has been attached to the occupation. The power of self-government should not be extended beyond the present limitations, unless it is established that the public interest demands it."[51]

Professional roles and scope of practice will have to be expanded in the coming years as interdisciplinary teams of health practitioners continue to develop and grow. This expansion will require each pro-

---

[47] Alvin Toffler, *Future Shock* (New York, 1970), pp. 403-17. Donald Schon, *Beyond the Stable State*, (New York, 1971).

[48] Toffler suggests that in the future "bureaucracy" will be replaced by "ad-hocracy" which will be more capable of dealing with the accelerating changes in society. Toffler, *Ibid.*, pp. 108-31.

[49] McLeod, *op. cit.*, pp. 57-113 examines this concept and presents his views.

[50] *Ibid.*, pp. 60-80.

[51] Ontario Government, *The Royal Commission Inquiry into Civil Rights*, (The McRuer Report), Vol. 3, section 4, quoted in McLeod, *op. cit.*, p. 80f.

fession to look anew at the way it regulates its professional members for the public good and in the public interest. The Report of the Committee on Healing Arts is very explicit: "It cannot be overemphasized that primacy of the public interest must be the regulatory structure. Where there is conflict between the interest of the public and the interests of the profession or group, the professional or group interests must yield to those of the public; but, to the extent that it is possible to do so by statute or regulation, conflict should be avoided. It would be folly to ignore or minimize the importance of pride in profession. ... At the same time, society can no longer afford to tolerate a total dedication by government of the right to guide, direct, and, in some areas, become directly involved in the affairs of the professions. The absence of any such guidance, direction and involvement can be blamed for the fact that there has been an absence of planning in a meaningful way for the new and increased role which members of the various professions and occupational groups are expected to play in modern society. The present problems of manpower and lack of complete harmony with relation to sister professions in an era of increasing teamwork in health care are but two illustrations of the effect of the abdication referred to."[52]

IV. The concept of the "Community Health Centre" has been emphasized in Canada following the Report of the Community Health Centre Project.[53] Hastings and his colleagues view the center as an independent facility or interdependent group of facilities providing a broad spectrum of high quality, accessible health services to individuals, families, and communities by a team of accountable health professionals. This health delivery system is perceived as a subsystem of the larger social services system.

The reasons presented for developing these centers in Canada are (1) economic: to obtain value for money spent on health services; (2) to reduce hospital bed utilization and acute bed/population ratio by alternative patterns of care; and (3) to increase productivity and effectiveness by teamwork, better deployment of staff, and utilization of human resources.[54]

Some critics argue that, "if the community health centre is to be an acceptable alternative or addition to the present health delivery system, it must demonstrate high quality medical care; free choice of

---

[52] *Report of the Committee on Healing Arts,* Vol. 3, p. 29, quoted in McLeod, *op. cit.,* p. 72.

[53] John E. F. Hastings, *The Community Health Centre in Canada,* (Ottawa, 1972).

[54] *Ibid.,* pp. 12-17.

physician; cost control; and/or a better by-product, i.e. a healthier community."[55]

The contention that lower hospitalization admission rates for health center patients produces overall savings for the health center, is refuted.[56] There is evidence, as well, that health centers are not economically viable when one looks at the provincial average *per capita* costs. However, the community health center approach may be an appropriate, albeit expensive, alternative for providing health care services in specific under-serviced areas throughout the country in order that governments may fulfill their promise of reducing inequities in health care delivery to all people.

The experimental nature of such community health centers must be emphasized. In the face of mounting pressure from public and professional [and even political] groups to blindly expand the centers, governments must accept responsibility for conducting studies that will monitor and evaluate scientifically their effectiveness.

There is much yet to be done in order to develop a comprehensive, coordinated, effective, efficient and humane health care system that will meet today's specific health needs and economic realities.

Concluding Remarks

Much health legislation has been enacted by all levels of government since the early days of Confederation. In those early days, Canadians were scattered over a large country, isolated in rural and frontier areas, or located in various-sized clusters in small towns and cities. Self-reliance was the attitude of the day and government intrusion into personal health matters was neither expected nor sought after, except during periods of national crises.

The move to the cities and consequent large grouping of population has accelerated during and since the Second World War. The mass media, electronic management of communication systems, increasing concerns for human rights and social justice are just some of the many factors at work that have raised the health care needs for Canadians into high profile among all political parties, social-political groups and among the Canadian people themselves. Programs and

---

[55] The Manitoba Medical Association, *Health Care in Manitoba as of To-day and To-morrow*, (February 1973), p. 47. The response by the various medical associations to the different provincial health reports makes very interesting reading and should not be overlooked by other professional groups.

[56] *Ibid.*, p. 47.

health systems in other countries have been observed and read about and the demands for health care services in Canada have increased.

As long as the economy was resilient, or appeared to be resilient, health programs were lavishly funded. One operating principle at the different levels of government appeared to be that of matching 'political' concern for human [voter?] needs with conglomerates of study trips, consultants, flow charts, programs, large injections of money, and so on. More money, more programs, more experts, more administrators, more recipients were thought to be the answer to health care programs for Canadians.

We in the western world have entered difficult economic times. Large infusions of money into programs will become increasingly scarce and will be questioned from all quarters. The time has come for objective external analysis of the mosaic of health care programs across Canada. They must be arranged dynamically within a sensible systems approach framework in order that all levels of government, social institutions and the people themselves can become a flexible, functioning, vital health care team.

The legislative healthscape outlined in this chapter is a manifestation of some of the concerns and reasons for the kinds of health service approaches we have developed in Canada since Confederation. We are in a period now when we must assess, for human and economic reasons, the kinds of directions we have taken and the kinds of directions we need to take now and for the future. The decisions Canadians made in the past, planned and unplanned, shaped their future and our present. The decisions we make now affect our present and our future.

So we must plan for the short and long term. We must vigorously assess our objectives in terms of the needs of all our people. New programs, expanded programs, more money? Is it possible that the thinking processes of the decision-makers and the beneficiaries are dulled by complex programs that have enveloped them? The time for the critical decision-making process by the real health care team is now. We can't afford to wait any longer.

7

Nurses and Political Action

HELEN K. MUSSALLEM, O.C., M.A., Ed.D.

- ...More than 104 000 nurses of the 170 000 registered
nurses in Canada are united in the Canadian Nurses'
Association, the largest association of health professionals in Canada. This association represents a numerically
strong and functionally essential unit in the field of
health. Nursing must naturally pursue these purposes
and objectives that, in this period of history, can be
advanced most effectively by political processes within a
democratic government. This is involvement in political
action.

In the long history of organized nursing in Canada, a number of
circumstances have combined to impose on the profession the necessity of political action on many fronts, and the continued existence of
these circumstances assigns to nursing a political role far into the
future.

Briefly, these circumstances can be set out as follows:
- The nature of our government—a representative government that in-
itiates, modifies and accomplishes by using information, persuasion,
acceptance, and implementation.
- The jurisdiction over matters of health assigned by the British North

America Act to provincial governments—themselves political bodies responsive to political processes.

- The inevitability and desirability of changes or modifications in our system of health care, which can be achieved only by political processes.
- The assigned and accepted responsibilities of organized nurses, the most numerous member of the health team, to the quality and progress of nursing care.

As far forward as it is possible to visualize, political action will continue to be necessary if nursing is to provide the quality of service in Canada that it hopes to provide. How could it be otherwise? The costs of health care now are met largely from public funds derived from taxes. The nature of the health care provided will, therefore, be determined by elected or appointed government people who must be responsive to the wills and wishes of the majority of the country's voting citizens. So, to achieve maximum effectiveness within its defined sphere of activity, professional nursing always must be willing and able to take the action necessary to have its position known, understood, and accepted by the electorate; and known, understood, accepted, and implemented by the elected—a situation that makes public relations the striking arm of political action. Indeed, the history of nursing in Canada presents an unending sequence of events in which nursing has found it necessary to engage in political action.

Democracy falls somewhat short of perfection but, by common consent, is the best form of government yet developed to satisfy the aspirations of men. The fuel that drives the vehicle of democracy is political action—the participation of citizens in a political process in a manner that aligns the strength of consenting members behind leadership in order to translate preferences and convictions into action. This translation rests on the premise that, to be accepted, a particular action must represent the greatest good for the greatest number. The democratic element in the process is that it enables the people themselves to determine what is best for most. The process imposes a number of responsibilities on its adherents. It presumes the existence of a level of information, intelligence, and understanding sufficient to bring objectivity to the determination of "what is best for most." It also imposes on leadership the responsibility, in fact the obligation, to construct in society that which is best for most.

Both the reasons and the necessity for nurses to be involved in political action are to be found within this context. Within broad limits, it offers the only route to corrective action within the profession and the only route to the kind of regimen that will enable the profession to operate with full effectiveness and efficiency within the framework of political forces affecting the profession.

The responsibility of nurses is quite clear. The field of health is their vineyard, albeit shared by other workers. But, as a classified organized group, nurses are the most numerous in the field. There are about 170 000 registered nurses in Canada. More than 104 000 of these nurses are united within the Canadian Nurses' Association, the largest association of health professionals in Canada. This association represents a numerically strong and functionally essential unit in the field of health. Its purposes and objectives are inseparably linked to the health and well-being of the Canadian people. Nursing must naturally pursue these purposes and objectives that, in this period of history, can be advanced most effectively by political processes within a democratic government. This is involvement in political action.

The response of individuals to participation in the political process is varied—ranging from outright rejection to toleration to enthusiastic espousal. In a large measure, this response is a personal one. But, regardless of the personal response, the political process is there to be used. Not using it, in fact, amounts to abuse.

In the context of state-provided health care, the link between health care and political action is inseparable. The *raison d'être* of nursing is health care. The quality of health care depends, to a large extent, on the nature of the nursing component determined by four elements:

1. Standards of education and preparation of those entering the profession.
2. The quality of care provided by the practitioner—a quality closely associated with education and preparation.
3. The number of nurses available—a consideration determined in modern times largely by the social and economic status the profession offers its members.
4. The milieu in which this care is offered.

If nurses are concerned about health care, they must accept responsibility for safeguarding these four dynamic elements of nursing practice. This can be achieved only by the participation of nurses in political action.

Politics and Action

In retrospect, it was the need for political action that inspired the founding of the Canadian nurses' organizations and gave them their purpose and meaning. A few of the early problems of nursing in the political arena have been satisfactorily resolved and have drifted into the limbo of history, but many are still readily identifiable and very much alive today.

A FEW OF THE ISSUES

One of the more enduring issues to confront nursing and one which, fortunately, now appears to be moving toward a satisfactory conclusion is that of educating nurses within, rather than outside, the mainstream of education.

An even earlier issue to command the attention of nurses was quality control through the processes of registering and licensing. This question was debated for several decades before satisfactory conclusions were reached, but it is now reappearing with a new dimension related to continuing education for competency to practice.

The social and economic welfare of members of the profession, with the connotation of unions, wages, working conditions, collective bargaining and strikes, has been, and continues to be, an issue of concern within the profession despite the social and economic advances made in this field.

A more recent example of nurses in action on the political front was the debate over the introduction of a new category of worker in the health field—the physician's assistant. This conflict now has been settled, at least for the time being.

In these particular cases, as in many others, the ability of nurses to mount and sustain an effective campaign of political action has enhanced the effectiveness of nursing and nursing care.

Education

The entry of nurses into the political arena for educational purposes predated the formation of the CNA. It began with the formation of the Mack Training School for Nurses at St. Catharines, Ontario, 1874, which was the first hospital-school established in Canada to train nurses. The strengths and weaknesses it exhibited were somewhat typical of the circumstances that were to give both strength and weakness to the hospital-school system for the next century. The Mack Training School introduced to Canada the concept of apprenticeship training for nurses, a practice which was valid at the time but led to difficulties later. Like the schools that followed, the Mack School was to encounter the self-defeating equation endemic in the service-for-training concept: it permitted to develop a system of hospital patient care under which a disproportionately large amount of the student nurses' time was devoted to service, leaving a correspondingly reduced time segment for educational purposes. It also created a readily available labor pool of student nurses: ultimately, hospital operation became so dependent on this labor pool that it came to be assumed that modern hospitals could not survive without it.

The long struggle for educational reform began in 1893 when 40 superintendents from leading schools in Canada and the United States got together to form the American Society of Superintendents of Training Schools for Nurses of the United States and Canada. This society, a forerunner of CNA, was able to exert some pressure on hospital managers and influence the better schools to provide lectures that could be attended by all students. However, the proliferation of mediocre schools continued; and, meanwhile, the Canadian groups withdrew from the alliance. Nevertheless, from 1893 until 1970, the efforts of the organized nursing profession in Canada to upgrade nursing education continued unabated in a wide spectrum of political arenas.

Just prior to the outbreak of the first World War, a combination of factors caused concerned individuals within the nursing profession to re-assess the "custodial" image of the nurse that had been taken for granted since before the turn of the century. These individuals gradually became aware of two facts: the percentage of eligible young persons entering the profession was declining and the standard of care offered by the nursing profession was not improving. At the time, several trends were becoming evident that inevitably would result in more strain on the ability of the existing system to cope with the needs of the public. These trends included the widening horizons of medical practice, growing public consciousness of the need to extend and improve the care provided by the state for its citizens, and public recognition of the need for improvement in all educational systems.

In 1914, a special committee on nursing education, in a report to the Canadian National Association of Trained Nurses—the immediate precursor of CNA—recommended the transfer of nursing education into the general education system in order to cope with the pressures that were becoming evident.[1] The next significant phase was a 1929–31 survey of nursing education in Canada, conducted by George M. Weir and sponsored by the CNA and the Canadian Medical Association.[2] The survey elicited a vast amount of information and the report

---

[1] Report of Special Committee on Nurse Education, the *Canadian Nurse*, 10: 10: 570, October 1914.

[2] G. M. Weir, *Survey of Nursing Education in Canada* (Toronto: University of Toronto Press, 1932).

based on this information became a springboard for political action. The basic conclusions and recommendations that emerged from it could be paraphrased as follows:

1. The abandonment of apprenticeship systems and standards.
2. The adoption of standards more characteristic of general education, as found in the modern teachers' college or university.
3. Integration of nursing education into the provincial education system.

The Weir Report recommendations closely paralleled the views expressed by nurses during the previous half-century, but the remedy remained elusive. In the next decade, nurses' organizations tried, in many ways, to effect the separation of service from education and, in 1946, the CNA biennial convention approved the establishment of a special school in an effort to demonstrate the value of this concept. This school, the Metropolitan Demonstration School of Nursing in Windsor, Ontario, operated from 1948 to 1952. In his report on the project, Arthur Lord stated that the objectives of the demonstration had been met. "The conclusion is inescapable," he said. "When the school has complete control of students, nurses can be trained at least as satisfactorily in two years as in three years and under better conditions, but the training must be paid for in money instead of in service. . . . "[3]

Of interest also is the influence of this demonstration school and its finding concerning nursing education on events in another political arena, the United States. According to Brick,[4] shortening the basic nursing education program and placing it in an educational institution provided the impetus for the movement to include nursing education in the programs of junior and community colleges in the United States.

In spite of mounting pressure for change and accumulating evidence of the pedagogical and economic desirability of change, little occurred in the control and financing of nursing education across Canada. Eventually, as a step toward improved educational processes, the CNA decided to finance a project to determine if national voluntary accreditation of diploma school programs was a feasible and desirable method of improving the quality of education for nurses. The study, a "Pilot Project for the Evaluation of Schools of Nursing in

---

[3] Arthur R. Lord, *Report of the Evaluation of the Metropolitan School of Nursing, Windsor, Ontario* (Ottawa, Canadian Nurses' Association, 1952), p. 54.

[4] Michael Brick, *Forum and Focus for the Junior College Movement: The American Association of Junior Colleges* (New York: Bureau of Publications, Teacher's College, Columbia University, 1964).

Canada," financed by the members of the CNA,[5] lasted from 1957 to 1959. A total of 25 schools of nursing, selected on the basis of size, control, type of program, location, and language of instruction, were studied by the author.

Data collected during the project were submitted to careful analysis by a national board of review. The results were decisive: a national program of accreditation was neither feasible nor desirable at that time. The basic reason was alarming: 84% of the schools surveyed failed to meet the proposed criteria for national accreditation. Thus, the first national survey of nursing education since the Weir study in 1932, arrived at conclusions distressingly similar to those reached by Weir a quarter-century earlier. To believe the figures was to opt for change.

The report, published in 1960, made three basic recommendations:
1. A re-examination of the whole field of nursing education be undertaken.
2. A school improvement program be initiated to assist schools in upgrading their educational programs.
3. A program be established for evaluating the quality of nursing service in areas where students in schools of nursing receive their clinical experience.

The latter two recommendations were implemented immediately, and serve as examples of the power of a profession to improve its standards of practice and, thereby, in a wider sense, improve the level of health care.

As a result of the study, the unsatisfactory state of nursing education received wide publicity, both within the profession, and beyond— in public, private, and government circles. Plans for implementation of the first recommendation were being considered when the Royal Commission on Health Services was appointed by Order-in-Council in June 1961. This Commission offered a further opportunity to the CNA to press on the political front for reforms in nursing education. The CNA fully exploited this opportunity to present its views and recommendations for change at the levels of political and administrative influence where convictions and recommendations could be translated into action. The recommendations ultimately made by the Commission have influenced the nature of health services for all Canadians.

In 1964, the first diploma program in nursing established within the educational system of any Canadian province was offered by the

---

[5] Helen K. Mussallem. *Spotlight on Nursing Education. Report of the Pilot Project for the Evaluation of Schools of Nursing in Canada* (Ottawa: Canadian Nurses' Association © 1960).

Ryerson Institute of Technology in Toronto. Isolated action on the educational front began to appear in other parts of Canada, but the first major breakthrough came in Saskatchewan where the minister of health appointed an *ad hoc* committee on nursing education in 1965. Nurses were the primary political force behind the resulting achievement of a transfer of the responsibility for nursing education to the minister of education and the setting up of a Board of Nursing Education, responsible to the minister of education. Jurisdictional authority for the transfer was embodied in an amendment to the province's Department of Education Act and in the Nurses' Education Act of 1966. This led to the phasing out of all hospital schools and the eventual inclusion of all diploma schools of nursing within that province's education system. Saskatchewan was the first province to commit itself completely in this direction. Quebec was soon to follow.

By the early 1970s, the development of basic diploma programs within the educational system was not so much a goal to be pursued, as a process to be improved. In 1964, only one of 171 initial diploma programs in Canada was conducted within the general educational system.[6] In the same year, 21 students were admitted to that program —less than 1% of the total admissions to diploma programs in the country. In 1973, 9 001 students were admitted to diploma programs outside hospital control and within the educational system. This figure represents 78.5% of the total number of students admitted to diploma programs that year. Between 1964 and 1973, the total enrollment of nursing students in educational institutions increased by approximately 429%. These statistics stand as a monument to the efforts of nurses at the chapter, provincial, and national levels to change educational processes.

WHY SO LONG?

The first steps in the re-direction of nursing education in Canada were taken in 1893, but the first tangible result was not visible until 1964— exactly 71 years later. Historians may be excused for wondering why it took so long for such a logical idea to bear fruit.

The reasons for this are both apparent and obscure. In the period between 1893 and 1964, the face and fabric of Canada changed remarkably in response to the pressures of events. In the interval, Canada experienced two major depressions and a number of minor ones; two world wars and participation in more limited conflicts. The

---

[6] Canadian Nurses' Association. *Countdown; Canadian Nursing Statistics, 1973* (Ottawa, 1974).

Canadian west was developed and populated, albeit sparsely. From a supplier of raw materials, Canada became an industrialized nation. Hospitals, schools, colleges, and universities proliferated and the concept of social security moved far away from those concepts existing in 1893. In effect, Canada was busy and on the move.

Against the background of a century of national turmoil, the proposals for changes in nursing education encountered deep-rooted resistance. Visible as the need was for university education for nurses, it has been sporadic and limited. As recently as 1964, only one in 46 nurses had received her education in a university setting. In 1973, this ratio had changed to 1:15 degree to diploma nurses. In an essay entitled, "The Development of University Nursing Education," M. Kathleen King delineates some aspects of the problems that have existed for university schools of nursing:

Throughout the first part of the century, organized groups closely associated with health care, for one reason or another, appeared to favor maintaining the narrow custodial image of the nurse. This coupled with the apparent inability or unwillingness of nurses to interpret developments in both education and service, further strengthened the accepted image of the nurse.

The situation was all the more unfortunate when translated from public confusion to government bewilderment. Since university nursing education has always depended on funds channeled through the provincial government, it is essential that the needs of nursing be interpreted clearly to this level of government. It was inevitable that through the lack of clear interpretation of the need for and the role of the baccalaureate-prepared nurse, there would be financial difficulties for university degree programmes.

The question may well be asked why, if the general public was confused, nurses were content to accept this situation. Over the same period other professional groups successfully recognized the need for evolving new educational approaches and interpreting these changes to the public. Unfortunately, the mass of nurses was apathetic and lacked understanding of both the need for, and the character of the change in basic nursing education controlled by the university. [7]

An educational program for nurses first appeared on a Canadian campus, the University of British Columbia, in 1919, about 15 years after the Graduate Nurses' Association of Ontario had requested such

---

[7] M. Kathleen King, *The Development of University Nursing Education*. In Mary Q. Innis, (ed.) *Nursing Education in a Changing Society* (Published on the occasion of the fiftieth anniversary of the University of Toronto School of Nursing) (Toronto: University of Toronto Press, © 1970), p. 73.

a course at the University of Toronto. The UBC program, the first baccalaureate degree course in nursing in the British Empire, led to a B.A.Sc. (Nursing). It consisted of two years' university study. The university assumed no responsibility for the quality of basic nursing preparation within the hospital. The decision was a breakthrough, but in some respects it was a limited breakthrough in terms of full acceptance of nursing as an appropriate university program with qualified staff who developed and controlled the entire program. In spite of its deficiencies and difficulties, this course—patterned after those already developed in the United States—became the prototype for many of the basic baccalaureate degree courses in other Canadian universities.

The first basic baccalaureate degree program completely under the control of a university was achieved at the University of Toronto in 1942. This meant that the curriculum for the new type of nursing course was planned, taught, and evaluated by a full-time staff of nurse educators employed by the university, and that the resources of the university were placed behind its development.

In spite of a somewhat slow start in Canada, basic degree courses have increased: by the early 70s, they were available at 22 universities. The number of graduates each year continues to be relatively small— only about 6% of all graduates from initial programs in 1973. In 1959, the first master's degree course in nursing was offered at the University of Western Ontario. By 1973, there were 6 universities in Canada offering master's degree programs in nursing and the number of students represented 8% of nurses enrolled in post-basic programs at universities.[8]

Although some progress has been made in this area, the slow development of university programs in nursing is recognized today as one of the most critical problems facing the nursing profession. There is general agreement that the key to improvement of both the quality and quantity of nursing education lies in increasing the number of postgraduate degree holders willing to accept teaching and research positions within the university health science programs.

Registration as a Political Goal

Of shorter duration, but equal intensity, were the efforts of the organized nursing profession to obtain legislation that would offer assurances of the quality of nursing being provided by nurses. The normal

---

[8] Canadian Nurses' Association. *Countdown; Canadian Nursing Statistics, 1973* (Ottawa, 1974).

processes to achieve this are registration and licensure—i.e., the compilation of a register of persons who meet the established requirements and the granting of a license to practice.

It is unnecessary to dwell on the abuses that can be generated by failure to control the quality of practitioners in the health field; or even by failure to eliminate the possibility of ambiguity or confusion in identification of the practitioner's qualifications; but, it is important to realize that registration and licensure are intended to protect the public and not to confer a special status up on nurses. Generally, there is agreement that professionals should police their own profession, but authority for the profession of nursing to guide its affairs was sometimes long in coming. Registration and licensure are the touchstones of quality control in the profession of nursing. Enabling legislation was first considered in England in 1874, but here the shadow of prestigious Florence Nightingale fell across its path. She did not endorse the idea of qualification by examination. Instead, she believed:

... standards would be levelled down by state licensing and that nurses would deteriorate if released from the control and supervision of their schools and given permanent status as registered nurses.[9]

Her conclusion was based on the opinion that character was non-registerable and that license and registration would stereotype mediocrity. However, in a letter to William Rathbone in 1891, she conceded that, after schools had improved to the level of higher standards of the superior schools, registration might be acceptable in 40 years.[10]

Miss Nightingale could not have foreseen the nature and speed of the events that occurred in the health field in the United States and Canada during the decades preceding and following the turn of the century. The proliferation of hospitals and schools of nursing over vast, sparsely populated areas, together with tides of immigrants from many different countries, caused critical conditions in the nursing field. Largely in response to these factors, the first nurses' alumnae groups in the United States and Canada were formed in the 1890s, including that of the Toronto General Hospital alumnae in 1894. In 1896, some of these groups formed the Nurses' Associated Alumnae of the United States and Canada, one of the main purposes of which was to secure legislation to differentiate between trained and untrained nurses. This organization first attempted to achieve its goal by trying

---

[9] Isabel M. Stewart, and Anne L. Auston, *A History of Nursing, from Ancient to Modern Times: A World View* (New York: Putnam, © 1962), p. 168.

[10] Edward Cook, *The Life of Florence Nightingale* (New York: Macmillan, 1942), Vol. 2, p. 364.

to control the caliber of all nursing schools, but this proved beyond the scope of a voluntary group. Instead, the member associations redirected their energies toward achieving state legislation that would ensure licensure of nurses after theoretical and practical examinations. At this point, the Canadian groups withdrew from the alliance with their US colleagues. This occurred because health legislation in the United States—and hence the proposed nurse registration acts—were under state control. To attain their objectives, the associations within the Associated Alumnae found it useful to incorporate, and, as such, could not include members from other countries.

Thus, for historical reasons, nurses' associations in Canada were left without a national organization. However, these groups, together with local, regional and provincial associations formed later, were the nucleus of the Canadian National Association of Trained Nurses (CNATN) the first national nurses' organization in Canada, that was formed in 1908.

In each province, the situations and the needs were different, but in all the provinces, the desire of graduate nurses to set professional standards in education and nursing care was the determining factor in the formation of provincial nurses' organizations. In each case, it was realized that the ultimate future of the profession rested with the nurses themselves, and that strength to press for new legislation could come effectively from small organizations grouping together to form numerically significant pressure groups. In Alberta, for example, the need for standards arose from the fact that there were three types of nurses whose preparation had varied greatly: graduates from well-established hospitals with effective nursing schools; immigrant nursing personnel from many countries with widely differing backgrounds, education, and experience; and graduates from small, isolated cottage hospitals, whose opportunity for exposure to professional training and education had been limited.

By 1912, the Edmonton Association of Graduate Nurses and a similar group in Calgary were endeavoring to unite to work more effectively for registration laws.[11] In 1914, a group known as the Graduate Nurses' Association of Alberta reported to the CNATN general meeting its progress in drafting nursing legislation.[12] The Alberta Association of Graduate Nurses was incorporated in 1916 and

---

[11] Canadian Society of Superintendents of Training Schools for Nurses. *Proceedings of the Sixth Annual Meeting, Residence, City Hospital, Hamilton, Ontario, May 23, 1912*, p. 25.

[12] Eleanor McPhedran, Report of the Graduate Nurses' Association of Alberta. The *Canadian Nurse* 10: 10: 634, October 1914.

among its objectives was a standard examination for registration—an objective accomplished in 1919.

By 1922, all nine Canadian provinces had passed bills for the registration of nurses. Newfoundland, then a colony of Great Britain, passed its registration laws in 1931.

Nurses have been forced to maintain continuing vigilance and political activity to assure that their rights in this area are not lost. For example, in 1971, two provincial governments, those of New Brunswick and Quebec, were considering legislation, that in each case, would have taken responsibility for registration from the profession and returned it to the government. In each case, effective action by the nurses' associations reversed the government position and allowed the control of registration and licensure to remain within the profession.

NATIONAL REGISTRATION

National—as opposed to provincial—registration of its members has been a continuing concern since the turn of the century. Even before provincial statutes delegating authority over registration were passed in each province, efforts were being made to permit Dominion-wide registration of nurses. One of the earliest of these was a bill proposed by a member of parliament from Toronto who asked the federal government to authorize creation of an Association for Trained Nurses of the Dominion. Although the bill received the approval of the House of Commons, it was rejected by the Senate. A similar bill, drafted in 1938, also failed to become law.

The Canadian Nurses' Association, as the national spokesman of the nursing profession, has a commitment to safeguard the standards of practice throughout the country. In 1932, following publication of the first national survey of nursing education, delegates to the annual CNA meeting appointed a Committee on Dominion Registration to "formulate some plan whereby a more uniform standard of RN examination may be maintained throughout the Dominion, taking into consideration the ... recommendations of the Weir report."[13]

For the next six years, the question was studied by this Committee and its successor, a 16-member body that included representatives of CNA and each province. This group proposed creation of a Canadian College of Nurses or Canadian Council for Dominion Registration of Nurses to permit voluntary registration on a national basis. The suggestion was, however, opposed by some provinces and the national

---

[13] *Report of the Committee on Dominion Registration of Nurses*. In Canadian Nurses' Association. Committee on Dominion Registration for Nurses. *Reports, 1934–1938*. Montreal, p.1.

organization decided the question should be re-opened when greater unanimity of opinion warranted further study.

Eighteen years later, in 1956, a CNA Task Committee on Special Aspects of Registration Requirements looked into the question again. This time the Committee recommended that instead of reciprocal registration the Association concentrate on a national accreditation program and adoption of a national system of licensing exams. The Committee urged provincial nurses' associations to demonstrate greater flexibility in the assessment and evaluation of nursing qualifications and recommended that the question of national registration be post-poned again.

The benefits of a system of national registration in terms of individual nurse mobility are obvious. The problems are also obvious. Some of the key elements included in the organization of the profession are: provincial rights to registration and licensure, and approval of schools of nursing.

Nevertheless, a significant alternative has been achieved. In 1970, the CNA established a National Testing Service to prepare examinations for graduate nurses seeking provincial registration. This service is available to all provincial and territorial registering and licensing authorities for both graduate nurses and nursing assistants. Although successful achievement in registration examinations is only one of the requirements to become a provincially registered nurse, the use of the same registration examinations in all provincial jurisdictions provides a nationwide standard for admission to practice. In many respects, this is not far removed from the concept of national registration.

Collective Bargaining

The appearance of collective bargaining as a working reality in the world of nursing created a situation that required action of a political nature on two fronts. As far back as 1944, the Canadian Nurses' Association accepted the principle of collective bargaining and added a rider that implied if the bargaining could not be done by the appropriate association, it should at least be directed by the provincial associations. This mandate remained in force, but relatively inactive, for almost two decades. In the early 1960s, a number of concurrent developments took place in the political-social-economic field that began to exercise an immediate influence on the profession with implications of a serious nature pointing far into the future. Even in retrospect, it is not simple to separate these events or assign them priorities based on importance but, in broad outline, they included the following:

The union movement was advancing in Canada on a broad front and one consequence of this process was that employee groups covered by the collective bargaining procedure tended to move upward on the economic ladder; those not covered were left behind. Most nurses were not covered and, as a result, lost ground in the socio-economic status race.

As the economic gap widened to the disadvantage of the nurse, a subtle but disturbing change in the social status of nursing developed. It is widely held that social and professional status are closely related to economics. In this case, as the nurses fell behind on the economic scale, their social and professional status appeared to decline. Coinciding with this trend were the increasing opportunities for young women in other professions and commercial occupations. The women's liberation movement had not yet appeared to accelerate this process, but the trends were readily visible. For the first time, it became apparent that the educated woman could choose to be something other than a nurse, teacher, or secretary.

The full effect of these and related circumstances was a measurable and growing decline in the percentage of eligible young women entering the nursing profession.[14] Statistical projections indicated that, unless the process was reversed, there would develop such a shortage of nurses as to jeopardize the ability of the profession to provide nursing care at the desired levels.

How to reverse this process? Clearly, if a profession is to be well staffed and respected, it must be well paid. Therefore, it became clear that the remuneration of nurses should be commensurate with their responsibility, and their working conditions competitive with those available in comparable occupations. In other words, improvement of the economic and professional status of nurses.

With the means of reversing the situation determined, it remained to be decided how this could be accomplished. Nursing leaders recognized that the process of a friendly, dignified request for improved remuneration was falling on deaf ears or, more probably, on ears that were being assailed by many similar, but more strident, demands. In fairness to the employers of nurses, it should be recorded that this was a period of militant labor demands from all quarters. Naturally,

---

[14] Helen K. Mussallem, *Nursing Education in Canada*. Royal Commission on Health Services, (Queen's Printer, Ottawa, 1964), p.21, (Table 8).

employers of nurses tended to respond first to the greatest source of pressure—the organized, unionized groups, capable of conducting collective bargaining. It became necessary for nurses to acquire the skills of collective bargaining.

Realization of this situation had a traumatic effect on many nurses. The conclusion—reached with great reluctance after many disappointing experiences—was simply this: Collective bargaining, with all it implied, offered the only viable route to competitive salaries and working conditions for nurses. If these were not made competitive, the supply of nurses would decline.

But—and this was a problem for many nurses—collective bargaining implied the threat and use of strike action. Although preferred terms were "withdrawal of service," or "economic sanction," they implied "strike" action. And, in the context of nursing care for patients, "strike" was an uncomfortable word for the majority of nurses. So difficult was this concept that, in 1946, the CNA passed a resolution stating it was opposed to any nurse going on strike at any time for any reason, and this resolution was not rescinded until 1972— a quarter of a century later. What alternatives were available?

A very difficult social-political problem was to obtain sufficient unity of opinion and cooperation within the profession to make the collective bargaining process effective. Suffice it to say that this was done, and, ultimately, collective bargaining was accepted by nurses— but, as a method of ensuring that there would continue to be a sufficient number of practicing professional nurses to provide quality of nursing care to Canadians.

Reaching this conclusion was difficult, but the difficulties did not end there. One in particular remained—the need to formulate labor relations laws that would make it possible for nurses to engage in the collective bargaining process. Such laws were far from uniform across Canada, but eventually solutions were to be achieved—through political activity by nurses' groups.

Other details remained to be sorted out. Some are still not settled. One such question is: Who does the collective bargaining agency bargain with: Since the advent of medicare, funds for this purpose have come from the public purse. But, various units are still interposed between the bargaining unit and the source of funds—municipal, provincial or, national treasuries. Since management bargaining units are not disposing of their own funds, the validity of their ability and authority to bargain collectively comes into question. This situation ultimately will be clarified, and this too will be accomplished by political action.

Physician's Assistants

A more recent example of aggressive political action in the world of nursing involved the case for or against the physician's assistant, a controversy that echoed throughout the media in the late 1960s.

The idea of introducing a new category of health worker in Canada, to alleviate the shortage of physicians, was borrowed from the United States where there was also a reported physician and nurse shortage. There, in response to a perceived shortage of health manpower, a course was developed at Duke University to prepare persons in a two-year course as physician's assistants. Those originally selected were men who had "a medical background but lacked the qualifications to become doctors." The Duke trainees were mostly medical corpsmen who recently had returned from the wars in southeast Asia. It was assumed they would, with their additional training, be able to substitute for physicians in remote US areas not served by a physician.

During 1968 and 1969, health services in Canada were engaged in a dialogue about the introduction of this new category of health worker. An article[15] and an editorial[16] on the subject appeared in the Canadian Nurse in January 1970. The article contained interviews with protagonists on both sides of the question and identified the divergence of views of medical and nursing leaders. The editorial in that issue took a position opposed to the introduction of physician's assistants.

Nevertheless, during the latter part of 1969 and early part of 1970, the federal government appeared to be favorably disposed to the idea and said publicly that programs to prepare physician's assistants, similar to those in the US, would be instituted in Canada. At this particular moment in history, directors of the national nursing organization were grappling with the problem of reported unemployment among nurses in all major cities across Canada.

In October 1970, the directors of the CNA, having studied both the unemployment and the physician's assistant situations, took a public stand against the concept of adding another category of health worker—the physician's assistant—in Canada. A statement was prepared, endorsed, and relayed to the Minister of National Health and Welfare, the provincial ministers of health, and the Canadian Medical Association. It also was publicized widely throughout Canada. The statement read:

---

[15] Carlotta L. Hacker, "A new category of health worker for Canada?" The *Canadian Nurse*, 65: 1: 38-43, January 1969.

[16] Virginia A. Lindabury, Editorial, The *Canadian Nurse*, 65: 1: 3, January 1969.

The CNA views with grave concern a proposal to fill gaps in health services by introducing a new category of worker, namely the physician's assistant or associate.

The CNA firmly believes that the health needs of the Canadian people can more effectively and economically be served by expanding the role of the nurse.

The CNA sees at least four areas in which immediate action could be taken to utilize nurses fully:

1. primary care for ambulatory patients;
2. continuing care for convalescent and long-term patients;
3. preventive care to preserve health;
4. care for patients requiring specialized services.

The CNA takes this position for the following reasons:

1. In general, the preparation and potential of the nurse is not now being utilized to its fullest capacity. In particular, a large number of nurses prepared in university schools of nursing at the baccalaureate level do not realize their full potential in the present health care delivery system.
2. Nurses constitute a large and ready pool of workers who with little or no added training could move in to assume greater responsibilities in relation to primary, continuing, preventive and specialized care.
3. Public health nurses already participate to a significant degree in the delivery of these services.
4. There are currently unemployed nurses in a number of Canadian cities who could quickly be available if new roles existed.
5. It would be less costly to provide short courses for nurses when necessary, than to fund entirely new programs for the preparation of a totally new category.

The CNA, therefore, believes that the physician's assistant should not be introduced and urges that a fair trial be given to expanding the role of the nurse.

The CNA believes that experimentation with various patterns of delivery of health care utilizing the nurse in an extended and more independent role is urgently needed. However, the CNA emphasizes the importance of proceeding jointly with the medical profession in these endeavors.

Evidence reveals that this statement, the wide publicity it received, together with subsequent numerous verbal and written communications on the subject, had an effect on the outcome of the debate. Position statements by provincial nurses' associations supporting the CNA declaration widened and deepened its impact.

Political action on the part of the CNA did not end here. CNA officials also met with the federal deputy minister of health to explain the association's position and to seek his support. As a result, the deputy minister agreed that his department would cooperate with the CNA, allied groups of health professionals, and the Consumers' Association of Canada in holding a National Conference on Assistance to the Physician: The Complementary Roles of the Physician and Nurse. This conference proved to be a milestone. Indicative of federal views on the subject was the fact that early in the conference, a senior official of the department of health stated extemporaneously that Canada would be calling on the US to assist in developing Medex courses—these to prepare physician's assistants. However, at the end of the conference, which had representation from doctors, nurses, consumers, and government officials from all provinces, the decision was reached that a new category of health worker—the physician's assistant —would not be introduced but, rather, the nurse would be more fully utilized along the lines set forth in the CNA position statement.

Although this was a cooperative effort, there is little doubt that action in the political arena taken by the CNA and the provincial nurses' associations influenced the course of events that led to the rejection of proposals to prepare physician's assistants.

One further political event should be noted. Realizing that the official statements were those of the nursing profession and recognizing that the whole medical profession's position on this issue should be explored, the Canadian Nurses' Association invited dialogue with the Canadian Medical Association to obtain that association's views. Subsequently, the CNA and the CMA agreed to form a joint committee, with equal representation from both associations. This joint committee on the expanded role of the nurse was charged with the responsibility of developing a position statement subject to approval by both associations. Another milestone was achieved when, in April 1973, the position statement was adopted by both associations as a statement of policy. It read in part:

. . . that improvements in the accessibility and effectiveness of Canadian health services can more appropriately be achieved by expanding the roles of the nurse rather than creating new categories of workers.

The full implications of this situation are still to be realized, but the political action of the moment brought about two specific results: the advancing idea of the physician's assistant was halted, and new opportunities were opened to competent nurses through a growing acceptance of an expanding role for nurses.

Political Action in the Provinces

By world standards, Canada has a distinctive system of nursing providing enviable standards of nursing care. This has not come about by accident. It has occurred because, at critical times and places in our history, Canadian nurses' organizations have initiated and carried out the political action necessary to maintain the kind of direction that leads to high standards of practice. The weight, prestige, and statistical support of the national organization have been helpful in these confrontations, but the initiative and brunt of these conflicts have been carried by the provincial associations—the shock troops of political action. Each provincial nurses' association has its own impressive record of achievement through political action.

The number and nature of these political engagements make it difficult to select any single event and any one province as being typical.

In the past decade there arose in Quebec, however, a sequence of situations requiring sustained political response to political developments that would shape the direction of nursing in the province—for good or for bad—and for years to come. As an exercise in marshaling and directing the full weight of membership numbers as a political force, of achieving unity of action, identifying pressure points, sensitive time periods, and of developing and using significant information effectively, the Quebec action of the late 1960s and early 1970s may be considered a classic example of intelligent and useful political action by a professional nurses' association.

THE QUEBEC SCENE

It began with Quebec's Royal Commission on Education, which offered an appropriate platform for expression of the convictions of the Association of Nurses of the Province of Quebec, (ANPQ, now the Order of Nurses of Quebec, ONQ) with respect to education reform. The report of the commission, known as the Parent Report, appeared in 1964. Among its more important recommendations was the proposal to establish colleges to provide all pre-university and technical education at the post-high school level. As subsequently established, there were two streams of endeavor: the academic, pre-university stream; and the vocational or technical stream. The technical stream would have the advantage of academic courses available in an academic environment to supplement technical or clinical training. The academic/technical mix of courses would be determined by the needs of the professions involved.

Nursing was one of the options that was to be offered in the new education units; hospital schools of nursing were to be closed and nurse education would move from the hospitals into the general education stream of the province. This proposal coincided with expressed convictions of the Quebec nurses' association, which threw its official support behind the new education proposals.

The enabling legislation for the new system was passed in June 1967. The first CEGEP's (*collège d'enseignement général et professionnel* —general and vocational college) were established soon after, and the first three nursing options were open for business in the fall of 1967. By 1970, the 41 hospital schools of nursing in Quebec were closed to new students, and initial diploma program students were enrolled in the nursing options.

Throughout the formation of the new programs, ANPQ maintained constant dialogue with government officials, mainly the department of education, to give emphasis to the organized nurses' wishes with respect to the new curriculum; the student/teacher ratio; arrangements for clinical instruction in hospitals and other health units; library requirements; qualifications, status, responsibilities and work load of nurses directing or teaching in the nursing options.

ANPQ appointed a staff advisor for the nursing options to work as liaison officer with the department of education. The incumbent of this position made these observations in her report to the 1969 ANPQ annual meeting:

... The philosophy of nursing, the aims for nursing sought within an educational setting and the structures of the nursing program all affect the realization of the advantages of the college system.

... Preparation, status, responsibilities and work load of nurses directing or teaching in nursing options are all relevant to the ultimate future of the options themselves.

... The dual role played by the Association and the department of education is an essential condition of success with regard to the content and quality of the educational program. [17]

MEDICARE

A health care system funded through public monies and administered by the government came to Quebec in October 1970. As it did elsewhere in Canada, it was to have profound effects on all health fields in the province, particularly in the area of control of health services and the health professions. The first involvement of the ANPQ with the

---

[17] Association of Nurses of Quebec, *News and Notes*, December 1969, p.7.

new health regimen began in July 1971 when the text of Bill 65 was received. This bill, an Act Respecting Health Services and Social Services, established new organizational structures for the operation and administration of all hospitals and health centers throughout the province, and centralized their control in the hands of the government.

ANPQ moved quickly to establish a study committee to examine the document, and in October 1971 presented its brief to a committee of the Quebec National Assembly. In its study of Bill 65, the ANPQ had noted with alarm that the status of nursing was obscure, and in its brief sought to have this situation clarified. However, when the bill was passed, nursing administration was still downgraded from its established status.

Unwelcome clarification of the projected lower status of nursing administration under the new hospital organization plan was received in May 1972, when the department of social affairs introduced proposed Regulations under the Act Respecting Health Services and Social Services. These Regulations proposed an organization chart that would place the head of the nursing department under the authority of the director of hospital services, and well below the rank of the director of professional services (formerly medical director).

In the next few months, the ANPQ carried out an active campaign of information toward legislators and members of the civil service in the health field. Some progress was achieved in November 1972, when the regulations that were adopted showed the head of the nursing department reporting to the general manager, but still not achieving the rank of "director." The ANPQ continued to lobby for support of its position: For nursing care to fulfill its potential under the new structures, it would be essential for the nursing branch to be on an equal administrative footing with professional services.

In September 1973, an amendment to the Regulations placed the "director of the nursing branch" on the same level as the "director of professional services." This, in effect, accorded to nursing administration full recognition as a separate entity in the hospital structure—as requested by the ANPQ.

In July 1974, the government introduced Bill 41, an Act to Amend the Act Respecting Health Services and Social Services. In it, the different management roles in hospital centers were specified and clarified, including that of the general manager and the directors of professional services, hospital services, and nursing. The Act reiterates that each hospital center shall have a director of nursing, who must be a member in good standing of the professional corporation of nurses of Quebec. This represented success for the ANPQ: the bill was passed on October 15 1974, 3 years to the day from the date the ANPQ made its first presentation on the subject to the parliamentary commission.

PROFESSIONAL CODE

In its continuing program to reorganize the social structures of the province, the Quebec government introduced Bill 250 in November 1971, establishing a Code of Professions.[18] While not dealing specifically with nursing, it was important to nursing because it set out methods of administration and criteria for discipline for all professions.

In December of that year, the ANPQ senior officers met with district and chapter presidents to solicit membership opinion to assist in preparing an ANPQ brief, and later that month the brief was submitted to the parliamentary commission studying the bill. It indicated that the ANPQ fully supported the principles expressed in the bill, but made several specific suggestions for clarification and modification of some of its provisions, which the nurses felt were essential to the efficient and effective functioning of their professional corporation.

THE NURSES' ACT[19]

Yet another significant piece of legislation affecting nursing was introduced by the provincial government in December 1971: Called Bill 273, it was a complete revision of the previous Nurses' Act. What it proposed would have drastically reduced the previously-acquired legal right of the ANPQ (under Bill 273 to be called the Order of Nurses of Quebec) to control the standards of admission to nursing education programs; to approve basic nursing education programs; and, to establish, and control the examinations for registration. In addition, the proposed legislation omitted certain legal machinery needed for the effective operation of the nurses' association.

ANPQ immediately launched a program to re-shape this piece of proposed legislation. What the nurses of Quebec were embarking upon, led by their professional association, was a major public relations effort in the political arena to ensure that the profession would, in the future, have the necessary legal tools to enable it to fulfill its function of providing the public with high-quality nursing care.

A full-fledged information program was set up, directed to the ANPQ members, members of the provincial legislature, members of the civil service involved with the new legislation, and the general public. It solicited the understanding and support of the ANPQ position with respect to Bill 273 and also for the Association's views on Bills 250 and 65.

---

[18] Statutes of Quebec, 1973, chapter 43.
[19] Statutes of Quebec, 1973, chapter 48.

Indicative of the intensity of the program is the following excerpt from a message signed by the Association president in the March 1972 issue of *News and Notes*:

A few weeks ago, we appealed to all members of ANPQ to support the Association with clear, informed and united thinking about the new legislation now pending to replace the present Quebec Nurses' Act.

We are convinced the time has come to carry your support of the Association one step further. We now urge all nurses of ANPQ to tell their respective members of the National Assembly that they support the Association in its position on Bills 250 and 273. This ANPQ position is expressed in briefs already submitted to the government and will be subject to examination and discussion this month before the parliamentary commission studying the legislation . . . [20]

In August 1972, a special general meeting of the Quebec association to discuss legislative issues was held in Montreal and in seven other centers connected by a telephone network. Its purpose was to give individual members up-to-date information on the proposed new laws, and to discuss what the individual member could do to help effect more viable legislation.

The problems still had not been resolved by early 1973. Lobbying and other activity by ANPQ increased:

- In mid-February, copies of the ANPQ brief to the parliamentary committee were presented personally to the 108 members of the national Assembly. A letter was addressed to each Member requesting support during discussion of the bills.
- During the following weeks, meetings with various members of the National Assembly were arranged by the ANPQ public relations officer for the senior officers and executives of ANPQ.
- A newsletter from ANPQ headquarters was established to keep senior ANPQ officers informed quickly of developments on the legislative scene. The first of these was issued February 26. The information contained in the letters was planned to be used to keep all ANPQ members abreast of events as soon as possible after they occurred.
- The senior executives and officers of ANPQ attended meetings of the parliamentary commissions involved with Bills 250 and 273. These meetings started on March 5 and lasted over a period of months.

---

[20] Association of Nurses of Quebec, *News and Notes*, March 1972, p.1.

- On April 18 1973, an Information Day was held in Montreal with eight other centers connected by telephone hook-up, to inform all ANPQ members of the most recent developments.
- As a result of the interest evinced at the local level, groups of nurses organized by ANPQ districts—and numbering in the hundreds—converged for one day on the legislative buildings in Quebec in a show of numerical strength and solidarity of purpose. As many as could be accommodated in the committee room attended the hearings to give moral support to the official position of ANPQ.

Activities continued on all fronts until, finally, in early July 1973, the ANPQ's secretary-registrar could write to the ANPQ committee of management:

Have we won? No doubt we have, since all principles enunciated by the Association were included either in our Act or in the Professional Code. Therefore, the legislator has given us all the tools necessary to fully discharge our responsibilities![21]

As an exercise in political action, the program was complete, coordinated, and effective.

Public Interest

There is no way of forecasting the manner and direction in which medicare will influence the practice of nursing. There are, however, certain self-evident aspects. The rise of consumerism is certain to exert forces for change on the nursing profession. Today's patients are consumers of health services. They consider their health care bill prepaid through their tax payments and they want to know that they are getting value for their money. The assurances of a closed profession which, from the point of view of the consumer, operates behind a barricade of professional mysteries, are no longer sufficient reassurance.

This comes as no surprise to an objective observer. Viewed from the outside, the policy statements and political actions of the health profession seem at times to fall a little short of being entirely altruistic. So, the role of the lay representative in the affairs of nursing is a useful one: specifically, it can provide assurances to other lay people—

---

[21] Association of Nurses of the Province of Quebec, *Latest News*, July 1973, p. 1.

the vast body of consumers—that professional nursing is indeed functioning in the interest of the public and the patient.

This situation already has been examined and satisfied in many provinces, including New Brunswick, British Columbia, and Saskatchewan. In New Brunswick, in 1971, the report of the government-commissioned Study Committee on Nursing Education recommended that, because of the possibility of a conflict of interest between the professional organization and the public it serves, a drastic separation of functions should take place and that these functions should be assigned to two separate government ministries. The purpose of this split was to ensure that the three areas of education, regulation and professional growth of nurses and nursing assistants would be dealt with in an objective manner and in a way "clearly and demonstrably in the public interest."

The solution contained in the report was debatable, but, the NBARN recognized the source of the problem as real and valid: a responsibility devolved on the association to demonstrate that it was dealing with provincial nursing matters in an objective manner, "clearly and demonstrably in the public interest." In effect, the report asked for watchdogs to guard the public interest. Two avenues to this end were immediately visible: one was to invite representative members of the public to participate in the decision-making; the second course, more simple and less effective, was to turn the matter over to the government, which presumably represents the public interest.

The organized nursing profession, like other organized professions, has not, in the past, been demonstrably hospitable to the idea of inviting laymen to participate in its deliberations in order to assure the public that its best interests were being served. But the NBARN had been farsighted in this respect and earlier had initiated action in just this direction. As a consequence, its political stance was valid and credible when it marshalled its forces to prevent the drastic solution proposed in the report and proposed to the government an extension of the public participation process already underway. The NBARN proposals for lay members on its council rang true with the government and satisfied the basic need to assure the public that the affairs of nursing were being guided in a manner consistent with the public interest.

It would be inaccurate to suggest that this political action set at rest all the political problems of the NBARN, but it did appear to satisfy immediate needs in a constructive manner. Nevertheless, the desire of the public to know that professional groups are functioning in a manner "clearly and demonstrably in the public interest," is one that will command increasing time and attention from all professional groups.

Foundations for Future Action

Historians will record that attitudes and achievements in the realm of health care moved more rapidly and further in the second half of the 20th century than they had in the previous millennium. Many elements contributed to this advance, including, of course, a rising material standard of living, that supported the general conclusion that a competent, modern society not only should, but could, guarantee health care to its citizens. As far as the western world was concerned, the movement started in Northern Europe, then spread to England and Canada. Significantly, it did not take root in the United States.

The concept of universal health care was regarded in some quarters with antipathy or suspicion, and inevitably these attitudes led to confrontation—between the political elements proposing universal health care, and the professional people who would be called upon to provide it. Nevertheless, the basic concept prevailed. The idea of universal medical care was incorporated into the political platform of every party in Canada.

Like most translations from theory into practice, the execution fell short of the visual concept. Gaps appeared in the system; additional gaps are still being identified and it can be assumed that more will continue to appear as the health care system responds to the demands for universal services. For the nursing profession, this evolution presents a continuing challenge to political action. Nurses can recognize the gaps in the health care system. They can identify with problems and deficiencies as they arise. They can indicate to those who are able and authorized to make the necessary changes, the best way, in the public interest, of filling these gaps. To do less than this is to abrogate the role of the nursing profession in seeking the best possible health care for our citizens.

In many respects, succeeding generations of nurses will find the identification and solution of problems affecting their profession easier than did their predecessors. For more than half a century, individual nurses have worked to create a national organization capable of supporting and protecting the profession and the public. Today, nurses "from Cape Race to Nootka Sound," have access to the accumulated resources of the CNA.

The Association has become a national repository for the information that is the key to effective political action. Some of these resources include a nursing library of international repute, a statistics department that can provide current information on more than 170 000 registered nurses and qualified research staff involved in the solution of current problems.

Changes in all phases of life, including health care, are inevitable. Beneficent changes in the field of health care will be those reflecting the knowledge and experience injected through the political action of nurses.

8

The Nurse's Role in Health Care Planning

HUGUETTE LABELLE, B.Sc., B.Ed., M.Ed.

- Planning is essential to make health care services available, accessible and relevant to all people ... and to assure this is achieved at the lowest reasonable cost. Consumers must be consulted at the "embryonic" stages of planning rather than being drawn in to comment on the finished project. Nurses, because of their special concerns for the well-being of the total individual within his physical and social environment, could be important agents to ensure planning is consistent with the multi-dimensions of man and society.

    The fact that nurses have not been involved may be interpreted in two ways: nurses may feel planners are reluctant to involve them, or planners may perceive a lack of interest on the part of nurses. Commitment and accountability form the basis for meaningful participation by nurses in health care planning.

As more nurses seriously consider sharing the responsibility of planning health care, a number of questions must be raised. Should nurses participate in the planning of health care? If so, what are some of the ways whereby this participation could take place and what impact would it have? What is the meaning of participation in the planning activity for nurses? In studying these questions, one must start from the assumption that planning for health care services is essential at all levels: unit, institutional, regional, provincial, national, and international. Planning is essential in order to make health care services available, accessible and relevant to the Canadian population, and to assure that this is achieved at the lowest possible cost. In the last three years, several reports[1] published in Canada have supported this position.

Why should nurses be essential partners in planning health care? The scope of nurse preparation, the length of client contact for each nurse and the continuity of care provided by nursing personnel would enable nurses to be strong client advocates. This advocacy can aid the consumer to actively participate in the planning process of health care and ensure that the needs and interests of the client are not overlooked or misinterpreted by planners.

Very often, consumer participation in planning is a major goal on paper, but in actual fact, the consumer is rarely consulted. In an examination of health planning in the United States, Krause found that:

The theme of citizen participation in planning grew with each program, while its actual absence remained constant. In short, the increasing demands for public accountability, participation and control of health services planning is being met with the increasing use of ideology as a symbolic, not real response to the demands. This process is the inevitable consequence of technocratic rationalization within a system where the inside technocrats work in mutual cooperation, or as agents for, outside interest groups, primarily concerned with the perpetuation of profits and the maintenance of their existing power and control over the system.[2]

---

[1] Castonguay-Nepveu Report, Province of Quebec, Commission of Inquiry on Health and Social Welfare, 1967, 1970 – 71. Manitoba *White Paper* on Health Policy, The Cabinet Committee, 1972. Foulkes Report, "Health Security for British Columbia," 1974. Mustard Report, "Health Planning Task Force Report," Toronto, 1974, Marc Lalonde, *A New Perspective on the Health of Canadians*, Government of Canada, Ottawa, 1974.

[2] E. A. Krause, Health Planning as a Managerial Ideology, *International Journal of Health Services*, Vol. 3, No. 3, 1974, p. 460.

If we assume that the situation in Canada does not vary greatly from the one identified by Krause concerning the United States, then one of the key goals for nurses as they share in planning should be the correction and prevention of a similar situation occurring in Canada.

If, by legislation or common agreement, consumers are invited to participate in decision making, then it is important to guard that this participation is not limited to tokenism. Often, such professionals as retired physicians, nurses or citizens who have previously served on health planning boards, are selected as ordinary consumers in order to participate in the planning process. This representation is obviously a misuse of the concept of consumer participation because it perpetuates the situation identified by Krause. It is very important that consumers be consulted at the "embryonic" stage of planning rather than being presented with the finished plan as a *fait accompli*. The nurse can attempt to protect the concept of consumer participation from becoming mere tokenism by acting as a mediator between planner and consumer in the formulation stage of health planning.

● Nurses can assist in assuring the return of responsibility for one's health, in great part, to the individual.

Nurses, through participation in planning of health care, can have an impact in developing a greater degree of self-reliance in individuals concerning their own health needs. Illich, in *Medical Nemesis*, claims that "the so called health professions have an even deeper, structurally health denying effect in so far as they destroy the potential of people to deal with their human weakness, vulnerability, and uniqueness in the personal and autonomous way."[3] This author also contends that the ultimate backlash of the hygienic process results in the paralysis of healthy responses to suffering. He states further:

. . . the proliferation of medical agents is health denying—it produces dependence. And this dependence on professional intervention tends to impoverish the non-medical health supporting and healing aspect of the social and physical environments and tends to decrease the organic and psychological coping ability of ordinary people.[4]

If this trend continues, the current theme in a few years may not be "de-medicalization" but "de-nursification" of society. Nurses who recognize this fact will encourage and help consumers to reclaim autonomy in respect to their own health.

● *A New Perspective on the Health of Canadians*, published by

---

[3] Ivan Illich, *Medical Nemesis* (Toronto: McClelland and Stewart, 1975), p. 40
[4] *Ibid.* p. 40.

National Health and Welfare, 1974, proposes one type of comprehensive approach to planning, organizing and evaluating health services.[5] The health field concept suggests that the health field could be mapped into four broad dimensions: lifestyle, human biology, the environment, and health care organization. Other authors[6] also support the concept of studying man as a unified whole in the context of his environment. .

Nurses, because of the special concern for the well-being of the total individual within his physical and social environment, could be important agents on planning teams in assuring that planning is consistent with the multidimensions of man and of society.

● In keeping with their long-time endorsement of the WHO definition of health, these same nurses could bring a special concern and emphasis toward maximizing well-being and optimum functioning of people as opposed to only minimizing suffering. Thus, health care planning would shift some of its emphasis from the "sickness model" to one of health support.[7] The identification of positive health indicators would be highly valuable in assisting planning from the basis of "health assets"[8] instead of initiating health planning from health problems. In this manner, good health may become as important as healing.

● Modern technology seems to have encouraged health professionals to adopt the "*technologic imperative*." This approach, as Fuchs[9] points out, has serious consequences because it guarantees all possible care to one part of the population while another segment is deprived of even minimal services. It is very easy to spend a greater part of resources on acute care services even when there is an increasing dilemma involving the financing of these services.

Nurses could help to alter this situation by assisting in planning

---

[5] Lalonde, *op. cit.*

[6] Ludwig von Bertalanffy, *General System Theory* (New York: George Braziller, 1968), p. 295. Hildegarde Siegel, "To Your Health—Whatever That May Mean," *Nursing Forum*, Vol. XII, No. 3, 1973, p. 286. Halbert L. Dunn, "High-Level Wellness for Man and Society," *The American Journal of Public Health*, Vol. 49, 1959, pp. 786 – 92. Monroe Lerner, "Conceptualization of Health and Social Well-Being," *Health Status Indexes, Proceedings of a Conference Conducted by Health Services Research*, Ed. R-L Berg, Hospital Research and Educational Trust, Chicago, 1973, pp. 1 – 6. Tapani Turolla, "A System's Approach to Health and Health Policy," *Medical Care*, September–October 1972, Vol. 10, No. 5, pp. 373–9.

[7] Walter J. McNerney, "The Missing Link in Health Services," *Journal of Medical Education*, Vol. 50, No. 1, January 1975, pp. 11 – 23.

[8] Murtle Kutschke, Unpublished Paper, Prepared for the Office of the Principal Nursing Officer, National Health and Welfare, June 1975.

[9] V. Fuchs, "The Growing Demand for Medical Care," *New England Journal of Medicine*, Vol. 279, 1968, pp. 190 – 5.

for a more equitable distribution of resources and services to popula-tions-at-risk such as the socio-economically deprived, those in rural areas, infants, adolescents, and the aged.

• Tancredi and Barsky[10] have produced an analysis of the way in which the health care decision-making process has become mechanized through technology. The planner is too far removed from the consum-ers' problems and tends to lose sight of human considerations when making decisions. This often occurs because of the diffusion of deci-sion-making responsibility that occurs in a bureaucratic hierarchy. "Some of the technological innovations themselves are designed to aid the decision-making process. Operations research and systems analysis attempt to point to the maximal arrangements of inputs for a given output and thereby mechanize decisions previously made on a more intuitive basis."[11] Operations research and systems analysis are, indeed, important tools in assisting planners to arrive at more accurate decisions. At the same time, when dealing with the moral and ethical issues that providers and planners of health care face (abortion, euthanasia, genetic control, for example), there is always a highly subjective element left in the final planning process. The caring, sup-portive and understanding capability of the nurse would provide a balanced decision between cold fact and those situations where it is difficult to judge right from wrong.

Briefly, the nurse's rapport with client and family, her caring capability and client advocacy are assets that she brings to the plan-ning process and the benefits of her contribution would be substantial.

How can nurses become more involved in the planning of health care?
Seeking representation. There are several ways of involving the nurse in community health planning in a systematic way. Simmons describes a five-level system of activity involving the nurse in the planning of health care.[12] He suggests positions starting from (1) staff planner for the chief executive officer of the institution; (2) appointed member of a long-range planning committee of an institution; (3) institutional representative of a community based planning group; (4) community member of a planning agency board or advisory committee; and, (5) sponsor or applicant for an institutional or community based demon-

---

[10] Lawrence R. Tancredi and Arthur J. Barsky, "Technology and Health Care Decision Making—Conceptualizing the Process for Societal Informed Consent," *Medical Care*, October 1974, Vol. 12, No. 10, pp. 845–59.

[11] *Ibid.*

[12] H. J. Simmons, "Community Health Planning—With or Without Nursing?" *Nursing Outlook*, April 1974, Vol. 2, No. 4, p. 262.

stration project. Certainly, this progression or "track" provides the nurse with the experience and knowledge to advance from institutional planning to the broader area of community health planning. In some instances nurses who are without previous experience in planning may become members on regional health councils, hospital boards, or provincial health councils. Lack of experience in previous levels of planning should in no way deter nurses from accepting the position and actively participating on the planning committee. Participation on unit and institution planning committees provides valuable experience in working with groups and in learning about the planning process.

The fact that nurses traditionally have not been involved in planning groups may be interpreted in one of two ways. To the nurse, it may appear that the planner is simply reluctant to extend an invitation to join in the planning process; however, from the planner's viewpoint, it may be perceived as a lack of interest or desire on the nurse's part to become involved in planning. As the first step toward correcting this situation, the nurse must demonstrate willingness and enthusiasm to occupy a responsible position in respect to planning. Nurses cannot expect to be automatically included in planning groups unless their initial signals are given to planners.

The nurse who is seeking representation on a board, council, or expert committee must be articulate, intelligent, and able to identify planning problems. She must demonstrate by her actions and ability that the nurse has a positive and unique contribution to make to the planning process. Without this genuine desire to become involved, lobbying for representation would be seen simply as seeking the enhancement of a particular professional group and the effort, consequently, would be doomed to failure.

In some instances, the qualifying requirements for representation on a multidisciplinary or expert committee may be particular attributes in a specialized field, rather than the fact that the individual is a nurse.

Some provincial and national nurses' associations have successfully obtained nurse representation at the regional and provincial level of planning. Special efforts are still required to obtain similar representation at the chapter level in regional and local community health planning.

Becoming knowledgeable about the planning process. When one participates in health planning, there must be knowledge of population characteristics, location, specific problems and needs, as well as clinical expertise. Health professionals, through readings, experiences and discussions with experts, must have a sound grasp of the planning process itself; otherwise very little can be accomplished.

Based on the WHO publication on health planning, the health plan is defined as "a predetermined force of action that is firmly based on the nature of extensive health problems from which are derived priority goals. The centre of this planning process is the analysis of alternative means of achieving preselected goals while facing a variety of constraints."[13]

Knezevich summarizes planning as providing the following:

... a disciplined approach to (1) force specification of objectives; (2) anticipate a set of long and short range futures; (3) identify alternative courses of action; (4) stimulate the use of sophisticated analysis tools or techniques; and, (5) improve rational decision making on resource allocations.[14]

This author further claims that multi-year programs and financial documents form the important outcome of the planning process.

Health planning, therefore, should guide change, provide for the optimum use of available resources and include the political realities of the situation. Those involved in developing a health plan should work closely with planners of such other community services as education, welfare, recreation, and agriculture, in order to develop a closely coordinated and integrated community plan.

Nurses who are involved in health planning should be aware of techniques that are used in systematic planning and be able to utilize this method of simplifying decision-making. The two most widely used methods in planning are "systems analysis" and "operations research." Simply defined, these are:

A *systems analysis* "attracts problems rationally by comparing alternatives for reaching an objective in terms of the cost and effectiveness of each option."[15] This technique presents a decision-maker with a range of choices rather than the "best" choice, while also emphasizing basic economic concepts.

"Operations research accepts specific objectives and assumptions and then attempts to compute an optimum solution."[16]

In health planning, all problems must be approached systematically and in so doing, the pragmatic aspects of the situation will be revealed.

---

[13] H. E. Hilleboe, A. Barkhuus and W. C. Thomas, Jr., *Approaches to National Health Planning*, World Health Organization, Geneva, Public Health Papers No. 46, 1972, p. 9.

[14] Stephen J. Knezevich, "Program Budgeting," *PPBS*, (Wisconsin: University of Wisconsin, McCuthen Publishing Co., 1973), p. 33.

[15] *Ibid.*, p. 174.

[16] A. C. Ethoven, cited in Stephen J. Knezevich, "Programs Budgeting," *PPBS*, (Wisconsin: University of Wisconsin, McCuthen Publishing Co., 1973).

Once accepted, how can nurses improve their participation in health care planning?

Doing one's homework. It always should be remembered that there is no substitute for informed participation. Arriving at a meeting unprepared, not having reviewed documentation, and bluffing one's way through a meeting will bring disrespect from colleagues. Preparation for a meeting may mean individual review of documents for discussion, consulting peers and colleagues of other disciplines, and/or consulting associations at the local, provincial, or national level. Such consultation brings a broader base of knowledge and greater capability for a comprehensive and analytical approach to document review.

Learning to work within a group. Learning to understand how and why we react to different types of persons and how we influence others is a prerequisite to successful participation in a group. If either the opportunity or the experience to learn about successful group activity has never presented itself, then it may be helpful to discuss one's contribution with a trusted member of the group. This may offer an insight into certain weaknesses and provide an opportunity to make a more positive contribution.

Positive participation. It is essential to develop the ability to give constructive criticism, which includes positive alternatives. Picking holes in documents that have been painstakingly developed, without providing positive alternatives to these criticisms, does nothing but alienate other members of the group who will, in future, be less inclined to invite that individual to serve on other committees or to review important documents.

Many decisions are made through informal channels prior to the beginning of formal meetings. One must be fully aware of informal channels of communication that may provide positive decisions. An informal lunch, the Christmas party, driving to a meeting—each instance provides a good medium for sharing concerns or expressing one's point of view.

Learning to live with consensus. As convictions are developed on certain issues, needs, or plans, it is sometimes difficult and painful to see another approach or set of needs emerge from group discussion. Sometimes, what does emerge will be so far beyond our point of compromise that withdrawal from the planning activity may be thought necessary. On the other hand, resignation may rescind any opportunity one might have had of exerting influence on future decisions.

One of the greatest assets when working with a group is to have the courage to advance one's ideas and the wisdom to know when to retreat. A planner also must learn to distinguish the important causes from the insignificant ones, and expend valuable energy accordingly. Arguing over unimportant points is like spending all one's time uprooting one tree while being surrounded by a forest. Arguing simply wastes time and creates opponents who might otherwise have been positive supporters for other issues.

A final admonition. The constant danger in planning, which is inherent in diffused decision-making, is losing sight of the object for which we are working, i.e., the client and community. The nurse participant should be aware of this constantly and help the members of the group to keep their primary objective in mind.

However, as nurses become more involved in planning, they should not allow their participation to become "a thinly disguised rationalization for funding of existing programs and for gaining power grounds for professionals with vested interests."[17] Participation in planning of health services, therefore, always should be for the sake of providing relevant services to the consumer, not to enhance the role of the nurse.

Commitment and accountability form the basis of meaningful participation by nurses in the planning of health care. Larger numbers of nurses must become involved in health planning at all levels.

Nurses cannot rely on the fact that the strength of their numbers, as the largest group of health professionals, or the fact that they are one of the key providers of health services on the front line, will automatically gain them entrance into the planning process of health care. In facing the challenge of becoming more involved in health care planning, the words of Derksen ring true:

Opportunities—do not arrive on a platter! Rather, they originate by creative and imaginative minds.[18]

---

[17] Krause, *op. cit.*, p. 459.

[18] George Derksen, *Opportunity in Northern Canada*, Vol. 1, No. 1, 1975, p. 8.

Biographical Sketches of Authors

Betsy LaSor

Education
>A.A., R.N., Pasadena City College
>B.S., California State University, Los Angeles.
>M.N., University of California, Los Angeles.

Work Experience
>Staff nursing in emergency room, surgical and psychiatric nursing, Europe and the United States.
>Supervisor, Psychiatric Nursing, Mt. Sinai, Los Angeles.
>Assistant Professor of Nursing, San Diego, California.
>Assistant Professor of Nursing, University of British Columbia, Vancouver.

M. Ruth Elliott

Education
>R.N., B.Sc., University of Alberta, Edmonton.
>M.S., University of California, San Francisco.

Work Experience
>Staff nursing in public health nursing and pediatric nursing.
>Head Nurse, Children's Hospital, Calgary, Alberta.
>Lecturer, School of Nursing, University of Alberta, Edmonton.
>Lecturer, School of Nursing, University of California, San Francisco.
>Lecturer, School of Nursing, University of British Columbia, Vancouver.
>Mental health nurse.
>Assistant Professor, School of Nursing, University of British Columbia, Vancouver.

Lucy Dorothea Willis

Education
>Graduate of School of Nursing, Toronto Western Hospital, (now the Atkinson School), Toronto, Ontario.
>Certificate in Teaching and Supervision (Nursing), University of British Columbia, Vancouver.

B.S., M.A., Teacher's College, Columbia University, New York.
Ed. D., University of California, Berkeley, California.

Work Experience
Staff nurse, Toronto Tuberculosis Hospital, Weston, Ontario.
Instructor, Moose Jaw Union Hospital and Saskatoon City
   Hospital; became educational director at the latter.
Director, Centralized Teaching Program, Regina Center, Regina,
   Saskatchewan.
Professor and Director, School of Nursing, University of
   Saskatchewan, Saskatoon.
Professor, College of Nursing, University of Saskatchewan,
   Saskatoon.

Shirley M. Stinson

Education
B.Sc.N., University of Alberta, Edmonton.
M.N.Ad., University of Minnesota, Minneapolis.
Ed.D., Columbia University, New York.

Work Experience
Public Health Nurse.
Associate Director of Nursing Service, The Hospital for Sick
   Children, Toronto, Ontario.
Teacher, Undergraduate and Graduate Programs, Research
   Consultant 1969-1976, University of Alberta, Edmonton.

Marguerite E. Schumacher

Education
R.N., Victoria Hospital, Winnipeg, Manitoba.
Certificate in Teaching, University of Western Ontario, London.
B.Sc.N., Western Reserve University, Cleveland, Ohio.
M.A., Ed.M., Teacher's College, Columbia University, New York.

Work Experience
Private Duty Nursing, Winnipeg.
General Duty Nursing, Winnipeg General Hospital and
   Vancouver General Hospital.
Head Nurse, Clinical Instructor, Director of Nursing, Grace
   Hospital, Winnipeg.

Evening Supervisor and Associate Director of Nursing Education,
Winnipeg General Hospital.
Advisor to School of Nursing, University of Alberta, Edmonton.
Coordinator, Division of Health Sciences, and Chairman, Nursing
Section, Red Deer College, Red Deer, Alberta.
Dean, Faculty of Nursing, University of Calgary, Alberta.

Isobel Kay

Education

S.R.N., S.C.M., M.T.D., England.
B.N., McGill University, Montreal, Quebec.
M.Ed., Toronto, Ontario.

Work Experience

Staff Nurse, Staff Midwife, Ward Sister, England.
Staff Nurse, Instructor, Jewish General Hospital, Montreal.
Head Nurse, Supervisor, and In-Service Education Coordinator,
Joseph Brant Memorial Hospital, Burlington, Ontario.
Director of Continuing Education, Associate Director of Nursing
Services, McMaster University Medical Centre, Hamilton,
Ontario.
Assistant Professor, Faculty of Health Sciences, McMaster
University, Hamilton, Ontario.

Dorothy Kergin

Education

B.S.N., University of British Columbia, Vancouver.
M.P.H., University of Michigan.
Ph.D., University of Michigan.

Work Experience

Public Health Nursing, British Columbia.
Occupational Health Nurse, British Columbia.
Instructor, School of Public Health, University of Michigan.
Associate Director, Associate Professor, School of Nursing,
McMaster University, Hamilton, Ontario.
Professor and Director, Associate Dean of Health Sciences
(Nursing) and Professor, Faculty of Health Sciences,
McMaster University, Hamilton, Ontario.

Margaret Boone

Education
> R.N., The Mack Training School for Nurses, St. Catharines
> General Hospital, St. Catharines, Ontario.
> B.Sc.N., Lakehead University, Thunder Bay, Ontario.
> M.S., Boston University, Boston, Massachusetts.

Work Experience
> Staff Nursing, The Hospital for Sick Children, Toronto, Ontario.
> Lecturer, Lakehead University, Thunder Bay, Ontario.
> Clinical Nurse Specialist, The Hospital for Sick Children, Toronto.
> Assistant Professor of Nursing, Lakehead University, Thunder
> Bay.

June Kikuchi

Education
> R.N., B.Sc.N., University of Toronto, Toronto, Ontario.
> M.N., University of Pittsburgh, Pittsburgh, Pennsylvania.
> Currently enrolled in the Ph.D. Program at the University of
> Pittsburgh.

Work Experience
> Public Health Nurse, Victorian Order of Nurses, Toronto, Ontario.
> Staff Nurse, The Hospital for Sick Children, Toronto.
> Pediatric Instructor, Vancouver General Hospital, Vancouver,
> British Columbia.
> Head Nurse, The Hospital for Sick Children, Toronto.
> Clinical Nurse Specialist, The Hospital for Sick Children, Toronto.

Mitzi I. R. Montgomery

Education
> R.N., Toronto General Hospital, Toronto, Ontario.
> B.Sc.N., University of British Columbia, Vancouver.
> M.S.W., University of Michigan.
> Ph.D., University of Edinburgh.

Work Experience
> Public Health, British Columbia.
> Clinical Nursing Instructor in Canada, United States and Europe.
> Family and Adolescent Counselling in Community Mental Health,
> British Columbia.
> Special Consultant to Minister of Health, British Columbia.
> Associate Director, Canadian Association of Social Work, Ottawa.

Helen K. Mussallem

Education

Diploma, Vancouver General Hospital, School of Nursing, Vancouver, British Columbia.

Diploma, Teaching, Supervision and Administration, University of Washington, Seattle, Washington.

B.N., McGill University, Montreal, Quebec.

M.A., Teacher's College, Columbia University, New York.

Work Experience

Active Service, Lt. (N/S) Royal Canadian Army Medical Corps, Canada and overseas.

Staff Nurse, Head Nurse, and Supervisor, Vancouver General Hospital, Vancouver, British Columbia.

Director, Pilot Project for Evaluation of Schools of Nursing in Canada, Canadian Nurses' Association.

Director of Special Studies, Canadian Nurses' Association.

Executive Director, Canadian Nurses' Association.

Secretary-Treasurer, Canadian Nurses' Foundation.

Huguette Labelle

Education

R.N., B.Sc.N.Ed., B.Ed., M.Ed., University of Ottawa.

Currently enrolled in Ph.D. program in Education, with major in Administration.

Work Experience

Director, Vanier School of Nursing.

Lecturer, University of Ottawa, School of Nursing and School of Health Administration.

Teacher, Clinical Coordinator, and Assistant Director of the School of Nursing, Ottawa General Hospital.

General Staff Nurse, Ottawa General Hospital.

Principal Nursing Officer, Health and Welfare Canada.

Index